Leading For Educational Lives: Inviting and Sustaining Imaginative Acts of Hope in a Connected World

Critical Issues in the Future of Learning and Teaching

Volume 10

This series represents a forum for important issues that do and will affect how learning and teaching are thought about and practised. All educational venues and situations are undergoing change because of information and communications technology, globalization and paradigmatic shifts in determining what knowledge is valued. Our scope includes matters in primary, secondary and tertiary education as well as community-based informal circumstances. Important and significant differences between information and knowledge represent a departure from traditional educational offerings heightening the need for further and deeper understanding of the implications such opportunities have for influencing what happens in schools, colleges and universities around the globe. An inclusive approach helps attend to important current and future issues related to learners, teachers and the variety of cultures and venues in which educational efforts occur. We invite forward-looking contributions that reflect an international comparative perspective illustrating similarities and differences in situations, problems, solutions and outcomes.

Edited by Pamela M. Denicolo (p.m.denicolo@reading.ac.uk - University of Reading, UK)
Founding Editor Michael Kompf † (Brock University, Canada)

Pamela M. Denicolo was the Director of the Graduate School at the University of Reading and an active member of the University Committee for Postgraduate Research Studies. Now Emeritus at Reading she is currently employed as a consultant on postgraduate research at the University of Surrey.Her passion for supporting and developing graduate students is also demonstrated through her contributions to the UK Council for Graduate Education Executive Committee, the Society for Research into Higher Education Postgraduate Network, and other national and international committees and working groups which, for example, review and evaluate research generic skills training and the concordance of UK universities with the European Code and Charter, produce a framework of skills for researchers over their full career and consider the changing nature of the doctorate. As a psychologist working particularly in the fields of Professional and Postgraduate Education, she has supervised more than 50 doctoral students to successful completion, examined many more, and developed and led Research Methods Programmes for social scientists in her current and previous universities. She was honoured to be appointed an Honorary Member of the Royal Pharmaceutical Society for her contributions to the education of pharmacists. Her lifelong interest in student learning, and hence teachers' teaching, led her to become an active member of the International Study Association on Teachers and Teaching (ISATT) and serving member of the Executive Committee for many years. Her research has been oriented by a commitment to understanding the way participants in learning processes construe their roles, situations and activities, through the use and development of Personal Construct Theory approaches and methods.

In keeping with Michael's spirit, the friends and family of Dr. Michael Kompf have established the, Dr. Michael Kompf Graduate Student Travel Scholarship, which will be administered and housed in the Faculty of Education of Brock University. Tax deductible contributions to the endowment fund for the award can be made by cheque to Brock University with the subject note: Dr. Michael Kompf Graduate Student Travel Scholarship, or contributions can be made online by going to: https://www.brocku.ca/onlinedonations/start.php?giving=BNBHighestNeed and clicking on the drop down box for the Dr. Michael Kompf Graduate Student Travel Scholarship.

Leading For Educational Lives

Inviting and Sustaining Imaginative Acts of Hope in a Connected World

John M. Novak
Brock University, Ontario, Canada

Denise E. Armstrong
Brock University, Ontario, Canada

and

Brendan Browne
Halton Catholic District School Board, Ontario, Canada

SENSE PUBLISHERS
ROTTERDAM/BOSTON/TAIPEI

A C.I.P. record for this book is available from the Library of Congress.

ISBN: 978-94-6209-552-6 (paperback)
ISBN: 978-94-6209-553-3 (hardback)
ISBN: 978-94-6209-554-0 (e-book)

Published by: Sense Publishers,
P.O. Box 21858,
3001 AW Rotterdam,
The Netherlands
https://www.sensepublishers.com/

Printed on acid-free paper

To Michael Kompf, colleague, editor, and friend extraordinaire,
who demonstrated continuously how to care, share, and dare.

TABLE OF CONTENTS

Acknowledgements   ix

Introduction   xi

Part 1: Educational LIVES Seen From an Inviting Perspective

  1. Education Matters, Really   3

  2. The Inviting Perspective   17

**Part 2: Imaginatively Leading, Managing, and Mentoring
      Educational LIVES**

  3. Leading From the Inside Out   39

  4. Managing and Mentoring Your Educational Self   53

  5. Leading Others   69

  6. Artfully Managing Conflict, Really   85

  7. Leading for Valued Knowledge   99

  8. Managing Educational Sensibilities   113

  9. Leading Educational Communities   125

10. Managing a Starfish   139

11. Leading Within and Beyond Schools   155

12. Managing Schools for a More Inclusive World   169

Part 3: Dare to Lead for Education

13. Hope for Educational Leadership   183

Appendix A   191

Appendix B   193

References   197

Index   203

About the Authors   209

ACKNOWLEDGEMENTS

We like to express our gratitude to family, friends, and colleagues who have supported and encouraged us in the writing of this book. Special thanks go to:

- Our editor, Michel Lokhorst for your ongoing support and encouragement.
- Dorothy Buchanan, Patrick Tierney, and Mark Poulin for your thoughtful comments, careful editing, and dedication to this project.
- William and Imogene Purkey for the sustaining adventures we have had throughout the world.
- Clio Chan, Peter Wong, and the Hong Kong Alliance for Invitational Education for making an inviting approach to leadership a way of life in Hong Kong and beyond.
- Billy Tate, who worked for peace in Northern Ireland in creative and courageous ways.
- Our colleagues and students at Brock University, particularly our international students, for your energy and enthusiasm in taking to heart new ideas.
- Colleagues, staff, students, parents, trustees, and community of the Halton Catholic District School Board.
- Linda, Natalie, Ivan, Michael, Mabel, Richard, Adeline, and Eddy Novak for being my inviting family.
- Tom, Anne-Marie, and John Armstrong for your unconditional love and ongoing encouragement.
- Sarah, Fiona, and Orla Browne for your inspiration, encouragement, and never-ending support.
- Betty Browne, who led invitationally and inclusively and by doing so inspired the next generation of educational leaders.

INTRODUCTION

Question: What do you get when you cross the perspectives of an American-Canadian philosophical teacher of leadership with a Caribbean-Canadian administration scholar and researcher and add in an Irish-Canadian storytelling practicing principal and supervisor?

Answer: Done well, a convincing and creative way to learn to lead, manage, and mentor for educational purposes in educational ways that combines philosophical defensibility, administrative savvy, and illustrative stories. Done poorly, well... we do not want to think about that.

Our book speaks to and about the growing number of educators (teachers, administrators, support staff, parents, and community members) throughout the world who wish to face the challenges and opportunities to lead in ways that feel right, make sense, and contribute to worthwhile practices. It is about a hopeful approach to education that can provide an ethical framework for leading, managing, and mentoring. Hope, as we see it, is not to be equated with wishful thinking, the mere yearning for something better. This is a much too passive and often unproductive view for people who seek to act thoughtfully in a rapidly changing world. We argue that the type of hope needed for educators trying to make a difference is a pragmatic virtue (Shade, 2001), an intentional and self-correcting way of living that revolves around persistence, resourcefulness, and courage in the face of relentless challenges. Show us someone who keeps trying, finds new ways to come at things, and does so in the face of risks, and you will see someone who possesses the pragmatic hope we are referring to. For those working in schools, this hope is focused on the possibility of bringing about an educationally desirable way to be in the world. In other words, everything done in schools should be directed to having people lead educational lives, to become lifelong appreciators and learners in all they do. This focus is creatively expressed and sustained in an individual's professional and personal life through a visceral understanding and commitment to living in an educationally satisfying and responsible manner. From this pragmatically hopeful perspective, an educational life is not only worth living, it is worth living well.

That's a lot to hope for but we stress throughout this book that pragmatic hope is the core to educational vitality because educational relationships are fundamentally about people and the caring and ethical relationships they establish with themselves, others, values and knowledge, institutions, and the larger human and other-than-human world. *Leading for Educational Lives: Inviting and Sustaining Imaginative Acts of Hope in a Connected World* emphasizes the special quality of relationships needed to appreciate individuals in their uniqueness and call forth their potential to welcome the present and seek to live more meaningful lives. We call this framework an inviting perspective and offer stories about real educators from around the world who try to put imaginative acts of hope into practice as they lead, manage, and mentor.

Examples of persistent, resourceful, and courageous educators are essential because there is a need to vividly present what makes working for educational living unique, important, and fulfilling. Rather than seeing battles for models of educational leadership, management, and mentoring as merely the struggle between adopting a business model or keeping business as usual in the school, we stress that both approaches go wrong if they stray from the ideal of leading for educational living. Certainly educators can learn from business practices, and there are many creative practices currently going on in schools. However, not seeking to go beyond the status quo of schooling or thinking that business-oriented approaches are the only viable alternatives for creative practice is to put in peril the distinctiveness and heart of educational life. We think this is too big a risk and offer a theory, model, strategies, and stories to come to grips with the core educational values, beliefs, and relationships with which we dare not lose touch.

Leading for Educational Lives: Inviting and Sustaining Imaginative Acts of Hope in a Connected World is divided into three unequal parts. In Part 1, "Educational LIVES Seen From an Inviting Perspective," we offer two orienting chapters. The first chapter argues for the uniqueness and ubiquity of an educational perspective and the ideals that sustain it. Ideals are seen as pragmatic tools to get more of what is considered of value. This educational perspective is then seen in light of a structure for systematically exploring the range of relationships encountered in moving from the inside to the outside, from the personal self into the world of others, ideas, and institutional and societal practices. Chapter 2 shows how the practicality of an inviting theory of practice can serve as an educational guide for creating and sustaining the relationships involved in leadership, management, and mentoring. These relationships are seen in light of the foundations of invitational theory, which provide the theoretical roots for practical application. Within this framework the democratic ethos presents an ethical viewpoint for working with others, the perceptual tradition supplies a psychological method for more deeply understanding how people make sense of situations, and self-concept theory gives a perspective on motivation that radically changes the nature of educational relationships. A series of mentoring questions are provided at the beginning of each chapter to set the stage for what follows. Each chapter ends with mentoring conversations to more deeply extend the clarity and application of key concepts and principles.

The foundations of the inviting approach combined with the Educational LIVES model point to the concrete possibilities for practice in the 10 chapters in Part 2, "Imaginatively Leading, Managing, and Mentoring Educational LIVES." The chapters in this section alternate between leading and managing for each of the relationships in the Educational LIVES model. Based on the idea of John Dewey that an educator must first of all be human and only after that professional, Chapter 3 examines the art of leadership and the inner person. The workings of the perceptual world and the self-system are explored along with the concepts of integrity and the fine art of developing an educationally orchestrating self. The next chapter,

"Managing and Mentoring Your Educational Self," looks at how the orchestrating self-monitors the active elements of educational wellness and the development of realistic and positive self-dialogue.

Moving outside of oneself to the realm of working with other people, Chapter 5 is appropriately titled "Leading Others." Since working with others is dialogical (not monological), the dispositions of a dialogical self are examined in terms of developing an inviting stance. This stance is then applied to the craft of inviting. If the craft of inviting makes everything seem simple, the next chapter opens up the complexity of human relationships with the task of providing a strategy for moving from conflict to conciliation. A "Six C" rationale and strategies are offered as a way to handle conflict in a principled and practical way.

Entering the realm of values and knowledge, the next two chapters explore what's worth learning and why, not a minor concern to those working in educational settings. Chapter 7, "Leading for Valued Knowledge," returns to self-concept theory and emphasizes the importance of self-concept-as-learner as a worthwhile goal for education. Learning that one can learn and seeing oneself as a lifelong learner are educational commonplaces. The chapter moves beyond the clichés to the process of mindful learning and disciplinary knowledge. One type of learning that educational leaders need to manage relates to ethical dilemmas, when right versus right issues come to light. A strategy for managing these types of issues is presented in Chapter 8.

Schools can be called "institutions" but we lose much of our educational heart when we do this. With this in mind the next two chapters look at the development of educational communities. Chapter 9 presents the "Inviting Family Model" for schools by contrasting it with the "Efficient Factory Model." What we as educators value plays out in the models we choose to embody in our institutions. Next, since schools are places with people, programs, policies, and processes going on, some principled way needs to be found to manage these "Five Ps." Chapter 10 provides such a strategy along with a way to invite change.

The final two chapters in this section using the LIVES model move the school outside its physical boundary. Chapter 11, "Leading Within and Beyond Schools," looks at deepening democracy through ethical savouring, understanding complexity, and improving human possibilities. Following this, the final chapter in this section offers some practical strategies to take the school outside its usual boundaries in the exploration of social justice locally and globally.

The concluding section of the book, "Dare to Lead for Education," is made up of a summary chapter that looks at what is involved in calling forth and sustaining imaginative acts of hope through speaking the language of inviting. Inviting leaders involved in calling forth and sustaining educational life for themselves and others learn how to care, share, compare, prepare, and dare in an often resistant world. It's not easy, but we think it is a worthwhile way to proceed and it has been put it into creative and sustained practice by educators around the world.

The approach we are presenting in this book is a theory of practice in process and is being further constructed even while this book is being written. The conversations the authors have had about the key concepts of this approach look at educational leadership inside and outside of schools, from those inside and outside of formal leadership designations. Our hope is that you will see the richness and possibilities of an inviting way of thinking about leading, managing, and mentoring for educational life. May the conversations continue. May you be a part of an effort to enrich educational practices and educational lives. Time to read on.

PART 1

EDUCATIONAL LIVES SEEN FROM AN INVITING PERSPECTIVE

EDUCATION MATTERS, REALLY

Education is much more than what happens in schools. As an activating ideal, education can be seen as an imaginative act of hope focused on the possibility of calling forth and sustaining the capacity and inclination to lead flourishing educational lives. Leading is about communicating and orchestrating a compelling vision for developing the rich context for such lives. Managing is about handling the daily challenges of sustaining this collective vision. Mentoring is about constructing relationships to guide understanding and participating on this journey. With this in mind, here are some questions to consider for those who wish to explore their leadership commitments:

Why did you become an educator?

What makes being an educator worthwhile?

How do you orchestrate institutional requirements and educational hopes?

Are you as idealistic about education as you once were?

Because being a lifelong educator is vital for educational leadership, it requires a reflective commitment to developing people, ideas, and adventures. This book is likely to call into question your beliefs if you:

- Think education is synonymous with what happens in schools;
- Feel that there is no hope for hope in education;
- Enjoy being in charge all the time;
- Are counting the days until retirement;
- Would not encourage your children to work in education.

This book is likely to build on your beliefs if you:

- Think education goes beyond schooling;
- Feel that without hope education lacks a sustaining energy;

> ### *About "Yes"*
>
> *I have thought a lot about my leadership path and where it began. Mrs. Carson sat down with me one day and asked me to be the teacher in charge when she was out of the building. I was a second-year teacher, unsure of my competency and cognizant of my place on the established seniority ladder. I wondered how I could possibly lead but recognized I couldn't possibly say no. Not to Mrs. Carson. Her invitation encouraged and inspired a young teacher to think outside of hierarchy and tenure. I said yes. I still can't believe I said yes. Yes was the best thing I ever said. Upon reflection, I realized that Mrs. Carson took a risk, too.*

– Enjoy working with people on co-operative projects;
– Are thinking of new ways to keep growing;
– Would encourage everyone to think about working for educational living.

In their not-so-humbly titled book, *The Truth About Leadership*, James Kouzes and Barry Posner (2010) make the claim that "everything you do as a leader begins with one word: *yes*" (p. 153). Yes, we agree, but with some qualifications. Not just any yes will do. What is required of educators who care about leadership and who are in it for the long run is to find a thoughtful, a defensible, and sustaining, "yes" to affirm. The position taken in this book is that leading, managing, and mentoring in schools in ethically defensible ways is about saying yes to a vision of promoting educational living for oneself and for others in all aspects of life. The idea of living educationally can be a liberating notion for educational leaders as it challenges the fictional supposi-

> ***About the Sustaining Vision of These Authors and This Book***
>
> *Underpinning this book is the idea that education is fundamentally an imaginative act of hope. Leading starts with developing a compelling vision for such hope. Managing involves coordinating the daily details of practice in alignment with this hope. Mentoring calls forth inviting relationships that guide the initiation of others into this evolving embodied hope.*

tion that a school leader should be omnipotent and all knowing. Educational living embraces the educational journey that hopefully never ends. We should always be learning, comforted by the knowledge that we can never know everything, which can be both humbling and empowering. Visions really do matter, even though they can be overhyped and then trivialized. Developed with an attentive integrity, visions point us in desirable directions, influence how we view life's possibilities, and shape habits we use in our daily practices. Artfully orchestrating the processes of leading, managing, and mentoring is a lot to hope for, and, ironically, a lot to hope with. This is a book for anyone who believes that it is desirable to be hopeful about people, ideas, and adventures through educational living. It is also for anyone who is willing to consider this possibility and to think seriously about it and its alternative (i.e., there is little hope for education). If it is true that "Where there is no vision, the people perish" (Proverbs 29:18) it is especially true that without an educational vision schools merely chase and often resent the most recent educational fad and are prone to becoming sites of honed cynicism. Our children, our schools, all of us, deserve better.

WORDS MATTER

This book is focused on these concepts: Leading, Managing, Mentoring, and Educational Lives. Leading, as we see it, is about:

- Developing a shared, hopeful vision that pays attention to the diversity of perspectives in the human community;
- Articulating that vision to a variety of audiences in such a way to pay attention to the aesthetic qualities of unique situations;
- Enrolling participants who can enjoy the process of extending that vision.

Of course there is more to leadership than this, but the vision articulated here forms the base for meeting the *structural, human relations, political,* and *symbolic demands* leaders have to face (Palestini, 2010). For example, leaders have to reach certain goals. *Structural leadership,* as Palestini points out in relating leadership to baseball managers, deals with the wherewithal and rationality necessary for "getting the job done." In the case of baseball managers, this simply means winning baseball games. School leaders who unreflectively accept the status quo will translate structural leadership into the task of raising test scores. That is considered the only game in town. This, however, just stays on the surface of the purposes of educational leadership. A key point of educational leadership, however, is to probe deeper and decide what is the job to be done and how should it be done.

The vision we work from is that the "job" (really the vocation) of educators is about inviting the development of educational lives. This takes us well beyond test scores. In addition, leadership is about working with people. *Human relations* leadership, Palestini (2010) shows, is about productivity through people, developing and managing players so you can win games. For unreflective school leaders who accept the status quo this means deploying your teachers and staff in the right way and making the right moves so the test scores go up. The vision we espouse here goes beyond using people for narrow ends. It involves an ethical commitment to people and developing co-operative relationships for shared growth. People matter, really. In addition, Palestini's baseball managers have to deal with reality, what actually is possible with the resources available. *Political leadership* focuses on honestly facing the reality and constraints of power relationships and the limited availability of resources. Baseball managers have to deal with what they have, not some fantasy league roster. For status quo school leaders this involves using the school's resources in the most effective ways so that test scores can be maximally raised, often working mostly with those who are likely to have the biggest numerical impact. From our perspective, educational leaders realize that being hopeful without being realistic is mere wishful thinking. Our approach is intended to provide a rationale for sharing and growing power while making educational choices in ethically defensible ways. Finally, leaders have to deal with people in their complexity and contradictions. *Symbolic leadership* for Palestini's baseball managers means attending to the intangibles that spur the motivation to carry on during difficult times. School leaders attached to the status quo will try gimmicks to motivate teachers to keep on working for the prescribed ends. The leadership we are promoting is not a one-size-fits-all formula aimed at merely motivating efficiency. Rather, it means to appreciate situations in their uniqueness while working with the ongoing motivation of people to call forth the positive possibilities that can emerge. This means going below the surface and facing life's ambiguities, confusions, and challenges with a creative and caring flair.

Managing, as we see it, is about:

– Making the larger vision a clear and present reality in daily practices;
– Doing good things, in good ways, for good reasons;
– Encouraging the development of self-correcting procedures.

Leading, with its emphasis on the visioning process and looking up, can easily become a very cloudy and dizzying affair. Managing breaks up the clouds by constantly asking the questions: So what? If we commit to a particular educational vision, how will we do things differently? Managing is an attempt to come down to earth without crashing. As John Dewey (1938) noted, moving from a traditional model to a newer model of education does not magically eliminate problems. Rather it gives you a new set of issues to deal with, a new set of challenges to consider. Managing takes seriously these new challenges by seeking to develop structures and activities that embody the spirit of educational living in people's professional and personal lives.

Mentoring, as we see it, is about:

– Extending the leading process;
– Connecting both the mentee and mentor to living educationally;
– Enabling the educational vision to deepen and refresh;
– Engaging the mentor and mentee in the process of constructing a dialogical theory of practice.

Mentoring can be essentially regarded as the transference of wisdom and guidance from the experienced to the rookie. With this in mind, mentoring is the process of building supportive and respectful relationships that guide individuals towards a path of increased understanding of self, role, and context. It is a collaborative process of learning together through different lenses and perspectives. Thus mentorship is a natural extension of the leading and managing processes in that it invites others to participate in the process of learning the art of constructing a vision and developing the principles and practices for managing it. It is also a natural extension of the learning process because it follows the educational adage that the best way to learn something is to have to teach it. Mentoring is a type of invitational teaching that sustains an educational vision.

EDUCATIONAL LIVING MATTERS

Leading for what? Managing how? Mentoring why? These questions naturally flow from a thoughtful reflection on the serious commitments previously implied. Are educational leaders merely to be enthusiastic advocates of the status quo? Is educational management nothing but applying business techniques to schools? Is mentoring simply about someone being coached to become streetwise regarding the workings of the "old boys" network? This may sound cynical but without a clarification of what educational life is, these are difficult questions to answer.

To get to the essence of the issue educators need a generative way of thinking about what education is. We take the perspective that it is important to focus not on the noun "education" but on the adjective "educational." As an adjective, educational describes a particular type of experience, a unique and growing way of coming to grips with life. Essentially, educational experiences are ones that enable people to do the following:

- Savour, or appreciate more of their daily experiences;
- Understand, or learn more about themselves, others, and the world;
- Better, or improve individual and collective life experiences.

In a fast-paced world that is pushing us to do more and more even though we may be finding that we are getting less and less, savouring seems both needed and out-of-place. That is why it is so important from an educational perspective. Savouring deals with the ability to slow down life, to live with eyes wide open, and to appreciate what we are presently engaged in. It provides the affective basis for deciding what experiences need to be extended. John Dewey (1934/1980), in his book *Art as Experience*, pointed out that the opposite of the aesthetic is the anaesthetic, that which numbs us to the world of rich experiences. Anaesthetic experiences are ones in which we merely go through the motions. Really experiencing something, according to Dewey, involves both doing and undergoing, taking an action and attending to its effects in the world and in ourselves. Savouring is what enables us to enjoy sunsets, friendships, travel, reading, and a host of other activities that provide support for understanding and bettering other aspects of our experience.

About Savouring

Out for dinner one night I was surrounded by accountants, CEOs, lawyers, and executives; friends who had, by financial and societal success measures, done very well professionally. The conversation turned to priorities, challenges, and disappointments. Of the eight, three expressed their ambivalence toward their work while the other five openly hated what they did. Four were actively seeking a new job within the same field. I listened quietly, reflecting on my day. As they complained about their bosses, partners, colleagues, team members, and prospects, I savoured the fact that a Grade 3 student came into my office to read me a story he had written, that I played soccer with students at lunch, attended a Grade 5 poetry reading in the afternoon, and connected with parents who were delighted with their children's progress. I savoured as they complained and I resolved to smell the roses more, not only to enjoy but to reflect and refine. Although there are many challenges, I recognize how fortunate I am to go to school every morning.

Increasing understanding is becoming more important as the world is getting more complex and connected. As Walter Truett Anderson (1990) noted, reality isn't what it used to be, things we once took for granted are being seriously challenged. Coming to terms with a more multifaceted and intricate world requires a commitment to intellectual substance and to self-correcting inquiry. If the word "understand" is taken literally, it means "to stand under." As we stand under something we can observe how the parts fit and form a working whole. Understanding, then, is about being able to note important details and connect them to a larger more unifying perspective. It is about becoming more complex in our relationships in the world (Davis & Sumara, 2006) in order to have more possibilities to work with for savouring and bettering our lives and our world we share. That is a lot, but there is more.

Educating is a moral practice because it involves intentionally influencing the lives of people (Starratt, 2004). It is about more than just making people skilful, providing them with technical know-how to function in a fast-paced consumer society, getting them to acquiesce to the status quo. That may make the world move faster but not necessarily better. As a moral practice, educating is meant to make people better. "Bettering," used here as a verb, is about improving the quality of experiences for more and more people. It is about going beyond the status quo in a responsible way. From the perspective of John Dewey (1916), the process of bettering experiences comes from understanding savoured experiences and constructing the means for their continuation and renewal. Our experiences become richer as we enjoy them and explore ways to make them better.

Although we live in what some call postmodern times, times when master narratives that provide definitive notions of right and wrong are being seriously questioned, striving to make a better world, a world where more people can live fulfilling lives, seems like a relatively uncontentious statement. At the very least, it would be hard in a democratic social order to find educators who would want people, as a result of their schooling experiences, to be unable to:

– Learn ways to appreciate and enjoy more of their life experiences;
– Learn how to comprehend more of what is going on around them;
– Learn to develop approaches for improving the quality of individual and collective experiences.

This vision of promoting educational living in schools through savouring, understanding, and bettering human experiences may seem idealistic, but ideals matter when they can be creatively and persistently connected to expanding real possibilities.

IDEALS AND INSTITUTIONS MATTER

The late Neil Postman (1996) noted that schooling without an end will be the end of schooling. By that he meant that those working in schools need to pay attention to the animating forces that direct where their schools are heading, especially in difficult times. Presently there are pressures to run schools more like businesses, with words like "customers," "competition," and "consumerism" emphasized (Norris, 2010). We see this as a diminishing of an educational perspective because:

– Students are not customers but participants in the exploration of ideas and skills;
– Learning is not primarily about competing but co-operating in self-correcting ways;
– Knowledge is not something consumed but is an active and thoughtful relationship to possibilities.

However, in spite of this still very idealistic talk that schools are not businesses, and students, learning, and knowledge are not consumer goods, schools are not the same as education. Schools are societal institutions and education is an ideal. Institutions and ideals can overlap, but each has distinct qualities and purposes. For example, to realize that love is not the same as marriage (but we should work to make it a significant part of marriage) and justice is not the same as law (but we should work to make it a crucial part of the laws we enact), and education is not the same as schools (but we should make it a part of the animating force of schools) is to note the distinction and relationship between ideals and institutions.

Distinctions matter. They can enable us to see differences that make a difference. Making the ideal/institution distinction is not a semantic nicety. It enables us to see that while there are institutional constraints on what we can do in schools, ideals can point us in a direction that moves beyond the status quo and is educationally defensible. Let's explore this further.

Ideals can be seen as experienced and defensible imaginings that serve real functions. Rather than being benign platitudes, ideals can connect with our deepest sense of what is possible and desirable. As an evoking aspiration, an ideal is not a static absolute that is possessed once and for all. Rather, it is an imaginative and lived hypothesis (a creative "what if") that is enriched through our encounters with real situations. In relationship to this book, the ideal of educating is seen as an imaginative act of hope which aims at inviting everyone to be able to savour, understand, and better more of their life experiences. For professional educators, however, this idealizing has to be done with institutional contexts in mind.

As human constructions, institutions such as marriage, the law, and schools, are dynamic forces that have their unique histories, rules, and relationships which have been influenced by political, economic, and social pressures. Schools, as such institutions, are complex entities that are pushed and pulled in many, often contradictory directions. For example, there are pressures on schools to raise test scores, solve deep societal problems, create happy well-adjusted children, among a myriad of other things, and to do this all with copious evidence so that taxpayers will know they are getting the biggest bang for their budgeted buck. However, although institutional cacophony can scatter educators, they still have to regroup in order to deal with what

Postman and Weingartner (1973, pp. 16–27) call the essential functions of schools. In other words, in whatever way a school may do it, it still has to:

- Structure time and activities;
- Define intelligence, worthwhile knowledge, and good behaviour;
- Provide evaluation, supervision, and role differentiation;
- Be accountable to the public;
- Be accountable to the future.

There are a variety of conventions educators can choose to carry out these essential functions. For example, some schools might have eight periods a day, have specialist teachers, and promote online learning as their most worthwhile intelligence. Other schools may have an integrated curriculum, longer periods, and focus on cooperative learning as their most worthwhile intelligence. The point is that although conventions may vary, some conventions will have to be used. What is important is that the conventions chosen are educationally defensible and practically workable to insure a defensible direction and successful implementation. Educational defensibility and workability involves the orchestration of ideals and conventions, infusing the ethically imagined with the necessary workings of the school.

ORCHESTRATING IDEALS AND CONVENTIONS MATTER

So here is the situation. Educational leaders have to artfully coordinate educational ideals and school conventions in such a way that it is not overwhelming or underwhelming. A situation is overwhelming if:

- Ideals are out-of-touch with institutional realities;
- Ideals are seen as mere verbal wordplay;
- Conventions go on as usual even if the ideals espouse change.

The point here is that if ideals are seen to belong to another world, they will be treated as such and ignored in this world. Out-of-touch ideals may touch off some occasional guilt feelings but will usually be ignored in the day-to-day workings of the school. Think in terms of New Year's Resolutions. An overly ambitious plan is easily ignored after a short period of time. Health clubs are usually crowded in early January but things return to normal a short time later.

On the other hand, the ideal/convention relationship can be underwhelming if:

- Ideals do not extend the ethical imagination of those involved;
- Ideals are seen as merely enthusiastic activators for the status quo;
- Ideals and conventions are both frozen in time.

Ideals that do not get us to reach higher, to build on that which challenges us to think beyond the present, have the effect of putting us on cruise control. Schools that operate at this level can be said to be "rusting" on their laurels. They put their status in the status quo. People get locked into the ideas that "this is as good as it gets" and they stop working at getting better. They are sinking into complacency and may never know it.

In order to lead change, it is important to connect with others to determine what is already being done well, see how it can be extended or added to, and collectively articulate where we are going and why. The status quo is both easy and stifling. The unrealistic idea is fantasy. People do great things. It is important as a leader to recognize, highlight, and utilize those great things by orchestrating the appropriate level of "whelm."

A situation is whelming if:

- There is a healthy tension between ideals and conventions;
- The ideal prompts movement in a desired direction;
- The conventions are self-correcting in unexpected ways.

The tension between ideals and conventions works best when the ideals build on imaginative extensions of that which we have found to be educationally worthwhile. Ideals return us to what brought us into education in the first place and add a savvied understanding of institutional realities to help us build a more sustainable goal to pursue. As Robert Nozick (1989) noted, an ideal is a pragmatic tool and should not be judged on whether we attain it, but whether it moves us in a direction we consider ethically worthwhile. Thus an ideal should stretch us but not break us. The ideal of educational living should also be seen in comparison with other operational ideals.

COMPARISONS MATTER

Richard Rorty (1989), a leading philosopher of the last part of the 20th century, pointed out that when discussing of beliefs, it is of limited conversational and social value to say, "I believe this and it is true." For Rorty, such remarks are show stoppers; they end a conversation. What can you add if someone says they have "THE TRUTH" on their side? Rather, Rorty suggests, it is more productive in a conversation to say, "I see it this way. What are the alternatives?" Following his lead, let us return to educational ideals and examine some alternatives to the vision of leading, managing, and mentoring for educational lives.

Neil Postman (1996), in his seminal book on education, *The End of Education*, makes the provocative claim that, "Without a narrative, life has no meaning.

> ### *About Whelm and Change*
>
> *As an educational leader, I need to be in touch with whelm and change. Changes seem to come so quickly in education. New initiatives, programs, expectations, and policies arrive from the board and the Ministry and are expected to be implemented into practice immediately. I need to be a better gatekeeper to be more in tune with stress to manage and mitigate the possibility of overwhelming staff. Having a vision and direction articulated at the outset of the year helps me maintain focus, even in the face of competing priorities that seem to arrive on a regular basis.*

11

Without meaning, learning has no purpose. Without a purpose, schools are houses of detention, not attention" (p. 7). In doing so, he is strongly asserting the importance of a guiding vision, an activating educational ideal for directing the activities of schools. The four ideals he presents and critiques are as follows:

- Economic Utility
- Consumership
- Technology
- Tribalship

Looking at these ideals as conversation starters, there is much that can be said, pro and con. These ideals are related, but each represents an important narrative about people's aspiration and education. *Economic utility* is about obtaining and keeping a job, with its emphasis on job training. Although there is something to the statement attributed to Mae West, "Rich or poor, it's good to have money," this vision of the purpose of schools sees their primary role as fitting people into the present economic system. Postman's (1996) critique of this vision is that it reduces people to what they do for a living. A democratic society seeks and needs more for and from its citizens. The emphasis on *consumership* in the second ideal tells the story that people are what they consume, with an emphasis on the bumper sticker wisdom, "Whoever has the most toys when he dies, wins." Of course we need to consume to survive, but the reduction of people to their accumulations seems short sighted, at the least. In a world with limited resources and great disparity among people, encouraging limitless consumption is merely exacerbating some of the worst aspects of the status quo. Michael Sandel (2012) points out the social importance of understanding *What Money Can't Buy.* Next, the ideal of *technology*

> ### *About Leading an Educational Life*
>
> *Leading an educational life creates an excitement for learning. As the principal, I am the lead learner in the community when I am taking courses, savouring conferences, and supporting and encouraging others to engage in learning opportunities. I love when parents ask me how my course work is going or when I speak with students about a paper or an assignment I am working on. Speaking with staff about engaging in learning opportunities or writing letters of reference for parents who are applying to teacher's college or masters programs are the fruits of leading an educational life. My active engagement in ongoing learning sustains and encourages others to do so. Staff members or parents going back to school or seeking various educational opportunities foster an educational culture that becomes infectious. It is exciting for students to realize that we're committed to lifelong learning together—students, teachers, parents, and the principal. The absolute joy is that it never stops!*

emphasizes running full-speed with the information-processing frenzy. Of course very interesting and amazing things are happening in the "information revolution." But is more better and is something important in the face-to-face connection of people being lost to inter-face to inter-faceness? Interestingly, in the last century Marshall McLuhan noted that we are at risk of merely becoming the sexual organs of our technology. Who is serving what becomes more than a speculative question. Finally, *tribalship* becomes an ideal because some groups are being over-ridden by an ever-expanding dominant culture. It is important to develop a voice to participate in the larger culture and some separation may be necessary at times (Kymlicka, 1998). The limitation of this perspective is that people are seen only as members of a subculture, which is often claimed to be a superior culture. This can have an isolating impact on individuals and groups.

We see each of these visions providing short-term incentives for some but lacking the deeper-seated educational purposes that unite people in their uniqueness and social responsibility. Each of these purposes is limited because it looks outside of educational experience for an end for schooling. Educational experiences are the beginning and end of the perspective we are advocating. We take the point of view that if you really want to get more out of experiences, it is necessary to get more into experiences. An emphasis on educational experiences is an emphasis on the types of experience that enable us to savour, understand, and better more of our own and others' experiences. Educational experiences are intrinsically valuable and provide the basis for continued growth. Developing, using, and growing through the habits of savouring, understanding, and bettering more and more of our experiences is what we mean by the pursuit of educational living. We build on the assumption that this educative impulse exists in all people and provides a valuational basis for all that goes on in schools. This is lot, but is it too much?

The pursuit of educational living provides an aesthetic, cognitive, and moral direction, but not the specific details for developing a shared educational ideal. It is a starting point and returning point for extended conversations and should be seen as a work in progress. Ideals work like that. They are not fully attainable ends but experiential, intellectual, and ethical means for pointing us towards living a more fulfilling life. From the point of view of John Dewey (1938), the best way to prepare to live educationally in the future is to work to live an educational life in the present. For educational leaders, educational living is not something to be delayed. It is the present grounding for future take-offs.

It is the work of educational leading to orchestrate conditions so that the educative impulse to savour, understand, and better more experiences can come to life. It is the work of educational managing to provide the self-correcting structures to stay on track. It is the work of educational mentoring to invite more people to participate in sustaining this educational vision. This has never been easy but it is even more difficult in an often fragmented world that cries for, but is suspicious of, unifying themes.

Working with the goal of educational living as a unifying educational ideal has a better chance of succeeding if it is seen for what it is: An attempt to increase the educational quality not only for students but for all involved with schooling (teachers, support staff, administrators, parents, community members, and others). Obviously, this is not an easy task and can, without much of a stretch of the imagination, be seen as overwhelming. Finding the right whelm level, orchestrating the celebration of successes while still keeping sight of the continuing challenges, is made manageable with the use of a heuristic structure for focusing efforts.

STRUCTURES MATTER

Educational leading, managing, and mentoring, as described in this book, are different from their counterparts in other contexts (business, non-governmental agencies, social services) in two ways. First, each (leading, managing, and mentoring) gets its momentum from the appeal of the desirability of the ideal of educational living. If we are right or at least on the right track, everyone has an educative impulse that can be tapped. If this educative impulse can be tapped, there is a basis for general agreement about educational directions and possibilities. Second, although educating is more than schooling, schools are envisioned as important institutions for educational aims. It would seem hard to find someone who in good faith would say that schools should not be educational. That would be like someone saying that marriage should not be about love or law should not be about justice. Institutions not vitally connected to their guiding ideals are a sham. For the ideal of educational living to be a reality in schools, educators willing to move in this direction need to be the following:

- Students (curious and attentive learners);
- Leaders (credible and informed developers);
- Managers (imaginative and determined strategists);
- Mentors (wise and informed guides).

This is a lifelong vocation that can be made manageable by using a heuristic structure based on the vital relationships an educator enters into everyday in schools. Heuristic here refers to a guiding framework that should spark individual insights. Viewed from a relational view of what is happening in schools, the process of educating involves a person or persons interacting with others so that something of value is learned. These relationships can be captured through the L.I.V.E.S. model which involves the following five relationships:

- **Lived** world (Subjective relationships with oneself and one's life possibilities);
- **Individuals** (Interpersonal relationships which function to call forth the potential of others);
- **Values and Knowledge** (Epistemological relationships with the veracity and significance of what is to be learned);

- Educational community (Institutional relationships with a school's conventional functions);
- Society (Ethical relationships with the creation of a more inclusive and flourishing social order).

These interactions occur in an institutional arrangement and are intended to advance a preferred type of social order. Connecting this generative framework to the vision of educational living, the relationships of educating involve a person, someone who has a subjectivity, who possesses a *Lived* world of memories, beliefs, and aspirations; working with unique *Individuals* in ethically defensible ways; so that *Values* and knowledge are examined, learned, and expanded; within an *Educational* community that is caring and self-correcting; and that is geared to promoting a *Society* that is just and flourishing. With some degree of prosaic licence these five relationships (LIVES) provide the basis for leading, managing, and mentoring educational lives from an inviting perspective (Chapters 3–10). However, before we go into that and the next chapter which introduces the inviting perspective for educational leadership, here are some questions and answers that can occur in a mentoring relationship regarding key points of this chapter:

MENTORING CONVERSATIONS

Q: What makes this conversation a mentoring relationship?
We are encouraging you to start to think about how things should be and how they can be and what role you can play in the process. As mentors, we want you to take a reflective approach to your current leadership, celebrate what you do well, and consider what you could do even better. We know you have reservations and potentially a very strong sense of the way things should be that might be based on the way things have always have been. We think there is more potential than the status quo suggests, and recognize that inviting leadership calls forth human potential in ways the status quo has never considered. We think, in fact we know that you are capable, talented, and interested in becoming an even better version of you so that others will become better versions of themselves.

Q: Isn't it too idealistic to have ideals?
We tend to not buy into the notion that there is a binary between ideals and reality, as if ideals are fantasy and reality is bleak. Ideals are grounded in the reality of contemporary schools, or at least they should be. The alternative to having an ideal is to be reactionary, simply lobbing back volleys as they come at you in the order they arrive. Leaders without strong ideals tend to move from situation to situation, reacting rather than using forward thinking. Having ideals means developing and articulating a vision not only of how things *should* be but how things *can* be. An ideal is something to strive toward. We should have a good idea of where we are going before we start the journey and certainly along the way. A leader plays a large role in the creation of collective ideals. To have ideals as an individual is important, and to have them as a leader who is able to share them with others who will work toward the same goal is even more so.

15

Q: Isn't there too much philosophizing in this chapter?
Perhaps. However, we think ideas matter and we enjoy considering how they influence action. We don't buy into the concept of the inert philosopher sitting on a rock pondering life's great mysteries inside his or her head any more than we would suppose that those who accomplish tremendous things do so with blinders on and a blank mind. Ideas matter because they influence action. Action matters because it influences ideas. This ongoing consideration is a dance that we are interested in pursuing and believe that reflective leaders should as well. If wisdom is found at the intersection of knowledge and experience, we would submit that it is the thoughtful reflection upon experience which informs knowledge and leads to wisdom.

Q: Will this approach work where I work?
An inviting approach to leadership is less about the context in which you work and more about you. That is what makes it so simple yet so challenging to live. Change is hard for most people and dismissing potentially important ideas is a great strategy to maintain the status quo and never have to change. We hear this all the time: "Sounds great in theory, but that could never work in the (insert: low income, middle income, high income, suburban, rural, urban, primary school, middle school, high school, university, social housing, etc.) area where I work." An inviting approach does not require a big staff meeting to rally your team before you can begin. It does not require promotional material, banners, or a press release. It does not require the blessing of your school board or district nor does it involve signing up to be part of a large group or organization. It can begin with simply opening your door and inviting people in. It can begin with the intentional consideration of the furniture in your office. It can begin with a smile and see where that leads you. It is not about finding the right context in which this approach to leadership will work; instead, it is about leading the change in whatever context you are in.

THE INVITING PERSPECTIVE

For an approach to take hold in schools it needs to resonate with an educator's deepest intuitions, provide a defensible intellectual position, and lead to creative and ethical practices. That's a lot to ask for but the inviting perspective aims to be an appealing, coherent, and useful theory of practice by focusing on the quality, consistency, and direction of the messages that are sent, with the aim of making schools places that intentionally call forth educational living for all involved.

How important is it to have a coherent perspective to work from?

Are immediate results the only things that matter in today's schools?

When you get down to it, is it really only "My way or the highway?"

Is it possible for all people to matter?

Because of the emotional, intellectual, and ethical commitment to be in education for the long run, these are important questions that need to be continually revisited to keep democratic and socially just practices alive. This chapter is likely to call your beliefs into question if you:

– Would prefer to work with things rather than people;
– Think leadership is really only about accountability for test results;
– Do not like having to explain your position on ethical issues;
– Feel that only some people really matter.

This chapter is likely to build on your beliefs if you:

– Find ways to enjoy working with people;
– Think in terms of linking means and ends;
– Grow through helping create mutual purposes;
– Are both activated and daunted by the belief that all people matter.

LEADING WITH INTEGRITY

Being an educational leader in the 21st century means facing conflicting demands and an infinite number of ways to be vulnerable. Lacking an integrated framework to operate from, it is easy to be pushed and pulled in incompatible directions. A thought-out integrated framework can provide educational integrity, a coherent and defensible position to operate from. Erik Erikson (1980), a key developmental psychologist of the 20th century, pointed out the tension between integrity and despair in the last stage of human development. If integrity wins out, a person's life has come together in a meaningful way, parts connect, and a depth and richness can be celebrated. If this does not occur, despair sets in because life has become Henry Ford's notion of history: "One damn thing after another," where a shallow fragmented existence is, at best, tolerated. Educators need the meaningful interactions to construct vibrant and coherent lives that seek integrity.

Having a consistent, coherent, and defensible position to operate from is important for all educational leaders. While some educational leaders may begin their tenures comfortable and confident, most do so unsure and afraid, suffering from a psychological phenomenon called the "impostor syndrome" in which individuals question their competency and ability to perform their role in relation to their perception of external expectations and impositions (Clance & Imes, 1978; Ferrari & Thompson, 2006). The impostor syndrome is grounded in the fear of failure and a lack of confidence (Kumar & Jagacinkski, 2006) and feelings of incompetence and self-doubt (Armstrong, 2009). Age, race, and gender can exacerbate these negative self-perceptions and can contribute to feeling unqualified for leadership. One of the authors began her tenure as a school leader as one of the first black principals in her school district while another of the authors became a school principal relatively young, 14 years younger than the provincial average. They experienced feelings of inadequacy and incompetence as well as a strong desire to fit in and to prove themselves as effective leaders. Relying on an integrated and ethically defensible leadership framework for making decisions contributed to the mitigation of feelings of incompetency and allowed them to answer to their internal prosecutors.

To operate with educational integrity is to work from a position that consistently integrates the whole person's:

- Feelings: What you are doing should connect with your deepest intuitions and emotions about what is meaningful, right, and important. Educators who cannot trust their deepest feelings get blown away and torn apart by the frantic present. Educators who do not step back and examine their deepest feelings, however, run the risk of becoming locked into knee-jerk responses.
- Thoughts: What you are doing should make sense and be able to be clearly articulated to different audiences. Educators who cannot speak to their deepest intuitions and school practices in an understandable and cogent manner run the risk of merely babbling to an inattentive audience of one or less.
- Practice: What you are doing should lead to imaginative and sustaining acts of hope. Educators who do not put their deepest feelings and thoughts into practice lose connection to both and are in danger of becoming divided and despairing in their work. They lose out in the long run and probably do not even do that well in the short run.

This chapter introduces the inviting perspective as a framework for leading, managing, and mentoring with integrity.

PERSPECTIVES ON PERSPECTIVES

Being a professional educator involves a commitment to people, ideals, and actions. People are to be appreciated in their uniqueness, and seen as evolving meaning makers in an ever more complex world. Ideals, as defensible guideposts, are the means to sustain positive direction and growth. Leading, managing, and mentoring that are anchored by a hopeful, reflective, action-oriented ideal have a much better chance to call forth and sustain imaginative acts of hope. The inviting perspective, made explicit in a school movement called Invitational Education (Purkey & Novak, 1996), offers an approach to integrating feelings, thoughts, and actions in an ethically defensible way

Invitational Education is an integrated system of insights, assumptions, concepts, and strategies for creating, sustaining, and enhancing truly welcoming and equitable schools. Centred on the conviction that the educative process is not a doing *to* process of technical manipulation but an ethical practice of doing *with* people, the inviting approach aims to call forth human potential to live educational lives. Schools are seen as message systems that send out positive and negative interpretive possibilities to others. These *"signal systems"* can be used to "summon forth the realization of human potential, and to identify and change those forces that defeat and destroy potential" (Smith, 2012, p. 3). The intention of invitational educators is to work together to create educational contexts in which people want to learn and want to be.

Any approach to working with people involves assumptions about what is important and how things work together. The inviting perspective, as an evolving theory of educative practice, is centred on the following five interlocking assumptions (Purkey & Novak, 1996, p. 3):

1. People are valuable, able, and responsible and should be treated accordingly.
2. Educating should be a collaborative and co-operative activity.
3. The process is the product in the making.
4. People possess untapped potential in all areas of worthwhile endeavour.
5. This potential can best be realized by places, policies, programs, and processes specifically designed to invite development and by people who are intentionally inviting to themselves and others, personally and professionally.

Assumptions without further examination run the risk of becoming mere romantic rhetoric or dogmatic drudgery. Because education is filled with pleasant-sounding unexplored slogans, it is important to look deeper into these assumptions.

Smith (2012) describes Invitational Education as an evolving theory of educational practice and a call to action. This means that it has grown from a focus on classrooms (Purkey, 1978), to looking at whole school environments (Purkey & Novak, 1984), to connecting with the world outside schools (Purkey & Novak, 1996), to providing principles and examples of ethically related online education (DiPetta, Novak, & Marini, 2002), and most recently to educational institutions around the world (Novak, Rocca, & DiBiase, 2006). The project of advancing, testing, and revising Invitational Education has come about as educators have put into practice, evaluated, and modified its key ideas. That is how a theory works. It is a way of thinking about a phenomenon, an aspect of existence, and articulating its underlying logic (Fairfield, 2012). In the case of Invitational Education, that phenomenon is how the communicative process influences the development of human potential. Following the thinking of Alasdair McIntyre (1981), a practice is a socially valued activity which contains its own standards of excellence that need to be maintained and extended for acceptable conduct to proceed and develop. An educational theory of practice, then, is a way of thinking about that which is intrinsic to the act of intentionally calling forth human potential to savour, understand, and better individual and collective experiences; it is a guide for inviting educational leadership.

For any theory to operate, it needs to make assumptions. As Wilfrid Sellars (1997) has noted regarding the Myth of the Given, there are no immaculate perceptions when it comes to theorizing or metatheorizing. Any theory, small or large, is mediated by implicit notions of what is real, important, good, and desirable. Theoretical constructs are not a given but a taken; that is, a theory is a heuristic framework imposed on experience in order to make it more understandable. The inviting perspective is no exception.

The inviting perspective focuses on the desirability of educational living. In assuming that all people possess ability, value, and responsibility (Assumption 1), the inviting perspective is an ethical way of communicating for the purpose of calling forth people to acknowledge the responsibility to work towards the development of human potential in respectful ways. People are not to be seen as objects to be shaped or as parts of groups to be recultured, but rather are to be viewed as human beings worthy of appreciation who are capable of understanding more about life and possessing the ability to make lives better.

> ### About the Collaborative and Cooperative Nature of the Educational Process
>
> *As a principal, I learned to embrace opportunities to highlight and build upon collaboration and cooperation within the school. I believed this could both encourage engagement by staff and parents. I took advantage of Curriculum Night each year for this purpose. Instead of simply identifying each staff member and role in the school, I purposefully shared the contributions each made to the school by publicly recognizing the often amazing ways in which each staff member gave to the community. The sum of the parts was exposed for both staff and parents to appreciate as staff members were recognized for their contributions and parents came to understand how the school was able to offer everything they were able to. A learning community does not happen by accident. By showcasing the contributions of staff members, I invited and challenged the parents to contribute their time and talents too.*

A teacher may meet with students individually to find out about them, their families, their hopes and dreams for the year and beyond, recognizing that there is no abstract "class," but rather a collection of unique, talented, capable, and, at times, mysterious, individuals. A school leader can do the same. Taking the time with staff members to connect and find out more about their lives, professional and personal goals, and hopes for the year and the future invites collective contributions to the school. Understanding what each staff member brings to the school from personal passions and talents to personal situations informs how each can contribute.

From the inviting perspective, people are not to be seen as isolated entities but instead need to be conceived as interconnected and intertwined persons in the process of constructing educational lives. Building on the collaborative and co-operative nature of the educational process (Assumption 2), the inviting process focuses on the dialogical nature of existence and the necessity to build doing *with* rather than doing *to* relationships. Ethically, people are not objects to be done *to* or done *for* but partners in the process of creating doing *with* relationships. Quite simply, people need to be emotionally and ethically involved in their life-relationships in order to have meaningful lives.

The idea that the process is the product in the making (Assumption 3) is the acknowledgement that what you do lives on in what follows. As John Dewey (1938) noted, means and ends are vitally connected. What you do and how you do it are both a part of the future that is being created in the present. Stated another way, present actions have future consequences. If this is the case, present ends become future means for later ends. And the process continues.

Sometimes leadership is described as being able to make tough decisions. However, the way in which the decision is made can be more important than the decision itself. Leadership is about relationships and relationships are based on shared values and priorities. Establishing leadership practices that make decisions which are consistently and defensibly person-centric can make the decision-making process simpler. Decisions made from a person-centric perspective establish an ethical foundation which can be respected by staff, parents, and students.

Realizing that there is much potential to be tapped (Assumption 4) is a recognition that people can become much more than they presently are. This is the basis for the belief in growth, the idea that each individual is only a small part of what he or she can become intellectually, emotionally, physically, socially, and morally. The process of connecting with the energies and interests of people through engagement with desirable social projects is the means to realize more of this potential. Educational hope is an energetic openness to, and pursuit of, these possibilities (Shade, 2001).

This energetic openness to the possibilities of appreciation and growth is seen in the realization that schools can be viewed as systems that can intentionally call forth human potential (Assumption 5). Just as everyone and everything in hospitals should be encouraging healing, so too everyone and everything in schools should be promoting educational development. Environments are not neutral, and neither are the people who inhabit them. People and places, among other things, are continually sending messages that are received, interpreted, and acted upon in the present and the future.

MEANINGFUL MESSAGES

Educational assumptions run the risk of becoming stale analytical lists of abstract thoughts if they are not linked to an activating metaphor, a way of imagining that brings ideas together. Building on the practice of inviting people to participate in a worthwhile activity, the following core definition of an invitation is offered to provide a unit of analysis for the communicative process:

> An invitation is the summary of the content of messages communicated verbally and non-verbally, formally and informally through people, places, policies, programs, and processes. Inviting messages inform people that they are valuable, able, and responsible and can behave accordingly.

At the school level, invitations are communicated by the way people greet one another; by the signs and pictures on the walls; by the rules and who makes them; by what is taught, how and when it is taught; by which students are placed in which classes; and by the spirit in which things are done. Messages in schools are both unique and ubiquitous and are integral to the formal and hidden curriculum. Attending to the quality and quantity of messages which call forth and those which shun human potential is vital in leading, managing, and mentoring. It provides educators with a framework to describe the communication process in their schools, a theoretical structure to explain that framework, and practical strategies for creating places where people want to be educated. This is just the tip of the iceberg. It is time to go below the surface and look at the ethical, psychological, and pedagogical foundations which provide grounding for this perspective.

LIVING FOUNDATIONS

The inviting approach is a part of a larger ethical project that attempts to promote human fulfillment. It is not neutral when it comes to what people are and what they can become. It takes a stand by seeing each person as having worth and needing to be given real opportunities to grow. In order to be applied in consistent and creative ways, its three interlocking foundations need to be examined:

1. Democratic Ethos: A commitment to the proposition that all people matter and individuals and communities have a right to participate meaningfully in deciding the guiding principles that control their lives.
2. Perceptual Tradition: A psychological and anthropological perspective that looks at events from the internal point of view of each person.
3. Self-Concept Theory: A model of human functioning that sees people as internally motivated as they attempt to maintain, protect, and enhance their self-system.

22

Each of these foundations can be viewed as a part of the larger project of inviting all people to lead educational lives.

Democratic Ethos

Democracy, as a social ideal, is much more than voting for representatives in public elections. Public elections are merely conventions of a deeper underlying ideal: that all people matter and can meaningfully participate in their self-rule. This participation, as John Dewey (1916) noted, is educative because people grow as they work to understand and appreciate the perspectives of others and learn to think more imaginatively and deeply about the consequences of social actions.

Democratic community and social justice are important concerns for theorists and practitioners due to glaring economic and academic gaps between dominant and minoritized students, growing pluralism, and the need to prepare all students to participate in democratic processes (Furman & Shields, 2005). It is easy to say that all people matter, but it is much easier in practice to favour the ones who are close to us, similar to us, whose power we seek to influence, or who we are naturally attracted to. The democratic ethos works to counter this tendency not merely through moral pronouncement, but more importantly, through the attempt to perceive more of our common humanity and fundamental connectedness. This ambitious inclusion project is made real, for example, as we see films which portray the richness and depth of peoples' lives that are very different from us, people with whom we would not ordinarily make contact. This project is made real by interacting with and working to understand people from different parts of our schools and communities, and by visiting places we would ordinarily not go. This project is made real by attempting to understand the consequences of our lifestyles on people throughout the world, something that we would often do not wish to consider. A school that

> ### *About Democratic Practice*
>
> *I learned about the democratic practice from a principal in a troubled part of Northern Ireland. When this school principal in Belfast was invited to the President of the Republic of Ireland's official residence to talk about the cross-community programs and projects that were taking place at his school, he insisted on bringing representatives from the entire staff. He hired a bus and invited everyone to join: teachers, parents, community leaders, educational assistants, and secretaries. He could have gone by himself and accepted accolades on behalf of the school but that would not have recognized the contributions of all. They saw themselves as a team. Anything that was accomplished was done so together. The democratic ethos was rich in this school and I will never forget the principal's actions in making that ethos real.*

23

promotes deliberative dialogue, inclusive respect, and social justice is working in harmony with the democratic ethos.

Evolving notions of democratic community based on Dewey's work are described as "the practice of deep democracy in schools, involving participation in deep democratic processes by all members of the school in the interest of the common good (Furman & Shields, 2005, p. 122). Deep here refers to going beyond the practice of merely voting to the process of learning to understand the underlying aspirations of all involved.

The Perceptual Tradition

If democracy emphasizes the social importance of all people and communities, the perceptual tradition provides a perspective for understanding the personal viewpoint of each individual. Rather than looking at people from the outside in, as objects to be inspected, the perceptual tradition looks at people from the inside out, as persons seeking meaning. From this point of view, at the moment of behaviour each person is doing what makes the most sense to him or her. There is no illogical behaviour when looking from the internal perspective. If, at the moment of behaviour, a person knew better, he or she would do better. A perspective that seeks to understand rather than blame others allows educators to come to terms with the meaningfulness of a person's actions and the seemingly illogical behaviour they may first perceive.

The educational axiom that we should seek first to understand and then be understood builds on the perceptual tradition. Understanding people from the inside out requires empathy, respect, and imagination. It amounts to reading behaviour backwards. Thinking in terms of the supposition, "What must a person be perceiving to be doing this now?" enables an "outsider" to move beyond his or her self-centredness to the realm of understanding others. In doing so, dialogical possibilities are opened and shared understandings can be constructed. Failing to empathically interpret others can result in misunderstanding, maladjustment, and continual conflict. In addition, appreciating the personal importance of a person's need

About Perception

My nephew was entering kindergarten and his parents were considering a special program for the next year. They called the principal and asked if there was a convenient time to come into the school to discuss the programs. She asked if she could answer their questions over the phone. When they asked about the two programs, she replied that curriculum information was available on the Ministry's website. My brother and sister-in-law felt disinvited—their questions were unwelcome. The questions might have been routine for the principal, but I knew by my brother's reactions that an opportunity to invite a new young family to contribute to the life of the school was lost.

for a stable worldview enables an educator to understand that often people are following the First Law of Rock Climbing: They do not let go of what they have a secure grasp of until they have a firm grasp of something else. Resistance to change or mere superficial adjustments are the usual results of those who ignore this need for grounding and secure alternatives. This perceptual tradition is most evident in looking at the core of a person's perceptual world.

Self-Concept Theory

If perceptions are people's psychological reality, their most intimate reality is their self-concept, the personal picture they maintain, protect, and enhance of who they are and how they fit into the world. This personal picture is a complex set of beliefs about what matters, how it matters, and why it matters about one's existence and is manifested when people use words such as "I," "me," "mine," or "my." So much of contemporary society is centred on the individual. The most popular forms of entertainment, technology, and media are focused on "I." The *i*Pod, *i*Pad, and *i*Phone do not have "I" in front of them by accident. Similarly, *my* family, *my* friends, *my* school, *my* country, and *my* future refer to valued relationships. The site that arguably started the social media frenzy was aptly titled MySpace. The sellers of technology ignore the personal at their own peril. Self-concept theory goes beyond the fashionably personal to the core of a person's identity.

From the point of view of self-concept theory, human motivation comes from within each person, not in the sense that if a person works at it he or she can motivate himself, but in the sense that each person is continually motivated to maintain, protect, and enhance his or her self beliefs. Good teaching, leading, and mentoring begin from the inside out, working with students' and staff's strengths and acknowledging where people are in terms of their knowledge, beliefs, and aspirations, their motivational groundwork. If this is true, educators do not have to motivate people but should shift their efforts to work with the natural energy operating within each person. Often when someone says that others are unmotivated what he or she is saying is that these others do not want to do what the person wants them to do. This is not a motivation problem but a compliance problem. Human energy and motivation are always there, even when they are noncompliant. If people were unmotivated, they would not be able to do anything, even provide resistance. Not having to worry about motivation enables an educator to work with others to overcome obstacles and proceed in a mutually positive direction. Not having to worry about motivation enables an educator to focus on inviting others to lead educational lives.

WORKING WITH INVITATIONS

A key component of invitational theory is that people are never neutral in their interactions with others. As Abraham Maslow (1968) noted, we are either forces for psychotherapy or forces for psychopathology. From the inviting perspective, we are

25

continually sending messages. Everything we do and every way we do it either calls forth or shuns human potential. The messages that are being sent and the resolve with which they are being sent can be viewed according to a four-level classification system for making sense of the communicative process of a school. Seen as a starting point for conversations, messages can be classified as:

— Intentionally Disinviting: Done with the purpose of diminishing another's sense of worth.
— Unintentionally Disinviting: Done without resolve but having the effect of diminishing another's sense of worth.
— Unintentionally Inviting: Done without resolve but having positive effects.
— Intentionally Inviting: Done on purpose for purposes that encourage another's sense of flourishing.

Intentionally Disinviting

Intentionally disinviting messages are offences of commission and omission. They are meant to put people in their place, and that place is not meant to be a location where any self-respecting person wants to be. Disinviting messages may be explicitly or implicitly communicated at the individual, system, and societal levels and they can be overt and covert. One of the authors still recalls her humiliation when her French teacher announced loudly in front of the class, "You would will never amount to anything." When she became an administrator, she was often shocked to receive similar reports from students and parents regarding overtly disparaging remarks. A particularly distressing case was a teacher who wrote on the report card of a student with learning disabilities, "This student is trying. Very trying." These psychologically toxic messages are intended to degrade and debase a person's sense of self and possibility by having that person see herself as incapable, worthless, or irresponsible. Aimed at taking the heart out of people, intentionally disinviting messages communicate, sometimes with subtlety and indirection, that some people are not to be included among those worthy of esteem. Often these elitist messages can be classified as racist, sexist, homophobic, or just plain cruel. Disinviting messages are also deeply embedded within taken-for-granted school structures and processes. Although metaphors such as community and family are commonly used to describe schools, schools are often structured as pyramids and not all people are welcome. Many hierarchical arrangements systematically reinforce disinviting messages that exclude

> **_About Disinviting_**
>
> *The first time I insisted on educational assistants (EAs) joining a case meeting, my hand was slapped. "EAs should not be at the table for these meetings," I was told. "Information presented will be shared with them as appropriate." Excluding a staff member who was intimately involved in the education of a student made no sense to me.*

staff, students, and parents from everyday processes that affect their daily lives and future possibilities. Case conferences in schools and social work bring together parents, teachers, speech and language, physical, and occupational therapists, and other professionals in support of students with various unique learning needs. These meetings are ostensibly set up to communicate with stakeholders and to benefit students. However, even at the high school levels, students are seldom included in these meetings. In her role as a principal, one of the authors insisted that students, irrespective of their (dis)ability, be part of these discussions and that their parents or guardians be invited or contacted for input. If we are going to be a community of learners committed to student success, insisting on standing on formality by imposing a hierarchy that excludes someone committed to the students' education is counterintuitive. We all have so much to contribute as part of our community of learners.

Obviously such messages can have an immediate and lasting negative effect on the person on the receiving end. However, another problem that lives on with the sender of the messages and the culture of the school in which such messages are transmitted is the justification of such negative practices. This justification sets the stage for such messages to be sent over and over. Ethically, the authors of this book do not see how such lethal messages can be justified. Intentionally disinviting messages contribute to student disengagement, failure, push out, and drop out. Cruelty should not be an accepted part of schooling. A lack of self-confidence by an educator can manifest itself in an approach to leadership that is reliant on external authority and compliance measures such as intrusive rules and micromanaged policies. In many cases blind rule following can lead to discriminatory practices that impact disenfranchised individuals and communities negatively. For example, a principal in an economically disadvantaged area refuses to let the kindergarten parents enter the school in the mornings with their children. When questioned about this practice she responded that her school needed to break the bond between the child and the parent because poor and immigrant parents had little to contribute to their children's education. However, intentionally disinviting messages need to be understood so that patterns and contexts in which they occur can be recognized and changed. If educators are unwilling to change, schools have the legal and ethical responsibility to remove them from contact with students.

I Am Intentionally Disinviting When...

- I use hierarchical position to reinforce institutional inequities.
- I use personal and role power to diminish and devalue others who are different from me.
- I enforce and create rules and processes that intentionally disadvantage and hurt others.
- I communicate orally and in writing with parents and students, and members of their community are unwelcome.
- I communicate despair rather than hope.
- I support deficit discourses that reinforce social injustices.

Here's what an intentionally disinviting perspective might look like:

I believe that the hierarchy within an organization is what contributes to the effectiveness of the organization. People need to know where they fit into the grand scheme of things and more often than not it requires them to be reminded of their place within the group. When I became principal, I was entrusted with the most important of all roles which is the effective running of a school. I worked hard to get to where I am. I took courses, extra degrees, and worked in the classroom and that has afforded me the opportunity to make decisions as the head of the school. My decisions are based on my experiences and my solid judgment and are not to be questioned. Insubordination gives the impression of weakness and the last thing any organization needs is for the leader to be perceived as weak. I am a strong leader—and will use every opportunity to reinforce this fact.

Each person plays a part in the organization under my direction. I have specific goals and objectives in mind for staff meetings so I appreciate when staff do not attempt to interject options or ideas because it may lead us away from my original objective. When/if they become principal of their own school, they can make the tough decisions but until then, I appreciate it if they do what I have asked them to do.

Everything comes through me because it is my job as the head of the school. If everyone simply does what I ask of them then the organization will work. I think committees and consensus are fine ideas in theory. Sometimes too much time is wasted discussing situations, ideas, and issues and less time is spent actually "doing." I'm a doer. I like to get things done and if you're not on board with me, then there's the door...

Unintentionally Disinviting

Schools are not neutral. They are shaped by societal assumptions and beliefs regarding what is valued and what should be pursued. These values and beliefs often lead to behaviours and curriculum practices that disengage and diminish others. One of the authors' students had a very bad accident and is now in a wheelchair. This student has encountered multiple physical barriers in schools for herself and other physically challenged students. These include access to washrooms, elevators, and other facilities that able-bodied individuals take for granted. In addition, in spite of the progress that has been made, girls and boys who choose to take traditionally gendered subjects may feel unintentionally disinvited by teachers' and students' comments and attitudes.

Intentionally disinviting behaviours by educators can be emotionally damaging but are less prevalent in comparison to unintentionally disinviting actions. This way of responding often represents being insensitive to people or situations, being out of touch with one's assumptions and values, and ignoring how one's actions are being perceived and acted upon. Being unable or unwilling to reflect on what one is believing and doing and the effects these are having often leads to prescribing work in schools that is perceived as lacking meaning and purpose. Students surrounded by what they sense as boring busywork, "drill and kill," super-competitive goals, or uncaring teachers and staff may choose to drop out of schools, either physically or psychologically. Not wanting to continually feel pain, it is easier to just leave.

Educators in schools that are unintentionally disinviting have to find ways to make explicit how the messages that are being sent are being interpreted and acted upon. Often this is difficult because not intending to do harm makes it difficult to see the harm that is being done. Frequently people will say something such as "I didn't mean it that way so they will have to learn not to take it that way," in an attempt to control the perception of others and to assuage their conscience. Perceptions, however, do not work that way. Dictating what people should perceive is a way to get them to be more resistant to what is offered. Learning to read behaviour backwards for both the sender and recipient of unintentionally disinviting messages is a good way to show respect for all involved in the communicative process.

I Am Unintentionally Disinviting When…

- I deny the value and importance of students' and parents' backgrounds.
- I assume a colour, class, and gender-blind approach to curriculum.
- I unconsciously communicate messages in my behaviour and curriculum that reinforce inequitable practices.
- I do not trust so I do things for others, not with others.
- I believe that if I want something done right, I have to do it myself.
- I am happy with keeping things going as they always have been done.

Here's what an unintentionally disinviting perspective might look like:

I know how valuable each member of the staff is because they are so talented and dedicated to their students but there is simply not enough time in the day to get everything done. I want to support them in their efforts to teach the kids so I try to take as many things off their plate as possible to allow them to concentrate on their job, which is teaching the kids.

Discipline is an office responsibility so I encourage teachers to send students down when they are misbehaving or disrupting. I want to know about each and every infraction so I can deal with it appropriately. I want teachers to concentrate on teaching. I must admit, though, sometimes I am astounded by the number of students who end up in the office. It takes up so much of my time at recesses, lunches, and in the middle of the day that everything gets pushed back to accommodate.

Sometimes the work seems to be too much and I admit that once in a while I allow my frustrations to surface. I feel that every teacher needs my leadership and direction so I try to involve myself as much as possible. Things can be hectic at times, but we're all working together for the benefit of our students so despite the hectic nature of the school, hopefully everyone recognizes that it's all worth it in the end.

Unintentionally Inviting

Educators operating at the unintentionally inviting level often do many things that work: they just do not know why. These habitually smiling people are often

29

the gregarious educators who have discovered things that are successful and keep repeating them. Often, when circumstances change, they are stuck because they are unable to explain the reasoning for what they were doing and cannot make the necessary adjustments. Being stuck, they often revert to disinviting levels of behaviour because they are frustrated when their "natural" way of educating no longer works.

I Am Unintentionally Inviting When...

- I send positive messages to others based on personality preferences.
- I welcome students and their parents because I am being polite.
- I listen to others because I am well mannered.
- I recognize that good things happen under my leadership but I'm not sure why or how.

Here's what an unintentionally inviting perspective might look like:

I like people and have always understood that people seem to like me in return. Some people are good with people and some are not. Ever since I was a child, I was always the leader of the group.

It seems like things work out most of the time because I have a great staff of teachers who are good at what they do. At times I question why I was given the opportunity to lead, but am happy to let them do what they do because they seem to do it well. I think they appreciate that. I like to talk to staff and they seem happy to speak with me. The development of rapport helps everyone to realize that I'm a good person who wants the best for them and the students. I hope they know that I will help them in any way that I can.

I'm a good public speaker. Words have always come easy to me. I notice that most leaders speak well so that would make sense in my case. I can usually come up with something that sounds good when talking with people or public speaking. I know that sometimes I am not prepared but thinking on your feet is an important part of the role of leader, so being able to improvise effectively is a sign of creativity and flexibility.

I appreciate the importance of the role of a principal in a school and will continue to do what I do which will hopefully empower the teachers to do what they do. If I can support and encourage them, I think the school will somehow improve as a result.

Intentionally Inviting

Operating at a consistently inviting level involves doing things on purpose for defensible ethical and pedagogical reasons that can be articulated to oneself and to a variety of audiences. This dependable and creative behaviour represents educational integrity in that it has been developed as a reflective way of working with people that shows appreciation for them in the present and a commitment to their future growth. Working with a pragmatic sense of educational hope, these educators demonstrate persistence of purpose, resourcefulness of means, and courage to respond to naysayers and cynics.

Intentionally inviting educators further demonstrate educational integrity because their feelings, thoughts, and actions reveal a deep congruence. Everything seems to fit and actions give the impression of flowing naturally. Often, however, underlying such seemingly effortless actions is a lot of reflection and rethinking of situations and past practices. It also needs to be pointed out that intentionally inviting educators are not without their flaws or limitations. Being mere mortals, they can be overwhelmed or "off their game." However, what sets them apart is that they find ways to grow through the tensions and setbacks they face. This persistence of resolve and personalization of approaches used is ignited by attending to the personal and professional needs of oneself and others.

I Am Intentionally Inviting When...

- I use formal and informal structures to routinize invitational and equitable practices.
- I continually ask questions that challenge disinviting structures. For example: Is our school invitational? What do we mean by invitational practices? Who is invited and disinvited? How do our structures and practices (dis)invite others? How are we complicit in these structures? How can we transform them?
- I reflect on how leadership is shared, how mentorship is focused on self and others.
- I engage all stakeholders in imaginative acts of hope.
- I create space and opportunities for the school community to reflect on and recognize invitational practices.

Here's what an intentionally inviting perspective might look like:

I like people and recognize the importance of relationships to education. The school is made up of individuals who collectively contribute to the success of the students and the culture of the community. I am constantly reflecting upon these relationships and experiences in order to find out what is working well and what can be improved upon for the future. My vision for the school is clear and growing and is shared with staff, students, and parents in recognition of the important role that each plays in the school.

Working together, we are supporting one another by reflecting upon practices— what worked and didn't work—and articulating ideas to one another in the spirit of collegiality and professional development. I respect the time and talents of the teachers so I am always looking for ways to disseminate important news and information without wasting valuable professional time with info items which can be distributed in more timely and effective manners. Staff meetings are a reflection of our priority upon professional learning communities and staff development.

I value the contribution to the goals of the school by each member of our learning community and continue to foster relationships. Each member has a set of skills and talents which they contribute to the whole, and that includes me as the leader. School leadership doesn't just "happen." It is the result of intentionally reflecting, refining, contributing, and valuing one another and articulating clearly to all stakeholders. There are many people who are good at what they do but can't seem to put a finger on why. Intentionality requires focus and consideration so that visions and goals are clear to everyone.

AREAS OF INVITING

Achieving invitational integrity requires the artful orchestration of one's personal and professional life according to principles and practices of ethical care and democratic practice. Because intentionally inviting educators are in it for the long run (Novak, 2009a), they realize that their resolve and creativity take training, discipline, and enjoyment. Long distance runners know that they can sprint when they need to but also realize that they cannot maintain that pace for a complete race. They have learned to pace and enrich themselves during their practices and their runs. Paying attention to the following four areas of inviting allows educational integrity to be sustained for the long run:

1. Inviting oneself personally: Attending to one's personal development and interests.
2. Inviting others personally: Developing a reliable social support group.
3. Inviting oneself professionally: Finding ways to grow in and through one's vocation.
4. Inviting others professionally: Applying a defensible theory of practice to one's work.

Each of these areas deserves a bit more attention now and will be expanded in later chapters.

Inviting Oneself Personally

If someone wishes to be intentionally inviting, it is because he or she thinks that this is a good way to be with people. One person each of us can never escape from is oneself. Try as we may, we are with ourselves every moment of our lives. So, if the inviting approach is so important to use with others, it is vital to use with oneself. Since the inviting perspective is a person-centred approach to life, each person doing the inviting needs to sustain his or her enthusiasm for leading an educational life. The old bromide, that if we are bored, we are probably boring a lot of other people, applies here. Inviting educators have a moral responsibility to lead interesting lives and one way to do that is to have a lot of interests, projects, and celebrations. If invitational educators think that the inviting approach means continually living for others, they will eventually learn to resent the others. Martyrs are limited in their longevity as inviters and are not around for the long run. In addition, paying attention to how one accepts or declines one's invitations to oneself encourages insight and growth regarding the subtleties of the inviting process. When Richard Rorty (1989) talks about the importance of being private poets and public democrats, he is talking about the importance of cultivating one's personal world.

Inviting Others Personally

The inviting approach is both personal and social. It recognizes the importance of each individual while also affirming our fundamental social connections. No person is an island. Each of us comes into existence because of a social connection and stays alive physically, psychologically, and intellectually through extending those connections. In hunter and gatherer societies, to be banished from a group meant great vulnerability. In our modern society, losing connection with others cuts us off from the sustaining nurturance needed to cope with and grow in a more complex world. Since the inviting process is a way of connecting with people, it is important to cultivate sustaining relationships in one's personal life. This means taking the effort to develop a solid support group of family, friends, and colleagues with whom one can share hopes, aspirations, fears, and frustrations. This is especially important in schools where the celebratory spirit can be kept alive by an imaginative social committee. While online networks/platforms increase possibilities, the need to remain connected can be enhanced by breaking bread together in face-to-face community and celebrating life events with real people in real time.

Inviting Oneself Professionally

Educators are intellectual workers. They are intimately connected with the world of ideas and are expected to invite the best ideas available. In a world where ideas are changing and expanding at an ever-accelerating pace, it is imperative that educators stay in touch with what is happening in their field and their profession. If one does not stay active in one's professional development, one runs the risk of becoming professionally obsolete, just going through the motions until the pension cheques start coming in. In addition, it is not only ideas that are changing; it is also that the people we are working with will not remain the way we want them to be. It was noted (Novak, 2002) that there is an old educational adage that says we think we have created great schools but they are sending us the wrong kids. This certainly can be the feeling of those who are out of touch with the nature of today's students. Surviving and thriving in today's schools means being involved in various professional certifications, doing research in one's field, and becoming a part of professional groups which can provide feedback on one's teaching and one's ideas. The availability of online training and development offers a multiplicity of possibilities.

33

CHAPTER 2

Inviting Others Professionally

To act and grow in education for the long run is to build on the sustenance and possibilities provided by the previous three areas of inviting. Following the key ideas of the LIVES model (Chapter 1), educators need to use their personalities, relationships, knowledge, organizational experiences, and social justice commitments to dependably call forth and sustain imaginative acts of hope in their schools and beyond. Being guided by the democratic ethos, perceptual tradition, and self-concept theory, educators have an ethically principled and psychologically useful way of thinking and acting. This provides a defensible theoretical base for one's sustained actions. In getting more concrete, the book *The Inviting School Treasury: 1001 Ways to Invite School Success* (Purkey & Strahan, 2002) provides specific inviting practices that have been used in schools throughout the world. Each of these practices is consistent with

> ### *About Inviting Others Professionally*
>
> *When talking about the fact that an inviting perspective is about more than being nice, a participant in a workshop remarked about an inviting drill instructor he had while in the US Marines. He said his instructor had high standards based on preparing soldiers to defend others and themselves in exemplary ways. The instructor was tough but his charges could see that he really cared about them becoming good marines. He respected his soldiers, and never took cheap shots, like some of the laxer drill instructors. His soldiers worked hard to become something they had signed up for. They felt valuable, able, and responsible as a result of accepting his invitation to "be all that they can be." After a long discussion, other participants felt they had a deeper understanding of the inviting process.*

the inviting approach and does not use bribes or coercion. These examples of inviting practices are not "best practices" to be rigidly copied but imaginative heuristics to generate ethical and imaginative ways of thinking and being in schools.

The thoughtful orchestration of these four areas along with the foundational principles of the inviting approach will now be connected to the LIVES model for use in guiding, leading, managing, and mentoring for educational life. We are always sending and receiving messages. Inviting leaders who are reflecting on how they are inviting themselves and others personally and professionally are aware of how these messages can be interpreted and how they invite or disinvite. School leaders can be guilty of trading and exchanging in the currency of busyness. Being busy can be unintentionally viewed as a badge of honour, as if a leader is only effective and engaged if he or she is busy. Unfortunately, this can be infectious. Others will follow a busy leader, running from here to there and back again, until the school is a whirling dervish of activity. If a leader is going to invite others to participate in the life of the school and encourage leadership in others, it should be a school life worth participating in.

MENTORING CONVERSATIONS

Q: What do you mean you are never neutral in your interactions? I work hard to be neutral.

All that hard work you put into being neutral is still sending a message. There is a line from the song "Freewill" from Rush that says "If you choose not to decide, you still have made a choice" (Lee, Lifeson, & Peart, 1980). We are always sending and receiving messages, whether as overtly as talking with someone with our arms crossed across our chest, rolling our eyes, or turning our backs, or as discreetly as our actions. Leaders recognize that they are never neutral. Leadership, by its very nature, is not about slipping through the cracks or hiding in the shadows. It requires shining a light on yourself, your decisions, and your values. It may be a lot to consider, but we think it is important to understand that your messages are not confined to announcements, emails, speeches, and mission statements. You are sending a message when you speak, both with what you say and how you say it. What you prioritize, how you make decisions, and the processes you employ reveal a great deal. How you interact with others and the set-up of your office and building all send messages. It is a lot to take in, but understanding the impact of the messages you are continually setting will hopefully make you reconsider the wisdom of the efforts you make to maintain neutrality.

Q: I'm only a new educational leader. How can I be expected to have so much deep integrity?

What is the statute of limitations on being able to say "It's my first day!"? Education is a deeply emotional vocation because we live to serve others and encourage them to lead educational lives as parents, teachers, and especially students. A parent who is upset about something that has happened to their child is doing so out of love and concern for their child. When they perceive their child to be wronged or not set up for success, they will not be afraid to say so and to question. Your "newness" is of little concern to that parent in that situation. Doing things on purpose for purposes that can be defended is not only good practice, but ethically defensible, which is fairly handy when dealing with an upset parent, student, or staff member. Educational leadership requires leaders to hit the ground running no matter what stage of their career they are at. The Grade 1 student who is new to the country or the family that just moved into the community or the Grade 4 student who is struggling with reading or the staff member who requires support and guidance require leadership now. We understand how daunting that can be. That is why an inviting perspective is so important—being thoughtful about how to become intentionally inviting will contribute to your ongoing reflection and refinement of practice, which will strengthen your ability to lead with integrity.

Q: How democratic can schools be? Even inviting schools?

We thought that people might get hung up on the term "democratic" as it brings up notions of decisions by consensus, voting, and political discourse. We recognize that leaders make decisions and there are times when the buck does indeed stop with them. We are not necessarily suggesting voting on all decisions large and small. What we are saying is that all people matter. A democratic ethos recognizes that all members of the organization play important roles in the efficient and effective functioning of a group, team, organization, or school. It is in this recognition that inviting leaders activate the very best from each member of the team. People want to be done *with* rather than done *to*. When they feel invested in the process and respected as vital team members, they are more likely to do what they do as well as they can. A democratic approach understands that the success of an organization is not all about the leader, but rather all about how the leader invites each member of the organization to contribute their greatest potential.

Q: Does the perceptual view mean that you have to accept and agree with how a person sees things?
We would suggest it is less about acceptance and even less about agreement as it is about understanding. Empathy is an important personal resource for educational leaders. Understanding where others are coming from—their background, experiences, goals, and expectations—is important to be able to invite. People have motivations for their actions and desired outcomes. The perceptual view encourages us to try to see things from another's perspective in order to develop a better understanding of their motivations, actions, and expectations. If you are too entrenched in your own views, opinions, and expectations, you will find it difficult to invite others fully. Just as we noted above, no one is neutral. Recognizing perceptual views helps you to respect others and their views. One of the authors was about to have a meeting with a parent group about the installation of a playground in the schoolyard. The school board strongly recommended against undertaking this project for a variety of financial, safety, insurance, and logistical reasons. The author went about researching all the reasons why it was a bad idea. The day before the meeting, he shared his research with a colleague. The colleague told him that he certainly had a lot of information about why it was a bad idea, but what about why it was a good idea? The author spent the rest of the time before the meeting researching all the positives and came to understand why the parent group had worked so hard to advocate for it. The parent group's time and effort was validated by a balanced approach and a thoughtful decision that weighed all the pros and cons commenced. Sometimes it requires the advice of a thoughtful mentor to get us out of our own perceptual fields.

PART 2

IMAGINATIVELY LEADING, MANAGING, AND MENTORING EDUCATIONAL LIVES

LEADING FROM THE INSIDE OUT

Leading involves more than pointing in an educationally desired direction. It also means imaginatively seeking out a direction and moving that way oneself because of one's embodied beliefs about educational ends. To lead with integrity for educational life means to be clear about the values that enliven one's sense of purpose and to develop a nuanced understanding of the complexities of reality, the paradoxical workings of the perceptual processes, and the expansive psychology of the self-system.

Do you really want to lead an educational life?

Are you clear in your mind about what really matters in schools?

Can an educator's personal and professional lives be integrated?

Is imaginative leadership divorced from reality?

Because of the deep-seated commitments to be in education for the long run, these are questions that need continual probing to keep the internal spark of leadership alive. This chapter is likely to call your beliefs into question if you:

- Think leadership is only about what you do to other people;
- Wish to be safe from difficult life commitments;
- Believe that leadership is about "playing the game";
- Are only your real self outside of the school.

This chapter is likely to build on your beliefs if you:

- Think leadership cannot get away from the personal;
- Realize that important life choices influence leadership;
- Believe that integrity can be developed in leadership;
- Are committed to being in education for the long run.

The chapter could easily be titled, "Leader, Lead Thyself." It is the first step in looking at leading, managing, and mentoring using the LIVES model: moving from the lived self, to relationships with individuals, to values and knowledge, to educational communities, and to the larger society and beyond. Leading one's self contains within itself the idea that if you intend to invite others to live an educational life, you have to be able to personally lead one yourself. There is no escaping the necessity to come to grips with what it means to be human and what it means to be an educator. These are crucial existential and professional issues. Professionalism is not a mask that covers a leader's character. Rather, leadership is a self-revealing process in which a person can step forward in professional roles to be challenged and to grow. This is especially true in becoming an invitational leader.

CORE AUTHENTICITY

The type of leadership we are focusing on in this book, invitational leadership, is too self-revealing to be faked on a regular basis. Authentic leaders "are distinguished not by their techniques or styles but by their integrity and savvy" (Evans, 2001, p. 184). Integrity, also described as "the fundamental consistency between one's values, goals, and actions" (p. 185), is critical to building the types of relationships that transform schools. In other words, people look to teachers and administrators not only for guidance but also to determine if their words are congruent with their actions. Are they worthy of trust? Do their actions speak louder than their words? Communicating a clear sense of their values and beliefs can be particularly difficult for new leaders, who often feel pressured to follow projected roles. Rather than acting on their own reflected personal values, they tend to conform to external expectations of what a leader should be and look like. Eventually a person's deeper values and feelings come to the surface; trying to suppress them requires too much effort. It would be like trying to hold a large beach ball underwater. You may succeed for a while but eventually the natural forces will win out; you will tire, and the ball will come shooting up. The same is true with deep-seated feelings, beliefs, and ideals.

The importance of personal ideals cannot be underestimated. Authentically pursued with the will and skills gained in the development of practical wisdom (Schwartz & Sharpe, 2010), personal ideals give someone something to aim for and work with in confronting and learning from difficult situations. Faking the pursuit of an ideal works against you in the long run, and it is not even that successful in the short run. Ironically, a superficial pretence can lead to overdeveloped sloganeering, buzzwords which you and everyone else grow tired of hearing and soon become the cynical residue of failed efforts. For example, the research of Kouzes and Posner (2010) lists "modelling the way" as the first exemplary practice of leadership.

> ### *About Authenticity*
>
> *Shortly after I was appointed principal, I started to think about the role as if I was creating a character in a play. I bought new suits. A principal wears suits, right? Ties, cufflinks too, I assumed. I found myself constructing a character based on what I perceived others expected rather than simply being myself and leading as the educator I was. It took me a while to embrace the fact that I was hired because of what I was to the profession as a teacher, leader, artist, writer, academic, husband, and father. I was not hired because I appeared capable of playing the character of "principal" in a play. I was hired because of who I was.*

Related to this, they point out that the highest admired characteristic of leaders is honesty. Putting the two together, modelling honestly, the leading of an educational life would be embarrassingly difficult to fake, even in the short run. Imagine trying to be perceived as being interested in appreciating more of life's experiences, being curious about learning new things, and being committed to taking ethical actions when you really do not care about any of these things or do not know why they are important. You would eventually be stymied because you lacked a sense of educational purpose. Your actions would lack integrity; they would not cohere with the words you used. The residue of cynicism would take over.

Stepping back and applying this once again to leadership research, Warren Bennis (1989) emphasized four crucial qualities of good leaders:

1. Positive other regard: Wanting others to be successful and making available personal and material resources for them to do so;
2. Balancing ambition, values, and competence: Making sure your personal goals, political principles, and professional capabilities are in equilibrium;
3. Wallenda effect: As in tightrope walking, focusing on what you have to do next to continue to succeed rather than concentrating on avoiding failure;
4. Emerson effect: Taking delight in what is happening around you.

Similar to be pretending to be leading an educational life, attempting to fake the leadership qualities that Bennis is emphasizing involves acting as if one took delight in others; as if one were not a demagogue, ideologue, or technocrat; as if one were an optimist; and, as if one really had a sense of excitement about life's possibilities. This is a lot of "as if-ing" and at some point, usually sooner rather than later, others will question your sincerity, honesty, and motives. A person who does this will appear as French novelist and diplomat Jean Giraudoux, who infamously said "The secret of success is sincerity. Once you can fake that, you've got it made." Personal leadership with an ethical focus needs to go deeper, and in a different direction, than this artful deception.

Rather than trying to fake the qualities of successful leaders or learn techniques related to successful individual educational traits but detached from educational purposes, the perceptual tradition, discussed in the last chapter, looks at the deep-seated dispositions at the base of behaviour. From the perceptual point of view, behaviour is just the tip of the iceberg. Beneath behaviour are more general perceptions about what is happening, what is possible, and what is desirable. Going deeper, underlying these perceptions are beliefs related to what Combs, Miser, and Whitaker (1999) call core dispositional aspects of leadership. These deep-seated beliefs involve the following perceptions about who a person is as a leader, how a person approaches challenges, and what a person is fundamentally about:

- Leadership Self: A sense that one matters and can make a difference;
- Approaching Situations: The belief that good things can happen;
- Sense of Purpose: The conviction that reaching for educational ends is worth the effort.

41

Each of these beliefs is based on convictions resulting from an examination of one's personal and professional life in order to act in intentionally inviting ways. This reflective process is not done once and then is done with. Rather, it is an ever-widening way of making sense of what life is about and where one fits in the scheme of things. Related to leading an educational life oneself, each of these beliefs involves developing the practical wisdom to artfully orchestrate the will and skill (Schwartz & Sharpe, 2010) to become the type of person whose advice one would seek and follow (Nozick, 1989). The will and skill to do this are not merely commanded to oneself then done away with. Rather, they have their roots in a nuanced understanding of reality, perception, and self. Working to more deeply understand what one should be committed to as a person and as an educational leader depends on perceptions of what is worth doing, the perceptual process itself, and the nature of the self which is doing the perceiving.

ESCAPING REALITY

Although this book is not a philosophical text, conceptual thinking, the making of clear distinctions, cannot be avoided. This is especially true for a book which emphasizes the importance of personal perceptions, imagination, and hope. Although perceptions are a person's psychological reality, they are not all there is to reality. To believe that there is no reality outside of one's perceptions is to live in a fantasy world, what philosophers call solipsism: that notion that "reality" is merely what goes on in one's head. Of course there is reality outside of one's perceptions. Almost anyone who thinks about it acknowledges that there were external events going on before he or she was born and events will be going on after he or she is gone. It's not all about us. Noteworthy here is the work of Peter Berger and Thomas Luckmann (1966) in their classic text, *The Social Construction of Reality*, who stress the importance of the realization that reality goes on within us (the psycho-social processes of making sense of our environments) and without us (the external workings of the social order). To relate this directly to educational leaders, to realize that there is more going on than what is presently in our heads is an invitation to grow and develop a more complex understanding of what is and what could be.

Educational leaders need to get real and be real. Related to the pursuit of educational living, this means to seek more intricate and diverse meanings within reality. Mihaly Csikszentmihalyi (1990/2008) has spent the last two decades describing the psychological process involved in seeking complexity, the ability to make differentiations within experience that are then reassembled in an ever more comprehensive framework. Put another way, people who are able to notice more things in the world can develop a more expansive way to interpret what they experience. They grow and possess the skill and will to keep growing. From this point of view, life is more like William James's series of flights and perchings in which we grow, assimilate our new perspective, and use this to continue to grow. Csikszentmihalyi talks about the ability to "express one's uniqueness, yet participating intimately in the complexity of the cosmos" (1997, p. 2). This lofty perspective of uniquely participating in the evolution of complexity is also applied to the world of business, where Csikszentmihalyi (2004) interviewed CEOs of successful companies who have worked to develop workplace atmospheres that enable people to develop ethical vocations with the joy of expanding themselves as they also respond to the needs of the larger society. These are realistic possibilities for people who want to develop an educational character, a character committed to the *telos*, the purpose, of leading for educational life. It takes desire and effort to learn to do this, especially in terms of one's own personal and professional lives. Escapists or defeatists need not apply, although, to be fair, everyone has to battle with these tendencies.

METAPERCEPTIONS

The development of educational character involves the focusing of impulses and habits to live more fully and openly in the present by learning how to savour, understand, and better one's own and others' experiences. This metaperceptual process involves perceptions about perceptions that enable us to take stock of what is happening within us as we try to sort out and live meaningfully in the world.

The perceptual foundation stressed in this book begins with the premise that people's behaviour is regulated by the differentiations and interpretations they are able to make at the moment of action. This differentiating process rests on the context of the situation and the beliefs people possess. Even though people want to realize happiness within reality, they do not possess "immaculate perceptions" of the reality they are immersed in. As Richard Bernstein (2010) points out, all perceptions are perspectival, coming from a certain vantage point. Learning to understand and to work with this perceptual mediating process enables educational leaders to have a richer understanding of themselves, others, and educational possibilities. With this in mind, here are eight key working metaperceptual principles and their application to educational leadership:

– *Perceptions can exist at various levels of abstraction.* Some things sound very good in the abstract but will not work in a particular context. For example, some leadership plans appear wonderful at the central office level but are filled with problems when implemented in different schools. The stories from educational leaders in this book reveal a variety of contexts, perceptions, and perspectives from within the reality of contemporary schools, all grounded in invitational theory. Realizing that educational ideas need to be born twice, first in one's head and then in one's actions, enables an educator to plan accordingly and give each its due. Failure to do this often results in what Daniel Kahneman (2011) call the "planning fallacy" (p. 249), the unrealistic expectation that the best-case scenario will ensue.

- *Psychological processes have a logic of their own.* Psychologic is not the same as deductive or inductive logic. An individual's perceptions of a situation may not follow strict rules of inference, because they are embodied with the person's unique history of meanings. Using disembodied logic to explain something to a person is often misplaced if the person doing the explaining does not have a feel for how the situation seems to the other person. Often policies that are planned to be logical and concise are perceived as out of touch by the people they are supposed to assist.
- *Perceptions are influenced by desires.* People are not neutral in focusing their attention. They attend to what they perceive will satisfy their wants and needs (more about this in the next section). If people did not have this filtered focusing process they would be overwhelmed by the sheer number of perceptual possibilities and would not be able to care for themselves. On the other hand, desiring to perceive something, to have it make sense and be meaningful is not the same as actually perceiving it. Perceptions that do not "click" create a sense of dissonance. Think here of not getting a joke in another culture, when everyone around you is laughing. Understanding something complex can be like a key opening a lock. Not all keys work but there is a feeling of relief when one does.
- *Different perspectives result in different perceptions.* Perspectives are influenced by personal factors such as gender, race, class, and culture, among others. Events can be perceived from many perspectives. This is especially true in a pluralistic society where people bring different histories and interests with them. Within groups there can be a "hardening of the categories," an attempt to demarcate boundaries and not let outsiders in. An example of this would be teenagers who create a language that excludes adults, and educators/professors who use acronyms and jargon (edubabble) to overawe parents and students. Being aware of multiple viewpoints does not mean that perspectives are incommensurable, containing no common ground. Rather, it takes imaginative effort to un-harden one's own perspective and learn to see new viewpoints. Literature, art, and film are ways to get a sense of others' perspectives and to broaden one's own. Related to educating, educators who are responsive to socio-cultural factors demonstrate a caring approach, deliver inclusive curricula, and build learning communities that achieve greater success with diverse learners (McMahon & Armstrong, 2010).
- *First perceptions can often be boxed-in perceptions.* People have a need to form a stable perceptual base because their worlds would be chaotic without such a base to rely on. However, perceptual anchorages also have a negative side because they can lock people into underdeveloped or malfunctioning ways of seeing things. Teachers' and administrators' positive and negative expectations of students have been shown to impact student behaviour and performance (Schramm-Pate, Jeffries, & D'Amico, 2006). Educators who do not understand or embrace difference are more likely to blame students and their parents for underperformance. This deficit perspective orientation often assumes an "if only" discourse. If only "those people" were as smart or good as us, they would not be

underperforming. This is a very distancing and demeaning standpoint, to say the least. Our experience confirms that people live up to or down to expectations. Under the right circumstances they can loosen the hold of initial perceptions and try on other ways of making sense of a situation. When it is said that education is a window to the world this means that students are introduced to ways of being and possibilities that they would not ordinarily encounter. Educational leaders can intentionally work to open more windows, their own included.

- *The future is the cause of behaviour.* This seems counterintuitive because we usually think that the past is the cause of the present. However, from the point of view of the lived world of the person, what we think will happen influences how we feel and what we do in the present. Our sense of what will happen is based on how we interpret the present situation in terms of the past. For example, there were people who thought the Boston Red Sox could never again win a World Series because they were so unsuccessful for so long. They were sometimes close but would always seem to find a way to snatch defeat from the jaws of victory. Then, in the 21st century, they won two World Series and people's perceptions of their chances are changed. (Now if this could only work for the Chicago Cubs or the Toronto Maple Leafs.) Related to education, unsuccessful reform efforts can lead people to perceive that nothing will ever change. Thinking nothing will ever change locks people into unresponsive boxes making it difficult for things to change. Self-fulfilling prophesies are hard to overturn.
- *Dissonances in proper doses can invite growth.* Dissonance deals with the tension between an expected perception and an actual perception. Based on the idea of hitting two adjoining notes on a piano, dissonance sends a haunting chill to the listener. What we do with the disturbance is one of the signs of educational character. To willfully ignore the dissonance or blindly hold on to the expected perception is miseducative. To inquire and test new possibilities is educative and will be done if the gains can be seen to outweigh the losses. Dissonance can be an invitation to grow but it takes will and skill to work through.
- *Perceptions involve what is present and what is missing.* What is present in situations influences what we consider to be normal and often goes unquestioned. For example, the television show *Mad Men* does an excellent job of showing what was the norm in the early 1960s regarding the diminished roles of women and other minoritized groups. The statement, "the silence was deafening," makes this point. When we learn to expect certain things, we notice when they are missing. This has strong implications for notions of social justice. Imagining a more inclusive world in the future enables us to attend to how the present conditions work for or against this goal.

These eight metaperceptual principles are only touching the surface of the intricacies of the perceptual processes. Taking them seriously enables educational leaders to understand that perceptions go beyond words, and so they are aware of the limitations of using only words to communicate. They also focus attention on the actual meanings people perceive in situations and point out the need to look for a variety of perspectives, while working to construct a shared perspective. In addition, these metaperceptual principles provide an understanding of the staying power of initial perceptions, memories, anticipations, and desires in influencing how people make sense of the world. Finally, creatively using dissonance and examining what is missing in any situation can be powerful sources of educational growth. This is a lot to remember but it becomes clearer when focused on the workings of the self-system.

UNDERSTANDING SELF-SYSTEMS

Perceptions are not free floating images waiting to be picked up by neutral observers. Rather, they are the result of active constructions of engaged people working to maintain, protect, and enhance their self-systems. Understanding the functional processes of the self-system gives educational leaders a deeper awareness of the inner workings of themselves and others. The psychological workings of this self-system can be depicted using William Purkey's (2000) spiral diagram (see Figure 1).

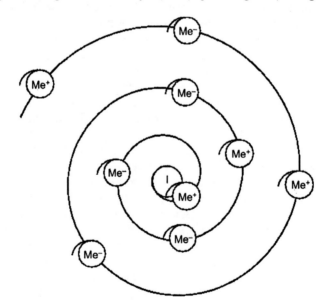

Figure 1. The self-system.

The self-system is a global structure comprised of three parts:

- The "I": Self-as-subject;
- The "me's": Self-as-object;
- The "+" or "-": Self-esteem.

At the centre of the diagram is the "I", which represents the live-connection to the world, to others, and to oneself that every person possesses. Usually called consciousness or awareness, this live-connection is what makes a person a person. Educational leaders who ignore others' and their own subjectivity do so at their own peril. Understanding, respecting, and connecting with the "I-ness" of more and more people is the practical ideal underlying the democratic ethos. Invitational leadership, with its emphasis on perceiving oneself and others as valuable, able, and responsible is the embodiment of this ideal and is manifested in the fundamental respect every person deserves.

Finding out more about each person on staff through the development of relationships helps inviting leaders to understand what contribution each person can make to the school. The teacher with a passion for painting or the educational assistant who runs marathons or the custodian who sings in a choir can all make immense contributions to an inviting school, perhaps in ways they had not even considered themselves. An inviting leader encourages the sharing of "I's" that make up all of the "me's" in the school. There are more dynamic interests, talents, and potential contributions in a school than may appear on the surface which inviting leadership can bring to the surface.

> ### About "I"
>
> *On occasion I have asked students to tell how they know another student in the class is not a top-of-the-line robot, one that merely looks and acts as they do. When they say this student will bleed when cut, they are told that top-of-the-line robots have a liquid red lubricant that will come to the surface when their exterior is punctured. They then usually say that the student has feelings, but are informed that outsiders cannot really see another's feelings and robots are programmed to portray mannerisms that can be interpreted as mad, glad, sad, or scared. After a few minutes the activity stops and is discussed. Students say that although they believe that other people have an internal world of memories, desires, and meanings, they realize that they do not have direct access to other's inner sanctum. This is an important realization and is necessary for the ethical treatment of people.*

The "me's" that surround the "I" represent the content of one's self-concept, the perception one has regarding one's identity and life possibilities. Each of the "me's" represents a perception of an attribute one possesses or a category one belongs too. For an example of the former, one can perceive oneself as interesting, humorous, and loving or dull, serious, and lonely. Regarding the categories, one can perceive oneself as a son or daughter, a leader or a non-leader, a Canadian or American. In addition, the closer a "me" is to the "I" the stronger its hold on the attention of the person. Things central to a person's existence such as gender, race, and competency influence strongly what he or she will attend to. On the other hand, "me's" on the

47

periphery are often ignored, but can come into focus when challenged. Because we and the world we live in are always changing, the "me's" change their proximity to the "I." Aging and new life responsibilities bring new "me's" into existence and rearrange the closeness to the centre of self of the other "me's." The idea of "putting away childish things" (Borg, 2010) can be interpreted as a rearranging of "me's" to meet new challenges. Learning to perceive oneself as a leader can involve this identity transforming process.

Self-esteem, the positive (+) or negative (-) evaluation of the "me's," is the third component of the self-system. We are constantly evaluating who we are and how we fit into the world. Rather than being neutral and distanced observers of our existence, we are active judges of our perceived strengths and weaknesses. Ironically,

> ### About "Me's"
>
> *A colleague was preparing a package for submission for a leadership position and asked for help with the resume. After looking through degrees, qualifications, and work experience, I commented "This doesn't tell me much about you. They want to hire you, not your degrees or additional qualifications or committee work experience. Those are important insofar as you have to have them to apply, but assume that everyone has them as well. You are so much more than the courses you have taken and your work experience. That is what makes you special and why they should hire you." The resume though good, did not pay attention to her 'mes'.*

we are not always fair judges of our accomplishments and possibilities, but our judgments matter and are real to each of us. For example, a person may be an excellent runner for his age but if he cannot beat his older brother in a 5 kilometer race, he may place a negative evaluation on self-as-runner, even though objectively he knows that he is a good runner for his age group. Depending on his competitive nature, this may be either close to or far from the centre of his existence. As was mentioned regarding metaperceptions, the logical is not the psychological, but the psychological is the personally lived reality that takes effort to move beyond.

Leaders wanting to be real have to learn to live with the psychological reality of self-systems in themselves and others. Returning to a metaperceptual perspective, understanding the operations of one's self-system means becoming cognizant of the subtle processes by which the "me's" influence the focus of awareness of the "I." One of the authors, in teaching the self-system to his class, talked about learning to address the various "me's" that are a part of one's identify. One of his students said she did this all of the time when she had a discussion with the "girls," her name for the various "me's" in her inner life. She said she tried to listen to each one and hear not only what "she" was saying, but how "she" was saying it and then tried to reach a personally informed decision. Although she said it worked for her and is a very personal way for her to listen to herself, we are hesitant about suggesting this as an approach for others.

THE IMPORTANCE OF EXPERIENCE

Understanding and comprehending the subtle and often ironic workings of the self-system make a person more complex and, in being so, he/she is able to note more and different things about people and interpret them in a more imaginative and integrative way. David Berliner (1986) has shown how expert educators are able to perceive much more related to educational possibilities than novice teachers. With more breadth and depth in their pedagogical perceptions they are able to use their practical wisdom to develop richer and more informed strategies for connecting with their students. Similar to expert chess players, they are able to see various possibilities and responses. Developing more complex perceptions is a vital part of an educational leader's growth.

Coming to a more complex understanding of the self-system also enables a leader to put polemical perspectives regarding the importance of self-esteem into perspective. For some, self-esteem is the answer to all the world's problems. If all people had positive self-esteem they would accomplish all their dreams and the world would be an idyllic place. For others, a focus on self-esteem is a distracter that either makes people weak, delusional, or self-absorbed. Either of these poles is an exaggeration. A healthy self-system does not mean a person will be able to overcome any adversity. Reality has a way of being inattentive to human needs. A healthy self-system, however, can help prevent a person from becoming his or her own obstacle to educational living, in addition to helping a person to learn from the external and internal difficulties faced. Being comfortable with one's self-system and attentive to its often subtle workings enables a school leader to become easier to relate to—a real person people want to know and work with rather than the archetypal, cardboard, and in some ways fictional version of a leader.

Related to research on educational leadership, Howard Gardner (1995) points out that leaders with a healthy sense of self are able to do the following:

– Reflect: Distance themselves from an activity to come to terms with its purpose and implications.
– Leverage: Rely on their unique personal strengths to work through difficult situations.
– Frame: Learn to learn from previous unsuccessful efforts.

This healthy sense of leadership self that Gardner describes is not an exaggerated sense of power nor a diminution of personal abilities but a positive and realistic perception of what one is and can be. Working to orchestrate such a sense of self involves an understanding of the workings of the self-system, along with an energetic openness to positive possibilities and the persistence, resourcefulness, and courage to try them out. As was said previously, this is not for the faint-hearted but it is worth the effort, even if not always successful. The next chapter shows some strategies for managing to orchestrate this educational leading self.

MENTORING CONVERSATIONS

Q: Don't you have to fake it sometimes as an educational leader?
Pretending to be someone you are not is bound to end in disaster. A confident leader recognizes what he or she does not know openly and honestly. One of the authors has a friend who is one of the brightest minds in the world, completing a PhD and post-doc work at the world's foremost institutions. During a conversation one day, he said "I don't understand that concept, can you walk me through that again?" The author had assumed that his friend knew everything given his sharp mind and academic pedigree. He came to understand that the more he knew, the more comfortable he became with how much he had yet to learn. His willingness to openly admit to a lack of understanding was liberating. Faking it is uncomfortable, and being able to do so for any length of time is unlikely. No one expects perfection. Celebrate what you are confident with, recognize what you need to know more about, and enjoy the pursuit of knowledge and experience—the intersection at which wisdom is born!

Q: How do you find confidence as a leader if you don't feel confident as a leader?
Confidence cannot be manufactured, unfortunately. It develops naturally over time through thoughtful reflections on experiences and refinement for future practice. Confidence is not knowing everything, but instead knowing how to find the answer. A confident leader does not project infallibility, but curiosity, persistence, and understanding. We all have feelings of inadequacy at times. The imposter syndrome posits that even the most outwardly confident and comfortable personalities can suffer from self-doubt. Finding confidence comes from embracing the fact that you can't and don't know everything, likely never will, but know where to find the answers when the time comes. It takes determination and persistence to constantly reflect, refine, and repeat in order to develop our leadership skills. Persisting in the face of self-doubt and resistance in order to refine our practice requires grit and determination.

Q: Doesn't paying attention to the inner world take us away from the outer world?
We are not suggesting anyone become utterly self-absorbed, but rather self-aware. Understanding self-systems helps us connect with others. Knowing strengths and weakness invites a collective approach to the leadership of the school as the contributions of all are not only respected and welcomed, but vital to our success. Leading for educational life takes on personal meaning when one is able to imaginatively choose this approach. Being grounded in this personal quest for meaningfulness enables one to invite others into more meaningful processes.

Q: Dissonance does not feel good. Why do you want me to hurt myself?
It is unrealistic to think that things will be good, harmonious, and balanced all of the time. Chaos can be positive and produce wonderful results. As leaders, we should

embrace ambiguity at times. One of the authors reflects on his leadership and recognizes how many of his proudest moments resulted from chaos. The final product was more than he could have imagined and only came as a result of letting go, trusting others, and embracing ambiguity. Over-planning and hyper-control can stifle creative and wonderful ideas that can turn good ideas into triumphs.

MANAGING AND MENTORING YOUR EDUCATIONAL SELF

Managing and mentoring for personal educational fulfillment involve making choices in order to artfully orchestrate savouring, understanding, and bettering experiences so they become more a part of one's daily life. As a start, this entails exercising one's imagination, constructing flow experiences, using realistic and positive self-talk, building habits of self-reflection, and taking a proactive stance to personal wellness.

What is needed to manage and mentor inviting and imaginative selves?

Can you talk with yourself in an inviting way?

Is imaginative educational living a realistic possibility?

How can you be both the provider and recipient of wisdom, experiences, and reflection?

Because of the persistence, resourcefulness, and courage needed to manage and mentor a fulfilling educational life, these are important questions to ask in order to develop a solid base for imaginative and optimistic action, practical wisdom, and ethical character. This chapter is likely to call your beliefs into question if you:

- Neglect the importance of daily life choices;
- Take no interest in what you say to yourself;
- Believe the body is separate from the mind;
- Do not think you can change your habits.

This chapter is likely to build on your beliefs if you:

- Value your ability to make ethical life choices;
- Want to improve how you talk with yourself;
- Have learned to mentor yourself and others;
- Use ideals to ground your leadership.

Invitational leadership involves trust, intentionality, respect, and optimism, centred around a caring core. In order to lead others, to live educational lives, it is important to manage and mentor oneself with these qualities in mind. Caring for ourselves, trusting experiences and reflections, respecting our own opinions, being optimistic about our ability to positively influence our own future, and doing so intentionally are vital to leading from an invitational perspective. We know more than we potentially give ourselves credit for and have a plethora of experiences to draw from and reflect upon.

THE IMPORTANCE OF CHOICES

Whether we like it or not, whether we are aware of it or not, educators are always making choices. Even to decide not to choose is a choice. Living educationally (i.e., teaching, administering, leading, and mentoring) is all about making choices. For the most part we do not give much thought to these choices and their impact on ourselves and others. This is because many of these choices are normalized within the school culture and are often seen as "the way we do things around here." Educators are often called upon to make choices such as: How do we challenge inappropriate comments and behaviours? Do we use policies to benefit students, staff, and communities? How do we choose resources that are representative of the students' lives? How do we include parents in decision making about their children? Though often operating below our level of usual awareness, these choices influence how we invite and value ourselves, how we structure schools, how we develop policies, how we select and sort students, how we decide on the type of curriculum we provide or do not provide, how we implement the pedagogical practices we choose, and the management and leadership practices we favour. Try as we might, we cannot avoid making decisions.

If the last chapter was about a leader leading oneself to come to grips with reality, perceptions, and self-systems, this chapter is about a leader intentionally managing and mentoring oneself to develop good habits necessary for educational living that are grounded in imagination and hope. Knowing what we should be doing and actually doing it are not the same things. It is often said that "the road to hell is paved with good intentions." Go to any health club in the first week of January and again the first week of February and notice the reduction in moving bodies. In a similar vein, embarrassingly, one of the authors has discovered that it was easier for him to show someone how to use a program on a computer than it was for him to use it himself. Developing imaginative and persistent personal managing strategies involves being aware of one's human foibles and making and implementing sound and creative choices to move them in positive directions. Inviting leadership involves managing and mentoring others as well as mentoring oneself. Learning from personal experience or from others who have developed sound judgment through experience, thought, and reflection is a way to pass on and mobilize personal, professional, and organizational knowledge and traditions to support and serve a better future.

DEVELOPING PRACTICAL WISDOM

The practical wisdom of developing one's own life strategies goes beyond reciting maxims and implementing formulas. Everyone is triple-dipped with "wise sayings" and "deep thoughts" as seen on greeting cards, bumper stickers, and bathroom walls. These guilt-inducing reminders of "constantly striving for success because you are worth it" are easily blocked out. This blocking out process is necessary for sanity but may lead to a tendency to feel that nothing can really be done regarding the habits of one's daily life, one's usual way of doing things. There is a feeling that we are condemned to be repetitious. "Been there, done that" attitudes promote apathy, disengagement, and cynicism. Cynicism we believe is unimaginative and cowardly.

Managing and mentoring invitational leadership requires educators to move away from the allure of cynicism and to develop and employ their practical wisdom in authentic ways. Similar to savvy, practical wisdom may be described as a combination of personal characteristics and professional competencies that successful leaders exhibit. These characteristics include, but are not limited to, common sense, craft knowledge, practical and emotional intelligence, interpersonal skills, and the ability to see, predict, and influence the "big picture." Practical wisdom that facilitates managing, leading, and mentoring requires educators to acquire deep knowledge about self, others, and physical and organizational environments. This requires moving beyond knowing what, how, where, and when to knowing why. Knowing why means understanding the rationale for an action. When grounded in our ethical values and supported by integrity, informed optimism, and imaginative action, practical wisdom can be used to facilitate authentic mentoring, managing, and leading of self and others. Although practical wisdom is acquired over time and with experience, it can be mentored using the strategies and approaches described next.

EDUCATIONAL LIFE STRATEGIES

So how is an enthusiastic but wise person to proceed in approaching educational life strategies? We suggest that a leader needs to be prudently passionate (Novak, 2009a). That is, a leader needs to view life strategies as a part of a developmental process, an initially simple way of moving to more complex possibilities. Perhaps the mantra for this prudently passionate approach is this: "What do we want? Change! When do we want it? In due course!" Surprisingly, this can work in many cases.

Managing and mentoring educational life strategies in a prudently passionate way can be seen as a developmental process using the following four steps:

– Awareness: Recognizing that there is an issue and realizing that a strategy or a series of steps exists that might be helpful in managing an educational life.
– Understanding: Grasping the purpose of the strategy and seeing how it connects with other parts of one's life.
– Application: Trying the strategy in a safe setting and becoming aware of and understanding deeper implications of the strategy.
– Adoption: Making the strategy one's own and habitually using it in creative and imaginative ways.

So what does this look like? Beginning with the negative, if someone is unaware of an educational life strategy, it is not possible to use it. Ironically, with so many sources for strategies available in our technologically connected world, there is so much to be both aware of and unaware of. Choosing to focus on a strategy means becoming aware of its deeper purpose and possibilities, and giving it personal meaning by connecting it with other important aspects of one's life. Strategies are not technically isolated skills but integrated ways of learning to engage and grow. Usually, when something has clicked, that is, when it makes sense to a person in terms of who he or she is and wants to become, then there is a willingness to try out the strategy in a safe setting. This is the initial part of the wisdom of practice: do not jump in over your head when you are just learning how to swim. Work in the shallow end and stay close to shore. After someone has tried, modified, and internalized a strategy, then he or she is beyond "learning that" (about the strategy) or "learning how" (becoming skilful in using the strategy) and is instead "learning with" the strategy (expanding oneself and the strategy). This approach for learning and managing life strategies, when internalized, becomes what leaders will model as they lead for educational living. Let us now look at this approach to self-management and mentoring in facing the dialectic of challenge and threat, the operations of the whispering self, and the goal of personal wellness.

SAVOURING DAILY LIFE

John Dewey's philosophy is centred on the importance of the concept of experience. For Dewey, experience represents one's live-connection with the world of people and things. Humans are not neutral observers of a detached world but connected participants in an ongoing development of activities and relationships. But this connective process goes beyond mere doing. What makes an experience educational is not only what the person does but also what a person undergoes as a result of the doing. Quite simply, an educational experience is one that has desirable qualities in the present and leads to future growth. It is one that leaves a good taste in one's mouth along with the wherewithal to gather additional healthy food. Taking this a step further, an educational experience is not merely what happens to you but what you do with what happens to you. Both doing and the undergoing require attention and imagination.

Leading an educational life creates an excitement for learning. A leader should be the lead learner in the community. Taking courses, savouring conferences, and supporting and encouraging others to engage in learning opportunities supports this participation in educational living. This participatory spirit can be infectious. Parents may inquire about how course work is going or students may connect with the fact that the teacher or principal is writing a paper for a course. Speaking with staff about engaging in learning opportunities or writing letters of reference for parents who are applying to teacher's college or masters programs are the fruits of leading an educational life. Active engagement in ongoing learning sustains and encourages others to do so. Staff members or parents going back to school or seeking various educational opportunities fosters an educational culture that invites growth.

In the same spirit as Dewey, beginning in the last quarter of the 20th century, Mihaly Csikszentmihalyi has deeply delved into the psychology of the personal construction of optimal experiences (1990/2008, 1993, 1997, 2004). He calls these optimal experiences "flow." Being able to create optimal experiences is a core component of savouring daily life and Csikszentmihalyi not only researches and theorizes about flow experiences but also provides insights for developing such experiences. What he offers is not a disembodied formula for attaining flow but a practical wisdom perspective that requires artful orchestration in which "the heart, will, and mind are on the same page" (1997, p. 28). Seeking sustained engagement as the core for fulfilling experiences, he further describes these experiences as containing:

- A challenging activity that requires skill: With too much challenge being overwhelming and too little challenge being underwhelming, practical wisdom involves finding the right "whelm" level that builds on the skills that a person possesses. With a task too challenging, it is necessary to break it in to smaller steps and develop appropriate skills. With a task lacking challenges, it is necessary to create ways to extend the skills already possessed.
- The merging of actions and awareness: The disjointedness of thought and action is one of the significant limitations to constructing fulfilling experiences. Being fully present in an experience by using one's skills at an optimal level enables heart, mind, and will to artfully come together and new possibilities for experience to emerge.
- Clear goals and feedback: The old saying that if you do not know where you are going, you will not know when you get there, applies here. Goals are ends that focus attention. Feedback provides information about what is going right or wrong and invites the necessary adjustment to keep an activity on the right track.
- Concentration on the task at hand: The inability to sustain attention makes it difficult to do anything requiring depth of engagement. Learning to develop clear and creative structures provides the direction necessary for accomplishing more complex tasks by counteracting the tendency to be distracted. A focused clarity is needed to overcome an overly roving mind.
- The paradox of control: Worrying about having to be in control is a distraction from being fully engaged. Getting beyond control issues enables a deeper connection with the purpose of the activity to develop and allows a richer interaction to take place. One gets out of one's head and into the dance of experience.
- The loss of self-consciousness: When energy is spent protecting an outdated image of the self, there is less attention available for full engagement in the task at hand. Investment in challenging activities takes a person beyond the self-protection mode and into the arena of creative possibility.
- The transformation of time: While a disconnected activity involves a person experiencing time as grains of sand piling up, in a challenging activity, one requiring skill and attention, a person is engaged with the intrinsic rhythm of the activity and time is simultaneously extended and shortened.

There is much talk in education about learning to be a self-directed learner. Often this means being expected to learn mandated disconnected procedures and skills that lack personal meaning or professional coherence. Csikszentmihalyi's attention to the qualities of optimal experiences gives educators an intrinsic goal to pursue: the artful challenge of orchestrating the fine balance between stress and boredom in all they do. With effort and practice, educational leaders can manage to have the world of work and play merge as they are engaged in constructing creative activities.

Educational experiences and flow activities are optimized through active awareness and practical wisdom. The process of self-mentoring and management is intimately connected to seeking to savour and be artfully challenged by one's daily activities. This moves a person away from being a passive responder to life's events to becoming a creative orchestrator of fulfilling experiences. It moves a person from being reactive to being proactive. Returning to the self-system of the previous chapter, a source for meaningful engagement can be developed by examining the significant "me's" of one's life and looking at the activities engaged in that "me" that contribute to or distract from this sense of a fulfilling experience. Rather than being lived by one's self-system, a person can creatively navigate within it to become a more alive and integrated person. This means deliberately paying attention to the conversations of one's inner life.

ATTENDING TO SELF-MENTORING

A mentee seeks to connect with the right mentor. Someone they can respect. Someone who makes good decisions, learns from experiences, listens, shares, articulates effectively and has time to commit to the relationship. Finding the right mentor is arguably the most important aspect to the development of a mentor/mentee relationship. What better place to start than within yourself? Connecting does not require scheduling, phone calls, or lunch dates, as you should always be available to yourself. Intentionally making that time and being present, however, is a skill worth working on. Mentoring oneself involves the recognition of the fact that you likely know more than you think you do and have more experiences to reflect upon and learn from than you might give yourself credit for. A mentor listens, guides, provides insight, reflects on experience, identifies key issues, and encourages creative approaches to decision making and planning. In order to be that to someone else, recognizing how to be all of the above to yourself is key. As the character Stuart Smalley played by Al Franken on *Saturday Night Live* said: "I'm good enough, I'm smart enough, and doggone it, people like me!" While the character is recognized as a satirical take on the proliferation of self-help literature and group therapy, he reminds us that we perhaps know more than we might even realize. Reflecting on our experiences contributes to our ability to lead and helps us to become our most compatible mentor.

An inviting approach to leadership involves doing things on purpose for purposes that are defensible. Being an optimistic, trusting, caring, and respectful person by nature is a wonderful thing. However, living invitationally requires more than a rosy disposition. Thoughtful reflection and consideration are required to do things on purpose. Living invitationally invites us to recognize the influence our actions and decisions have on ourselves and others. It is not enough to acquiesce to our perception of our initial nature. We can and should be thoughtful about our decisions, practices, and impact and commit to intentionally respecting ourselves and others, being optimistic on purpose, reflecting on our caring core, and trusting ourselves and those around us to similarly commit.

Mentoring yourself intentionally requires thoughtful reflection and consideration of events, decisions, and activities that influence who you are as a leader and person. It would be hard to develop an optimistic organization when you are not optimistic yourself. Cultivating respect for others starts from within. When you live the way you want to lead, your leadership is more likely to resonate with others and invite their contribution to the organization.

Leading intentionally has an element of openness to it as you reveal to others the emphasis you place on reflection, positive self-talk, and consideration of outcomes. As a leader, you are looked at as a model and for direction. Thoughtful consideration of what that means in your context will help determine how that manifests itself in your everyday reality. One of the authors has found that the intentional formation of daily habits contributes to his ability to self-mentor. When presented with challenging decisions or difficult situations, he asks himself "Am I taking my own advice?" and "Would I mentor someone else in the same way as myself?" Being a mentor to others has a degree of simplicity to it because a third-person objective position can be free from bias, ego, and emotion. By intentionally asking self-mentoring questions, one can force oneself to consider situations as objectively as possible. (And when he takes his my own advice, he finds that he can be a pretty good mentor to himself!)

It is entirely possible to be a caring, optimistic, trusting, and respectful person without ongoing reflection or extensive self-awareness. Living intentionally, however, requires awareness and commitment to thoughtful reflection and self-talk in order to reasonably anticipate outcomes. Having goals and desired outcomes requires consideration of the best way to achieve them. An intentional approach to leadership requires self-reflection and honesty about how things have gone, are going, and can go in the future.

PROBING INNER CONVERSATIONS

To be an educational leader it is important to learn about learning. This learning process is importantly personal as educators attend to the inner conversations of their life. The Socratic injunction to know thyself takes on concrete form when attending to what we say to ourselves, listening to how we say it, and seeing how inner conversations influence the quality of the educational life we experience on a daily basis. This is called attending to the "whispering self" (Purkey, 2000).

Often, it seems because we think no one else is listening to our internal dialogues we take liberties with what we say to ourselves about ourselves. At times we may be unnecessarily harsh and unrealistic with ourselves but allow such practices to continue because we think that is just who we are and change is out of our control. That is a passive approach to inner experiences, a denial of personal responsibility, and is out of synch with the intentional stance that leaders need to help modify habits in themselves and others.

Regarding one's sense of self, every person is an information processor and a character constructer. That is, one's sense of self is informed by the messages one receives and interprets, in addition to being formed by the messages one chooses to send or not to send. In the more intricate case of self-talk, each person is his or her message sender, receiver, interpreter, and developer of patterns of behaviour. This being the case, the importance of realistic and positive self-talk becomes paramount as one's inner life is self-evaluated and extended through the actions chosen. Unfortunately, what can happen in the inner sanctum of one's private world is that unrealistic, inappropriate, or unduly negative patterns of self-talk can take on an unseemly life of their own in public. It seems that often people will say things about themselves in public that they would not say about their worst enemies. Surprisingly, this public attack on ourselves may actually be a form of arrogance because what we are subtly implying is that we can understand how mere mortals can make mistakes but somehow that does not apply to us.

Realistic and positive self-talk is not a retreat from the difficulties of life but rather is a way of facing situations with more of our inner resources working for us. There is no guarantee that things will work out for the better in any situation but there is a better chance that they will if we are not working against our self. Having the odds more in one's favour is more likely to happen if one is aware of and rethinks several of the distortions noted by Paula Helen Stanley (1992, pp. 231–237):

- All-or-none thinking: Believing things are either black or white; if everything you do is not totally good, you must be all bad. In reality, situations can be viewed from many perspectives.
- Overgeneralization: Inferring too much from too little; if at first you do not succeed, you never will. In reality, human action is rarely narrowly determined.

> ### *About Inner Conversations*
>
> *I was playing tennis with a friend who would loudly berate himself every time he missed a shot. I had just developed my thinking about self-talk and went to the other side of the net and said to my tennis partner, "Stop talking like that about a friend of mine." My partner looked confused and said, "Hey, I'm talking about myself." So I replied, "And aren't you a friend of mine?" There was a silence and then my friend said, "I'll tell you what. I'll keep quiet if you stay on your side of the net." I complied with this suggestion and the match was a more enjoyable activity for everyone involved.*

- Mental filtering: Looking only for details that confirm your beliefs; spotting a lack of enthusiasm as a sign of total rejection. In reality, situations contain both positive and negative indicators.
- Mind reading: Accepting your first thought about what others are thinking of you; thinking you really know what is going on inside others' heads. In reality, people's thoughts are often not readily apparent and can be easily misread.
- Fortune telling: Feeling that you know what will happen in the future; claiming to be right about alternative scenarios. In reality, knowledge of what will or could happen is, at best, hypothetical.
- Magnification: Exaggerating the significance of an event; believing that what is important to you is important to everyone. In reality, it is not all about you.
- Emotional reasoning: Believing that your first thought is your final thought; feeling negative is proof that bad things will happen. In reality, emotions provide a first but not final indication about what may be happening.
- Labelling: Overgeneralizing about yourself; putting yourself down with statements like "total loser" or "quitter." In reality, everyone is a mixture of qualities.
- Personalization: Taking ownership of another's moods or actions; feeling yourself to be the total cause of another's difficulties. In reality, there are multiple reasons for others' difficulties.
- Blaming: Feeling others are the total causes of your moods or actions; believing another person makes you do something. In reality, we participate in the development of our moods and possibilities.
- Catastrophizing: Expecting the worst things to happen; exaggerating "what if" statements. In reality, the worst thing that can happen is relatively rare.
- Double jeopardy: Punishing yourself for your cognitive distortions; feeling that distortions make you an unreliable person. In reality, everyone makes distortions; it's called being human.

Interestingly, it is often very easy to spot these distortions in others and, in the abstract, with oneself. Obviously, the real challenge is to detect oneself in the actual process of distorting realistic and positive possibilities.

Self-talk is an automatic process that can have negative or positive outcomes depending on how we choose to dialogue with ourselves. Consequently, intentional management of internal conversations is an important part of self-mentoring and it looks to a first principle for framing possible actions. Borrowing from medicine, the initial step is to "first do no harm". Stopping the negative then allows the following things to develop (Stanley, 1992, pp. 237–239):

- Becoming an avid listener to your self-talk: Paying attention to what you say to yourself and, more importantly, how you say it. You will be surprised at what you hear yourself saying.
- Separating fact from fiction: Acting as a good researcher in examining the evidence for one's self-indictments. Evidential thinking has a way of grounding accusations in fact and reasoning.

- Treating oneself with the same respect given to others: Realizing that if it is worth doing to others it is worth doing to oneself.
- Using the reframe: Appreciating that there are always many reasonable ways to look at any event.
- Avoiding the extremes: Staying away from words such as "always" and "never" when referring to your actions. Notice, we have avoided saying "never use always."
- Getting a perceptual check: Requesting from others their observations or interpretations regarding something that occurred.

The above are guidelines and suggestions about where to begin and what you might do to manage wisely the habit of positive and realistic self-talk. Mentoring positive self-talk skills such as self-dialogue and respect, visualizing, reframing, and keeping perspective increases our ability to manage our internal thoughts and emotions while we negotiate the external landscape.

BECOMING REFLECTIVE PRACTIONERS

Managing and mentoring self-talk allows us to engage in critical reflection on our personal and professional lives and to interpret and deliberately act upon our experiences. In *The Reflective Practitioner* (1983), Donald Schon builds upon Dewey's notion of experience as education by suggesting the importance of reflecting upon experiences in order to inform future practice. Schon distinguishes between the reflection "on action" and the reflection "in action" as important practices to informing decision making. Reflecting "on action" is a traditional approach to reflective practice in that the experience has occurred in the past and provides fodder for thoughtful evaluation and assessment from the distance of time. A situation is analyzed, considered, and evaluated for the purpose of cataloguing for future consideration or planning. In contrast, reflection "in action" is similar to Csikszentmihalyi's flow experiences in that consideration, evaluation, reflection, and decision making occur while the action is taking place. Reflecting in action allows for a change in direction while the conclusion of the experience is undetermined at the time of reflection. Reflection in action is similar to flow in that a heightened sense of consciousness is required to allow for the simultaneous processing of the experience itself and the reflection on it. As we mentor ourselves, we are aware of our own experiences, how they influence our decisions and future actions, and how we can draw on our own incredibly vast catalogue of ideas, theories, and perspectives that we have developed and refined over time and in innumerable situations.

Engaging in and sustaining imaginative acts of hope requires focusing on the past, present, and the future. While reflection *on* and *in* action are important parts of management and leadership practice, our inner conversations must also involve reflect *for* action—imaginatively and realistically examining possibilities for consolidation and growth to maintain excitement, and to open up new possibilities for learning.

TRUSTING ONESELF

It is hard to inspire others to trust you if you do not trust yourself. Trust is developed over time as it is earned through experiences, decisions, and relationships. The most intimate relationship we can develop is with ourselves as we connect what we do with the decisions we make regarding who we think we are and who we want to be. We have relationships with ourselves we have been developing our whole lives. Ironically, we know ourselves better than we know anyone else, whether we know it or not. As mentees hope for mentors they can trust, we must begin with ourselves. If we cannot trust ourselves, how can we expect trust from others?

We all have more experiences to reflect on than we may initially realize. Each new situation provides opportunities for reflection as we develop a vast collection of learning experiences. Trusting ourselves to sort through and apply them appropriately is part of developing trust in ourselves. An inviting leader seeks to learn from experience and from others. Trusting oneself is paramount. Mistrust leads to second guessing, analysis by paralysis. Trust does not necessarily ensure "getting it right," but it does recognize the influence that we have on ourselves to make decisions and engage in situations for the right reasons. A mentoring self reminds us to trust ourselves and our decisions, as respectful, optimistic, caring, and intentional manifestations of inviting leadership.

Trusting oneself does not necessarily mean inflexible decisiveness. Leaders are often given credit for being decisive and unafraid of making a decision. Making a decision should not be lauded on its own. Making a defensible decision is much more important. An inviting leader considers, consults, and reflects, trusting in himself or herself to make decisions and inform direction from an ethically defensible perspective. Assume you're a good person interested in developing the organization by developing people, places, policies, procedures, and programmes and start from a trust in that perspective. Mentoring oneself means listening, reflecting, and encouraging trust in one's own competencies, decisions, and intentions. Not a bad place to begin.

Leadership can be lonely, as doing the right thing does not always mean doing the most popular thing. Others will attempt to influence and encourage for reasons which may not be congruent with your perspective. It is in these situations that trusting oneself is so important. A mentoring-self encourages trust in oneself as we learn from experiences, reflect on the future, and learn to rely on the mentor we know the best: ourselves. This self-confidence comes from a reflective sense of self-competence.

RESPECT ONESELF

If you don't respect your own capabilities and intentions, it is hard to respect those of others and to develop a culture that does as well. Leadership hinges upon relationships, and relationships are fostered through respect. When mentoring oneself, a healthy respect for your own ideas, experiences, contributions, and intentions is important if a culture of respect is going to be created. You have lived experiences that contribute to your decision making and those experiences are valid. You lived them. They contribute to you, your decisions, intentions, and goals. It is best to recognize that and respect what you bring to the table as a leader.

We've all had situations where we are at a meeting, silently sizing up everyone at the table assuming they have much more experience, better ideas, and more qualifications. One of the authors remembers vividly entering the first class on the first day of his PhD studies scanning the room and assuming that everyone else was smarter, more qualified, and experienced. As time went on he came to appreciate the gifts and talents that others brought to the program as well as his own. Mentoring a respectful self recognizes and values the unique contributions you bring to the table.

Even if you are a newcomer, it is also important to recognize what you bring to the table is of important value. Mentoring a respectful self involves the recognition of the many abilities you have and respecting your unique perspectives and talents. Respecting yourself does not happen by accident. It involves listening to your whispering self and intentionally evaluating and recognizing what makes you a leader. It is often more than what each of us gives ourselves credit for.

THOUGHTFUL OPTIMISM

It is often said that attitude is infectious. It is amazing how leaders influence the organization and individuals in the simplest of ways. Kind words, a smile or well-placed compliment can make a tremendous impact on a situation or individual. Leaders understand the impact of hope and work toward the cultivation of a culture that is optimistic about the future. While individual situations can be challenging and stressful, an invitational leader does not lose sight of the big picture and the hope that setbacks are minor and detours and diversions only add to the experiences that contribute to the goals of the organization. Inviting leaders welcome the input of others and invite participation in the leadership of the organization. Inviting leaders also call forth leadership in others. If we allow ourselves to become caught up in how hectic our lives are, we run the risk of making educational leadership seem unappealing and stressful. We can reply to innocent queries with horror stories of long hours, volatile situations, and under-appreciation. The reality is much more hopeful. There is a tendency to enjoy sharing how busy we are with one another in a game of one-upmanship as we take pride in proving how much more robust we are than others. This does not inspire others or invite them to embrace leadership. A hopeful perspective is infectious. Initiating such optimism from within requires reflection and positive and realistic self-talk. It should be noted that optimism does not mean the belief that good things are bound to happen. Rather, it is the practical wisdom that good things have a better chance of occurring if we are open to the positive possibilities in situations.

MANAGING PERSONAL WELLNESS

Being a leader involves not only the heart and mind but, more importantly, the development of the whole person. In order to continue to grow with the opportunities and challenges involved in living in a complex society, an educational leader needs a plan for being in it for the long run. A personally inviting plan enables a leader to draw from his or her deepest resources and work with the surrounding energies to make educational living a reality. Such a plan for wellness, the idea that you do not have to be sick to get better, can be developed by using the systematic approach suggested by Donald Ardell (1986) in his classic book, *High Level Wellness*. From Ardell's perspective, managing for personal wellness involves:

− Personal responsibility: Taking ownership for one's life by choosing to dispute negative and unrealistic self-talk in addition to working to create the challenging but not overwhelming conditions for flow experiences to occur.
− Nutritional awareness: Developing an awareness of the long-term nourishment value of what one eats and why one is eating this type of food by slowing down the eating process in order to savour, understand, and digest better foods and enjoy a higher quality life.
− Stress management: Learning how to manage the normal reactions of anger, depression, and anxiety so they do not become overwhelming by working to change distress to *eustress* (Seyle, 1974)—that is, positive stimulation.
− Physical fitness: Engaging in regular and enjoyable activities that promote strength, flexibility, and endurance by paying serious attention to the old adage, "If you do not take care of your body, where will you live?"
− Environmental sensitivity: Becoming receptive to the more-than-human world (Abram, 1996) by attending to the impact we are having on the world (Goleman, 2010) and the impact the world is having on us.

This seems like a lot to expect from educational leaders: to manage our personal lives for flow possibilities; to develop realistic and positive self-talk; and to create lifestyle habits for personal wellness. We would argue that educators should become leaders because they care enough to offer themselves to the larger purpose of educational living. Though a degree of care for the students, staff, and parents can be assumed, it can also be developed through reflection and positive self-talk. It can be easy to become wrapped up in the day-to-day realities of school leadership, but mentoring oneself involves positive self-talk and a whispering self that places care at the core of all decisions. It takes practice but it can be done and it is worth the effort.

MENTORING CONVERSATIONS

Q: Does every choice I make in my daily life affect my educational leadership?
We are more than the sum of our parts. While we would not suggest that you agonize over daily choices or the routine and mundane, we do suggest an intentional approach to decision making in situations large and small. From a "don't sweat the

small stuff" perspective, there are situations and decisions which do not, or at least should not, have significant impact on yourself as a person and a leader. However, there are other choices you make which might. What we are suggesting is a thoughtful, considerate approach to the choices you make and recognition of the impact they have on you as a person and a leader, and on others. When we recognize that we are always sending messages, our everyday interactions take on profound meanings, meanings we perhaps didn't realize were profound before.

Q: How long does it take to develop practical wisdom?
Practical wisdom develops with each new experience as long as you are thoughtful and reflective. Wisdom is the intersection of knowledge and experience. Without an intentionally reflective approach to ideas and situations, the world can blur by and turn into one thing after another. Taking the time to reflect on practice, reconsider, refine, and move forward is a powerful way to develop practical wisdom. Understanding how to do the right thing the right way comes with experience. Experience means very little without thoughtful reflection. If, as stated above, wisdom is found at the intersection of experience and knowledge, wisdom will develop over time as you encounter new experiences and gain the knowledge that comes with thoughtful consideration. Perhaps that's why those who are revered as wise usually have years under their belts. That does not mean that age is a precursor to wisdom, but rather that experiences contribute to the acquisition of wisdom. Start now.

Q: Is prudent passion an oxymoron?
We would not make the connection between passion and impulsiveness. To be passionate is to care deeply about something. To be prudent is to consider all the options and plan accordingly. Individuals can be passionate about travel and live to explore new and exciting places. Those same persons may spend a long time planning for the next excursion, considering options, and doing their research in order to get more out of their experience. Their passion manifests itself in their deep dedication to putting the right things in place for a successful experience. We can be passionate about education and educational leadership, and that passion can lead us to the thoughtful consideration of how to do it better. Passion does not mean flying by the seat of our pants and improvising. In fact, we might suggest that passion might compel someone to be thoughtful and considerate about how to make the experience better.

Q: How can I trust myself and question my self-talk?
Sometimes we do things without effortful thinking. We can get on autopilot and go about our day-to-day lives without reflection. There can be times when this is good. Taking time to relax and decompress is an important aspect of mental health. We are suggesting that we be more in tune with ourselves more regularly in order to understand how we talk to ourselves and how helpful that self-talk is. Being critically reflective means recognizing negative self-talk for what it is and developing ways

to turn negative thoughts into more fruitful possibilities. Engaging in the reflective process is the first step and we would suggest enough to allow you to trust yourself. If you are this far in this book and reading these questions, we suspect you are serious about a self-evaluation. Take inventory on your self-talk and determine how helpful it is to your work as an educational leader. You may be surprised at how supportive you are of yourself, or how challenging you are making things for yourself.

LEADING OTHERS

Leadership is about developing and deepening connections with others. The previous chapter discussed the importance of self-management and mentoring oneself. This chapter explores how inviting leaders work *with* and *for* others to foster authentic relationships that create inclusive approaches and democratic environments that endure. Connecting with others in a way that develops sustained educational leadership practices throughout a school begins with an inviting stance. By establishing "doing" with relationship with others, leaders can prepare, interact, and follow through in a manner that brings to life inviting ethical principles. Working on the craft of inviting others in a systematic way provides opportunities to develop deeper, more collaborative relationships.

What is the role of symbols in the communicative process?

How do dialogical relationships develop?

When can being intentionally inviting with others be systematically practiced?

What are the ethical responsibilities of assuming an inviting stance?

Because ethical and co-operative relationships are the lifeblood of any educational organization, these are questions that need to be asked to maintain the integrity of the interactions taking place. This chapter will likely call your interpersonal habits into question if you:

- Think trust can be legislated;
- Conceive of leadership primarily as badgering and bartering;
- Feel that the knack of working well with people is an inborn trait;
- Think that leading others is about following pre-set formulas.

This chapter is likely to build on your beliefs if you:

- Believe that working with people is about developing trust;
- See the necessity of mutuality in leadership;
- Feel that the art of working with people can be cultivated;
- Think that leading others is more about the orchestra than the conductor.

The ethical leadership stance underlying this book emphasizes the importance of developing relationships that show appreciation for each person in the present and that call forth potential for future growth. Building on the importance of the perceptual underpinnings of human relationships, this chapter connects the qualities of an inviting stance with the goal of habitually operating at an intentionally inviting level.

THE PERCEPTUAL CORE OF INTERACTION

In the previous sections we emphasized the importance of self-perception, the picture people have of who they are and how they fit into the world. This perception of fitting into the world primarily involves connecting with a world of people and social institutions. An inviting perspective recognizes the basic human need to be recognized and builds on this in an ethically defensible way. John Dewey (1922), in his classic text *Human Nature and Conduct*, noted that people are social through and through. Being human in a world with other humans is a complex, dynamic endeavour that involves a person attempting to make sense of others' present sensations, memories, anticipations, habits, hopes, and desires by ways of symbolic interaction. Put another way, rather than operating as a stand-up comedian doing a practiced monologue, relating to others in a human way is more like being thrown into improvisational situations that imaginatively build on symbols and referents. Situations and interactions do not always go as planned (Thank goodness!) and being open to others involves humility and courage.

LIVING COMMUNICATION

Living in the realm of human meaning-making, the communicative process is more roundabout and elaborate because each person is involved in encoding and decoding messages while being immersed in contexts that are open to innumerable interpretations. To simplify what really happens when one person is communicating with another, it helps to think of the communicative process this way: The initiator needs to read a context and to encode a message using symbols that are thought to have reference to the receiver's perceptual reality. The receiver assumes a context and decodes the message by connecting it to his or her perceptual field and infers the intentions of the initiator while sending back a verbal and/ or nonverbal message to the initiator. Because each person is not a blank slate, the complexities involved in this seemingly simple process can easily become incalculable. When so many things can so easily go astray, it is no wonder that we often have a failure to communicate. To overcome this communicative failure, people may respond in a dictatorial, impositional manner, often expecting others comply without question. The old saying, "When I say jump, don't say why, say how high?" certainly makes some things much easier. As educational institutions become more efficiency-focussed and bureaucratic, they have adopted similar doing-to approaches. This is the epitome of a "doing to" or even a "doing in" relationship. People are seen as objects to be used for preordained purposes, which may or may not be for their benefit. Power *over* messages (i.e., "My way or the highway") ensures at best merely compliance. At worst they breed anger and resistance. Fortunately, for educators and their peers and students, there are more imaginative and ethical ways of connecting with others. There are ways of dialogue, of "doing with" each other.

It is dangerous and destructive to the morale of a staff to introduce a new idea or initiative by deferring responsibility to outside authority. A group of people are not as likely to engage thoughtfully in a new project when we say, "The board wants us to do this" or "The Ministry has this new initiative." "Doing-with" encourages shared responsibility and mutual contribution. The success of an undertaking can be impacted tremendously by the way in which it is introduced. This takes practical wisdom, skill, and will.

The open-ended nature of the communicative process can be disconcerting because senders of messages do not have control over how their messages are interpreted. This is especially important when considering the communication tool. Electronic messages can often be misinterpreted based on what the reader is feeling when visual cues are unavailable. Rather than the message being dependent on the sender's gestures, the tone and emotion of an email is often influenced by the receiver's perceptions of words on a screen. Face-to-face communications such as body language, tone of voice, facial cues, and other nonverbal indicators are much more likely to be clearly received. When a personal connection is not possible, picking up the phone or using face-to-face technologies to speak personally is preferable. At least in that situation, there are more opportunities to clarify what is said.

IMPORTANCE OF RELATIONSHIPS

Doing-with relationships are enhanced when they are rooted in a perceptual approach to working with people. First articulated in the 1940s by Carl Rogers, George Kelly, and Arthur Combs, while they were in the Psychology Department at Ohio State University, doing-with relationships are focused on how individuals perceive situations. Dissatisfied with mechanical ways of conceptualizing people and ethically short-sighted strategies for manipulating change in the behavioural psychology of their day, these theorists developed ways of thinking about a person from the inside-out, from the way things looked from his or her perspective. While Rogers developed a person-centred approach to counselling and Kelly created a personal construct psychology, Combs ultimately combined with Donald Snygg to generate a perceptual approach that has been revised several times (Combs, Richards, & Richards, 1976; Combs &

About Relationships

I was preparing a leadership candidate for an interview when the penny finally dropped for me regarding the importance of relationships. We went through potential interview questions: parent conflict = relationships, student discipline = relationships, board politics = relationships, setting direction = relationships, special education = relationships. The ability to develop, grow, and maintain effective relationships is perhaps the most essential leadership trait worth considering, developing, and mentoring.

71

Snygg, 1959; Snygg & Combs, 1949) and applied to teacher education (Combs, 1982; Combs, Blume, Newman, & Wass, 1974), helping relationships (Combs, 2006; Combs, Avila, & Purkey, 1978; Combs & Gonzalez, 1997), and educational leadership (Combs et al., 1999). Combs's approach to working with people can be starkly contrasted to behaviourism: humans are not objects to be stimulated and conditioned but people to be understood by means of empathic interpretation of how a situation is viewed from the person's perspective. This broad perspective to understanding people was used by Wasicsko (1977, 2005) who employed Combs's work to look at dispositions of successful and caring educators. He noted that at a fundamental level they see themselves, others, purposes, and frames of reference in the following ways:

- Themselves: a sense of being identified with those with whom they were working. Feeling connected to others enables educators to think in terms of "us" rather than "them."
- Others: a sense of people as being able to learn important things. Seeing others as having multiple learning possibilities permits educators to build on people's interests and unique ways of making sense of events.
- Purposes: a sense of a people-oriented way of viewing situations. Viewing situations in a people-oriented way allows educators to focus on the humanness of events, on the thoughts and feelings in perceived particular situations.
- Frame of reference: a sense of thinking long term. Seeing events from a long-term perspective makes possible to educators the ability to think of the life-effects of learning something, the difference regarding what is learned and how it is learned.

So, rather than being neutral or manipulative in their relationships and seeing others as fundamentally unable to attain anything but short-term objectives, Wasicsko paints a picture of the connected educator who identifies with people who are able to learn lasting meaningful concepts, skills, and attitudes throughout life. This orientation is based on a sense of empathy, a belief in people's ability, a personal focus, and a consideration of a duration that transcends specific, isolated behaviours. All of this sets a doing with tone in everything an educator does.

Stances That Connect

People-oriented perceptions are a good place to start but ultimately perceptions have to be translated into actions if they are to make a difference. Empathy is achieved by investing in others' lives. Taking the time to connect with staff in real and caring ways contributes to the development of empathetic interpretations of others and situations. Knowing where colleagues come from each morning and what they go home to every evening (family commitments, passions, goals, etc.) contributes to empathic relationships.

The inviting process is a social action and, as such, involves rules and skills. It helps to view it as playing tennis. A basic rule in tennis is that a person is not allowed to cross or even touch the net. Each player has control on his or her side of the net. This is to be respected if the game is to be played with integrity. Next, in preparing to make a shot a player takes a certain stance towards the ball. Although each stance is individual, it needs to follow certain principles if the player is to have sufficient focus, efficiency, and leverage. It should be noted, however, that even the best stance does not guarantee a successful shot. It merely puts a person in a position to make a sound connection. Similarly, the inviting approach to working with people involves communication in which players cannot go over the net but can develop the proper focus to be in the game and have a chance to make solid contact so that something of worth is offered and occurs.

The helping perceptions of seeing oneself as identified with others, seeing others as able to learn important things, being people-oriented, and having a long-term frame of reference are put into play through a stance that shows respect for the net, supplies optimal focus, and provides the energy for appropriate leverage. This stance is centred in a caring core that radiates through trust, respect, intentionality, and meliorism. Each of these needs elaboration.

- Care: Without a core, attributes are free-floating, nice-sounding abstractions. From the inviting perspective, care is the glue that holds everything together. Building on Nel Noddings's (1984, 2005) ethics of care, the inviting stance is about extending the caring impulse, the desire to meaningfully connect with and participate in another's presence and growth. For inviting leaders, this involves receptivity to the other's perspective and a commitment to their educational well-being. Noddings points out that this requires taking the attention away from oneself and listening for the interests and meanings conveyed by the other. If leaders cannot de-centre themselves, get beyond the "it's all about me" disorder, they cannot be disposed to be authentically identified with the unique individuals they interact with and see how they can learn things as meaningful to their lives. This care manifests itself in a person's warmth, empathy, and positive regard (Schmidt, 2013).
- Trust: The social nature of people means that they are fundamentally interdependent in a living and lively system of human messages. As such, each person's ability to learn and grow is vitally connected to the authenticity and competence of those around him or her. Invitational leadership is a collaborative process that depends on establishing trustworthy patterns of relationships that are sustained over time. Without trust, everything is questioned and everyone retreats to a superficial or defensive posture, what Hargreaves and Fullan (2012) call contrived congeniality. With people not "in it together," they are pulled apart and time, energy, and positive possibilities are lost. From an inviting perspective, trust comes from the memory of messages received, interpreted, and successfully acted upon. The quality, quantity, and authenticity of one's invitations live on and through the trust that is built between and among people.

73

- Respect: The inviting approach to leadership is a doing-with process. This means not crossing the net and recognizing that each person has the ability to accept, reject, hold in abeyance, or negotiate the messages that they receive. People possess volitional needs, the ability to decide what is happening and what this means to them. Ignoring this is to disrespect their personhood. Related to their social nature, respect involves an appreciation of each person's uniqueness and his or her contribution to meaningful groups. Looked at from an ethical perspective, this means that invitational leaders need to contest practices that exclude, insult, humiliate, or subject others to prejudicial or unjust treatment. As stated earlier, the democratic ethos builds on the idea that everyone matters. Respectful treatment of all is the everyday manifestation of this commitment. Purkey and Strahan (2002) have noted that respect is the key to inviting positive discipline in schools.

As a school administrator, one of the authors worked with students, staff, and parents to use a 3Rs approach ("Respect for Self, Respect for Others, and Taking Responsibility") as a way to build an inclusive and ethical community. These precepts were used to guide conversations regarding school issues related to planning, decision making, and discipline and to inform short-term and long-term actions.

- Intentionality: Although good things can happen by accident, counting on such occurrences to happen on a regular basis is irresponsible. Luck has its limitations and liabilities. The purpose and direction of the inviting process involves being responsible in initiating and modifying what is done and how it is done in educational institutions. Being intentional means being proactive, getting inviting activities started, and having the persistence and resourcefulness to sustain them over the long run. This involves learning from one's mistakes and

About the Inviting Stance

I recall being at an off-site meeting, having left the school in the care of the principal-designate or teacher-in-charge, when a call came from her about a situation unfolding at the school. As a new principal, the overwhelming urge was to leave the meeting and go back to solve the problem. Colleagues suggested leaving to take care of it but I had told the designate that she was in charge and her judgement was respected. A decision had to be made whether to return to the school and address the problem personally or to intentionally live out the respect and trust I had professed. Returning to the school would undermine all the professed trust and respect not only with her personally but also for her amongst the rest of the staff. So, I talked her through the situation by asking questions and supported her decision, confident that she had everything under control. The situation was handled just fine and the principal-designate continued to grow in confidence as a result.

modifying what one knows and is willing to try. Creating a dependably inviting environment can happen in many ways. Connecting this with a large and growing frame of reference enables an educational leader to be determined and yet flexible in his or her intentionality.

- Melioristic Optimism: This is the thinking person's alternative to "NOPE": Naive Optimism (the belief that good things have to happen) or Pessimistic Entrenchment (the belief that bad things are bound to happen). Quite simply, melioristic optimism is the belief that good things can be made better and bad things can be made less bad through thoughtful consideration of what is happening and what is possible. Connecting with the concept of hope, melioristic optimism is the realistic assessment that good things have a better chance of occurring if one approaches them in a positive and thoughtful manner. Just as we do not want a foolhardy airline pilot who thinks he or she can fly through any conditions, we do not want an educational leader who feels any risk is worth taking. A realistic sense of what is possible along with a critical and creative sense of how possibilities may be attained provides a leader with a wider horizon of possibilities to work with.

The inviting stance supplies an ethical and shared orientation for putting perceptions into action in a sustained, self-correcting way. When this stance is applied to the craft of inviting, it provides a more structured guide to sustained action.

SUSTAINED ACTION

The inviting approach is an artful blend of dispositions, thoughts, and actions. The helping dispositions get to the heart of the matter: education, as a social activity, is about deepening connections to self, others, and life. The thoughts that inform the inviting stance promote an ethical way to approach situations. With a caring core, a leader has a thoughtful place to work from. Acting in a creative and caring manner in approaching ever more complex situations is enhanced through the development of the craft of inviting. It is here where the rubber meets the road. Real things happen as a leader develops the skill of being ready; doing with; and following through.

Being Ready

With the key value of intentionality, a leader has it in mind to do things on purpose for purposes that can be defended. The idea of planning thoughtful action, being proactive, takes place even before people meet. It happens outside and inside, in the ways a leader arranges the environment and prepares her- or himself.

- Preparing oneself. Although the inviting approach is about systematic and sustained caring actions, these actions have their core in reflected personal feelings. The ability to recall what it felt like to be invited or disinvited in one's own schooling experience is a way to empathize with the new people who will be coming into similar situations. Picturing what we want our students, co-workers, and community members to experience and remember from their involvement in our schools is a good way to maintain focus on what really matters in education. This is a way to kindle the desire to be a beneficial presence to others and oneself. In addition, preparing oneself involves the willingness to come to terms with one's prejudices and blind spots. It is here where a critical friend (Branson, 2009) can be of great help. A critical friend is a chosen colleague who you can share your joys, frustrations, and questions with and who wants to understand you and suggest ways for you to grow. The key point is that reflection does not have to be a solo activity. A leader is more apt to expect and plan for good things to happen if he or she has given it a sound perceptual check and nurtured the desire to care with others who share similar inviting values. Sometimes these others have to be from outside one's home setting so the importance of maintaining membership in organizations with kindred spirits can be a way to develop and sustain the creative spark necessary to work from an inviting stance. While formal mentorship programs and various professional development opportunities exist in most school districts, connecting with others professionally outside requires an intentional commitment to do so. Attending conferences, seeking out courses, and connecting with professional organizations open up doors beyond the confines of individual school boards.

– Arranging the setting. It seems obvious to say that invitations take place in, well, places. True enough. But they also take place through places. Workplaces send messages regarding the care, creativity, and co-operation that are going on

> ### *About Being Ready*
>
> *I remember walking into what would become my daughter's school to register her for kindergarten. I had never been in the building before and made my way up to the office. The secretary appeared busy and flustered and while it may indeed have been her 40th registration already that year, it was my first. I quietly completed the paperwork and hoped that I was making the right decision to enrol my daughter there. A lack of personal preparation for greeting people for their first visit to a school sent up red flags about the preparation and concern of the school leadership for other things. At schools I later worked in, the staff were ready for Kindergarten registrations recognizing it as an opportunity to welcome new families to join the community. We began at the front doors where we set up books, chairs, and toys for children while parents filled in forms. We had coffee available for parents to enjoy as they familiarized themselves with the school. Parent volunteers greeted and connected with new parents. Setting the stage was a relatively simple gesture to do but sent the most important message of the priorities of the entire community.*

in them. Some environments are neglected, dull, and isolating while others are personal, imaginative, and inclusive. Creating the former is easy; just do nothing and disorder will take care of itself. Perhaps some unintentionally inviting things will occur but, most probably, will not last. Developing a people-friendly work area that is clean, comfortable, and clear of unnecessary interruptions sends the message that people are important here and they are entitled to feel both comfortable and stimulated. A work environment that is alive arouses the senses. It can be filled with living plants, colourful art work, fascinating conversation, and good smells. Having places for sharing good and tasty refreshments can be a way to "break bread" together, a time-tested way to bond. One leader always has a supply of bottles of water around and begins each meeting with a toast and celebration of good things that are happening in people's lives. In our visits to inviting schools around the world, we have been impressed with the wonderful designs of workrooms, offices, and classrooms. Imaginative acts of hope shine through the persistence and resourcefulness of encouraging surroundings. The setting is something we have the most immediate control over and can send the strongest signals, yet can be so often overlooked. An inviting office is considerate of the stories the paintings on the wall tell, the books on the shelf and the priorities of the inhabitant such as family, local projects, and education. The set-up of the work space which allows for conversations and invites others in sends a clear message to all staff and visitors.

Doing With

Being ready gets one prepared to interact with others in ways that demonstrate the qualities inherent in inviting relationships. These qualities are extended when some specific strategies are put into practice. Below are seven sequential suggestions that enable a leader to show thoughtful and systematic attention to key interpersonal processes necessary for cultivating inviting relationships.

- Developing goodwill. Good feelings and trust between people are essential parts of inviting relationships. Looking for good possibilities in all situations, even if eventually proven wrong, is better than the alternative. "When you prepare for a fight, you'll be in a fight. When you assume the best in others, you'll rarely be disappointed." While these good feelings between people can happen on the spot, usually they take time to develop. This development is negated when someone violates confidentiality, acts in a distant, judgmental manner, or does not follow-through on promises. Even closer to our embodied homes, one's body language sends a variety of messages formally and informally. Disinviting messages can be unintentionally extended through tone or voice, facial expressions, and gestures. For example, when someone is not at ease with a person they may not make eye contact, sound stilted, and exaggerate hand motions. Becoming aware of such actions can come from a critical friend

77

who can enable a leader to develop ways to move to a deeper comfort level. In addition, the appropriate use of disclosure can be an invitation to share and grow together.

- Reaching beyond one's comfort level. It is only natural to like to be around people who like you or who are like you. If these groups are narrow, this negates the principle of democratic ethos that everyone matters. Intentional leaders find ways to expand the circle, to include more people in their comfort range. This is particularly important because invitational leaders need to become better informed by connecting with a variety of people in and out of schools to hear what they are saying and thinking about what is and what should be going on in their school. Inclusive leaders avoid being perceived as having favourites or limiting their range of contact. On a practical level, this can be done by preparing a checklist with the names of people in the school to see who may be being unintentionally ignored. We have talked with administrators and teachers who have used this to systematically be in touch with more and more people, who they would have probably missed if they did not have a systematic reminder.

- Perceiving personal and social contexts. In order to go below the surface of behaviour to the personal meaning of situations, a leader has to attend to how contexts are being perceived by the people involved in a situation. For example, often when people say they do not care, what they may be really meaning is that they do not want to be hurt again. Sometimes, but certainly not always, a disgruntled cynic is really a derailed idealist who is looking for a creative and sustainable spark to get back on a hopeful track. Assuming the best could in fact re-rail the idealist. In looking at the nitty-gritty of personal communication, it is important to realize that people may seem to be showing agreement when they actually may not know what they are agreeing to or may not understand the implications of their agreement. This is especially true in dealing with multicultural situations where people have learned to be polite and nod their heads to things they do not understand or agree with. Listening to the emotional meanings that underlie the words people use and restating aloud what you think they are perceiving is a good way to deepen comprehension for

> ### *About Doing With*
>
> *I knew a principal who felt his high school was getting too large and he decided to systematically invite students to have cake with him on their birthdays. He worked out a plan so that birthdays on Saturday, Sunday, and holidays were included. Students could share positive experiences with everyone who came or could talk with him in private if they had other concerns. He said it took a while for students to get used to the idea that he would listen, but he felt that, except for the personal weight gain, it was worth it. He felt he got a much better sense of what his students felt about their education and their lives.*

all involved. To go a step farther, Jurgen Habermas (1981) notes that distorted communication occurs because others may not comprehend, agree with, trust the sincerity, or concur with the appropriateness of what is being said. This is a lot to consider but invitational leaders learn how to work through these distortions.

– Constructing life-affirming invitations. For an inviting message to work, it needs to be accepted. For it to be accepted, it needs to be perceived as meaningful, as something of worth. A recipient of an invitation is more likely to take the time and interest to accept an invitation if he or she feels that the extender has taken the time and interest to extend a thoughtful, personal message. Many invitations are not accepted because they are seen as "one size fits all" comments, ignoring the uniqueness and capability of the receiver. This is particularly true of praise. Our colleague, William Purkey, notes that many teachers are "dead cat" praisers, meaning that whatever a student brings in, including a dead cat, will elicit a global, positive response. Such messages, often communicated with a mechanical, saccharine smile, seem rehearsed and lack the authenticity to be taken seriously by anyone without a desperate need for approval. A life-affirming invitation, on the other hand, is often based on the recognition of the meaningfulness of the efforts someone has put forth and the legitimate successes of these efforts. To acknowledge such personal effort is a concrete manifestation of professional appreciation.

– Making sure the message is received. In the Thomas Hardy (1891/1965) book, *Tess of the D'Urbervilles*, there is a tragic miscommunication. Tess writes a letter to her fiancé revealing an indiscretion in her past. She then puts the letter under his door and tells him that if she sees him smiling the next day, she will know that he forgives her and nothing else needs to be said. Sure enough, the next day he is smiling and nothing more is said until it is discovered that the letter never reached him because it slid under the carpet. Much sadness and heartbreak occurs as a result of Tess not making sure the message was received. From an inviting point of view, it is the responsibility of the extender to see that an invitation is actually sent, received, and acknowledged. In addition, it is essential that the extender let the receiver know what is being agreed to when, where, and how. This is not only important for leadership, but good advice for any relationship. There is a story of a married couple arguing publicly when one says to the other, "When we are talking, I am assuming that the information exchanged is understood. In the future, please tell me when you stop paying attention so I can re-visit the conversation!" Communication is a reciprocal relationship. It only works when both parties are equally engaged in sending and receiving messages. On a personal note, another one of the authors, during his graduate student years, was talking for an extended period to another student, when she suddenly said, "Are you asking me out?" He said, "Yes," and she said, "Then you better tell me when and where so we can be at the same place at the same time." In this case the demand for clarity by the recipient enabled a date, and later a marriage, to occur and still continue.

- Working out alternatives. There is no assurance that even the clearest, most life-affirming invitation possible will be accepted the first time it is extended, or maybe ever. Clarity in the inviting process does not guarantee acceptance, but it enables the extender to see what can be negotiated. In the inviting process, the sender and receiver have different roles. The sender, on one side of the net, decides the conditions for extending an invitation while the receiver, on the other side of the net, decides the conditions for acceptance. The conditions can be open for negotiations so that new possibilities can be considered and agreed upon. This dialogical process needs to be seen in contrast to the broken-record training technique promoted in assertiveness training courses. The broken-record technique is a one-sided mechanical approach intended to get the other person to comply, while the dialogical approach is an attempt to arrive at an imaginative amending and restatement of a more acceptable possibility. Getting to the realm of the concrete, a direct way to get to an acceptable invitation is to ask the other person, "If you will not accept this invitation, let me know one that you will accept." When the receiver becomes the hypothetical extender, new possibilities and understandings can develop.
- Living beyond rejection. Even if you have developed goodwill, reached beyond your comfort level, perceived the personal context of the receiver, constructed a life-affirming invitation, made sure it was received and understood, and worked out possible alternatives, the receiver of the invitation can still say no. Dialogical processes are open-ended and the final results are not guaranteed. Certainly, being rejected can hurt. Certainly leaders may seriously question an approach that may leave them professionally and personally vulnerable. Certainly having guaranteed successes would make one's life easier. However, stepping back and examining the process may provide a deeper understanding of what really happened and why. For example, it might be that an invitation was not actually rejected but a person really needed more time to think about it. This can happen, and often does. Non-acceptance is not the same as rejection. Still, there are times when an invitation is clearly rejected. What to make of this? Well, first of all it is important to realize that saying no to an invitation is not the same as rejecting the person who extends the invitation. There are many reasons why a person may reject an invitation that have nothing to do with the extender of the invitation. Many things are happening in people's lives that are unknown and unreachable to others. It is not all about the extender of the invitation. One final twist, a rejected invitation may make it easier for a person to accept a later invitation. That should count for something.

FOLLOWING THROUGH

Returning to the tennis analogy, the inviting approach starts on the sender's side and next moves to the receiver's side. The culmination of the approach comes back to the point of origin where the invitation is responsibly fulfilled and the process reflected upon. This involves the final two steps:

- Fulfilling responsibilities. The inviting process is an ethical approach to working with people in dialogical ways. As an ethical responsibility, the sender needs to make sure that when an invitation is accepted, what was offered is made available. Not to complete the invitation is not only unethical, it can be doubly disinviting. It communicates to the receiver that he or she is not important enough for you to follow through on what was promised in addition to being foolish enough to believe you. Such irresponsible behaviour on the part of the sender, in which action does not follow what was promised, contaminates the inviting process and makes it more difficult for a person to accept future invitations. What may have started out as something kind soon becomes something cruel. With that in mind, it is important for the sender to be clear on what is being invited and what is required to responsibly complete the invitation. Returning back to the ideal of inviting educative experiences, leaders need to invite themselves personally in terms of attempting new learning experiences so they can have a personal sense of what they are inviting others to do and become. In this respect, the personal experience of leading an educational life connects intimately with the ideal of professionally leading for educational lives.
- Reflecting on the process. This final stepping back is, first of all, a time for re-examining the whole experience. If an invitation has been accepted and ethically completed, the experience should be savoured. When you get right down to it, this is why you are an educator, to appreciate people in their uniqueness and participate in their growth. Invitations make this happen and should serve as a reminder of the success that is possible. On the other hand, if an invitation has not been accepted, it can provide a learning experience for getting wiser about the inviting process. Perhaps the invitation was unclear or too much too soon. Perhaps the receiver did not have the time, skill, or interest to act on the invitation. What might be done differently? Who might I discuss this with? As an active participant in an evolving theory of practice, what have I learned about myself and the process of inviting that I might use as I grow in the craft that calls forth and sustains educational lives?

Calling forth and sustaining others in their participation in the process of educational living is about the simplicity that lies on the other side of complexity. There is so much involved in the educational communicative

> ### *About Reflective Leadership*
>
> *Reflective leadership not only contributes to my ongoing pursuit of wisdom, but it is a humbling experience as well. I am not as interested in being a decisive decision maker, as I am with making the right decision. A reflective consideration may reveal flaws in my decision making, which is important if I'm going to make better future decisions. Shining a self-reflective light on the process requires the acceptance that I am not always right, but my goal is to improve with each experience.*

process that it is easy to get confused and overwhelmed. Learning to articulate one's commitments and developing an inviting stance are ethical ways to begin. Using that stance as a base for developing the craft of inviting takes one to new levels of complexity. The simplicity called for here means to get to the heart of the practice of inviting educational leadership. It means blending one's personality, commitments, and deepest thoughts to working on developing doing with relationships. This commitment is called forth in the process of managing conflict, which we will look at in the next chapter.

MENTORING CONVERSATIONS

Q: How do you know if someone trusts you?
You will know if someone trusts you if they support you without interfering, if they value your opinion enough to allow it to influence their own, and if they seek your counsel for ideas and support rather than simply affirmation of their own. You will know you are trusted when you are given projects to run with and the latitude to do so in creative ways. If someone trusts you, you will recognize their presence as support rather than oversight. Many leaders may find living trust in practice to be difficult. Trust requires a degree of comfort with ambiguity and the recognition by the leader that his or her vision may not be the best vision in the end. A lack of trust usually accompanies a lack of self-confidence. A trusting, confident leader tends to be a better mentor to others by encouraging and supporting rather than instructing and informing. If your approach to leadership is "If you want things done right, you'd better do it yourself," you likely have difficulties trusting others. Trusting others allows more to be accomplished and increases the likelihood that others will continue to contribute to the organization in meaningful ways.

Q: Do I have to trust people absolutely?
Trust is about relationships. You have different relationships with different people based on your shared experiences. We talk a lot in this book about developing wisdom which comes from the intersection of knowledge and experiences. Trust develops over time and strengthens with each situation. Trust can also be eroded based on experiences as well. Our assertion is that inviting leadership starts from a trusting core and builds from there. We assume that people are capable, willing, and able to contribute something of worth to the organization. Starting with trust accelerates the development of the relationship. Think of a relationship as a 100- meter race. At the beginning of a relationship, everyone is in the starting blocks. To begin the relationship by trusting others, a leader can begin at the 20-meter mark. Trust allows us to hit the ground running. Since we're already running, trust will encourage others to accelerate because they are recognized for doing good things and assumed to be trustworthy. The concept that trust can only be earned places us back in the starting blocks, forcing us to accelerate from nothing. Recognize where you are along the race, be wise based on your experiences, and continue to move forward with each relationship, even if you have been knocked backward.

Q: How can I develop an inviting stance if I'm not sure that I agree with everything implied in it?

Upon writing, reading, editing, and re-reading this book, we recognize that we are espousing a lot of ideas connected to practice. It might indeed seem overwhelming, especially if the ideas in this book are entirely incongruent with the way you are leading or the way you have always thought leadership is supposed to be. Start with what you connect with. If there is an idea or suggestion you would like to try, start there. We have talked to many leaders who have shared their enthusiasm for the ideas in this book, as well as potential skepticism about their ability to implement in their current situation. That's okay. At least they are considering their leadership and contexts and reflecting on how to live and lead better. We have suggested ideas as simple as leaving your office door open as a way to start. Find the most reasonable and immediately implementable ideas in this book and start there.

Q: Are there some basic things that should be a part of any inviting environment?

A thoughtful consideration of the messages being sent and received is the starting point for the consideration of any inviting environment. What does the front garden say about the care and detail that is taking place inside the school? How is the front entranceway, foyer, and office an inviting place for staff, students, parents, and guests? How does all formal communication—from the signs within the school, outside the school, on the website, or newsletter—reflect inviting practice? A reflective audit of the messages being sent is a great start as well as a useful ongoing practice.

ARTFULLY MANAGING CONFLICT, REALLY

Even when people intentionally practice invitational leadership, conflict does not vanish. It can, however, be managed in ways that exemplify the basic principles of the inviting approach and, in some cases, can be growth-producing for all involved. Rather than fighting fire with fire in an already heated situation, principled strategies at different stages of tension can redirect the energy toward positive solutions. In addition, philosophical differences can be approached in a way that builds on authentic conversational questions.

Are invitational leaders above conflict?

Should disagreements be avoided?

Can conflict be growth-producing?

Is it possible to reach agreement in every situation?

Because of the care and good sense needed to handle incendiary situations, these are questions that need to be addressed if educators are to come to terms with disagreements. This chapter will call your beliefs about conflict into question if you:

– Think that the only good conflict is one that disappears immediately;
– Feel philosophical conversations produce nothing of practical use;
– Enter into conflict attempting to convince the other side you are right;
– Rely on your position of authority to produce the outcome you want.

This chapter will likely build on your beliefs if you:

– Think conflict is a natural part of organizational life;
– Think conflict management can be dealt with proactively;
– Think philosophical conversations can build respect for complexity and diversity;
– Rely on your principled stance to influence mutually acceptable outcomes.

In many people's minds, the picture of a wonderful day means that the sun needs to be is shining. Likewise, in many educators' picture of a wonderful school, everyone is smiling. However, pictures give limited perspectives because they are only a snapshot, a moment in time, without a past or future, usually taken because people are posing what we want to project. Certainly, sunny days and smiling faces should be appreciated, but they are a limited picture of what makes a wonderful day or school. School leaders are faced with conflict on a regular basis. We live in a fast-paced, multilayered, often cloudy world where reaching agreement on important issues can take serious effort, and even then not occur. Amidst this complexity, confusion, and conflict, it is important to have a workable perspective on what to do when the sun is not shining, people are not smiling, and differences arise. An inviting perspective recognizes the reality of conflict and intends for leaders to use an approach to conflict resolution that cultivates win-win situations. Managing conflict from an inviting stance is not only possible but is also where the rubber meets the road. When that road is slippery and filled with bumps, it is very important to have a well thought-out plan for manoeuvring. This chapter provides a principled strategy for dealing with individuals many would rather not face.

INTERPERSONAL TENSIONS

Conflict is almost always emotional and particularly so when it involves cherished values and professional territory. Ignoring the highly emotional aspect of school leadership can spark conflict. Normally sensible and rational individuals can quickly turn emotional and unreasonable and others respond in kind. The tension of being rubbed the wrong way also provides the possibility for new ways of functioning and seeing things. When interpersonal tensions are handled well, more complex relationships with deeper understanding and respect can come into being; handled poorly, relationships are destroyed, people are hurt, and organizations become toxic. Understanding and addressing conflict is essential to leading, learning, and mentoring.

Using the Six Cs

Dealing with conflict is about respectful resolutions, not winning or asserting one's dominance. The foundational values of an inviting perspective are of most importance during times of conflict, as respecting others, trusting their intentions, caring about all involved, and being positive about the outcome contributes to working resolutions. The challenge for invitational leaders is to use the principles of the inviting stance to effectively deal with

About Conflict

When I was taking a principal's qualification course, one of the instructors, a principal at a high school in a neighbouring board, announced to the class "Most of you should not be here. An enormous amount of a principal's time is spent dealing with conflict. Most people are conflict-averse and will do anything to avoid it. You cannot be a principal and avoid conflict, so think long and hard about whether you should be sitting here or not. The odds are the most of you are not cut out to be a principal." We all sat in stunned silence. Despite the instructor's warning, all of us completed the class. While I might disagree with the instructor's sweeping dismissal of the majority of the administrative candidates' ability to effectively manage conflict, I do agree that she was right about conflict.

interpersonal tensions. With this challenge in mind, the "Rule of the Six Cs" was created, tested, and modified over the last two decades (Novak & Purkey, 2001; Purkey & Novak, 1996; Purkey, Schmidt, & Novak, 2010). The Six Cs uses a graduated approach to addressing conflict. This practice-oriented method for dealing with difficult situations has the following goals:

- Settle conflicts at the lowest possible emotional level: making available a wider range of perceptions.
- Use the least amount of energy: saving effort for other tasks.
- Demonstrate respect: showing the integrity and commitments of the inviting principles.
- Learn and grow in the process: finding the educational value in what did and did not work.

The rule of the Six Cs is to begin with the lowest possible C and commit oneself to it as long as it is viable and only move up to a higher C when necessary. The Six Cs represent six separate and increasingly firmer ways for dealing with challenging situations. Each of the Cs and its focus can be briefly described as follows:

1. Concern: Identifying latent and actionable causes of uneasiness.
2. Confer: Using a nonthreatening communication style to make a request.
3. Consult: Working together to review what has happened.
4. Confront: Providing a clear warning of logical consequences.
5. Combat: Following through on sanctions.
6. Conciliate: Reaching out to start afresh.

How we perceive and approach conflicts has an impact on their outcomes. The underlying psychological observation is that it does not take much effort or thought to throw gas on a spark, but the result is predictable: a large fire that can cause a great deal of damage. A leader sets the tone and direction in an educative atmosphere. A manager puts out fires that can still occur. With guiding principles, understanding, and skill, heat can be managed, possibly put to good use, and more people can stay in the kitchen. Let's now go through each of the Cs and see the reasoning involved and the questions that need to be asked in order to function at the appropriate invitational level.

Concern

The beginning of conflict resolution is a caring response revealed through a genuine respect for the situation, those involved, and the potential for a positive solution. School leadership viewed in a mechanical way is simply a job that presents difficult and complex problems to be solved or silenced. Invitational school leadership embraces the individuals who contribute to and are affected by conflict and endeavours to contribute to positive change.

With care being at the core of invitational leadership, identifying the issue and committing to its resolution is the first stage in the process. The concern stage is the first of the Six Cs because it sums up an invitational perspective by intentionally caring about and respecting those involved, trusting their intentions and capability to resolve an issue, and being optimistic for the future. A concern refers to a reflection as to whether something needs to be done in an uneasy situation if we are to be professionally responsible to others or personally respectful of our own feelings. When there is a potential conflict, when you are rubbed the wrong way and feeling tense, a very helpful first step is to determine what the conflicting issue is and whether taking action is the necessary or the wise thing to do at this time. How can simply identifying concern resolve conflict? While many people chose to ignore conflict at all costs and hope it will go away on its own, identifying the conflict often reveals the elephant in the room. Pretending a situation does not exist or is not a conflict also communicates a lack of respect for those involved, and the organization as a whole, since unresolved situations can irritate and disrupt a community. Invitational leaders care about relationships and recognize the impact a conflict can have on those directly involved as well as the larger community. A concerned leader essentially says: "There is an issue; this is what it appears to be; this is what can be acted upon."

Quite simply, at this stage it is useful to pose this question to oneself: "Is this a matter of concern, latent or actionable, or merely a preference?" Actionable concerns require immediate attention. Something needs to be done, now! Quite simply, these are matters of safety, welfare, morality, or reasonable personal annoyance. For example, the emergency exits in a school are blocked by chairs. This is not something that needs to be taken home and reflected on. A specific, measured action has to be taken for the safety and welfare of everyone. A latent concern, on the other hand, is something that you notice that might be a problem, so you will keep an eye on it. For example, if a colleague has started coming late for meetings, you might observe if this is a continuing problem before deciding to take action. A preference, on the other hand, is something you would personally like to see happen but realize that it is outside of your realm of responsibility or power to change. For example, a colleague keeps retelling old, self-indulgent stories that are neither interesting nor funny. This may annoy you but you realize that no one is really hurt or endangered by what is said.

Being able to recognize an actionable concern, a latent concern, and a preference and acting accordingly can mean the difference between calm, assured leadership and hectic, stressful fire extinguishing. Here are some things to think about in deciding if something is a preference or latent or actionable concern:

– Does the situation involve a legal, moral, or safety issue?
– What else might I need to know before I take action?
– Can I really do anything productive about this?
– Can this be looked at in any other way?
– Is my concern due to personal prejudices or biases?

One of the author's favourite Ashley Albright cartoons shows a picture of a deep and serious reflective person with furrowed eyebrows on a mountain top asking himself:

"Who will take care of the world after I am gone?" Dealing with whether something is really a concern and finding out it is not can be a very liberating feeling. Many, but certainly not all, potential conflicts can be effectively dissolved at this level. For those that cannot, it is time to move on to the next C.

Confer

One of the signs of being a professional is the ability to demonstrate complex understanding and skills when facing challenging situations. This is a key part of what the professional education of educators is intended to be about. In working with people for educational purposes, it is especially important that professional educators go beyond what the unreflective person would do. Natural instincts and customary ways of behaving can take care of many situations, but not all. What makes conflict so confounding is that the usual ways of doing things are often counterproductive. They can add heat to a fire when a less inflammatory way is required. Invitational leadership aims to achieve voluntary participation in an ethical process seeking to call forth educational living. This is not always easy, but it is much more difficult when you are out of control yourself.

This second C begins by calming yourself and then displaying this self-control and active listening throughout the process. In a conflict, all parties want to be heard and respected. We rarely, if ever, convince the other person that we are right and they are wrong, yet we often find ourselves valiantly attempting to do just that. Actively listening to words and emotions, demonstrating empathy, and having the other person feel that they are being heard can contribute to a positive and collaborative resolution.

The conferring process begins with an informal conversation done in private. Privacy is vital because the aim of the conference is to have a relaxed and non-threatening meeting where your concern can be expressed in a respectful way. Essentially, you need to let the other person know what your concern is, why it is a concern, and what is proposed to resolve the concern. Following this, you need to get agreement from the other person to go along with what is proposed. Nothing more, nothing less. To do this, a method called the "3+++wish? approach" was developed (Purkey et al., 2010). This approach represents expressing three honest positive messages, letting the person know what is requested, and asking the question: "Will you do this for me?" For example, returning to the case where your colleague keeps coming late for meetings, it would go like this: You would meet in private and say to your colleague, "I enjoy working with you, you have much to offer our group, your creative insights have been of great assistance and your coming late to our meetings disrupts the efforts of our group. Could you please come on time? Will you do this for me?" The three positive messages do not all have to be verbal. They do, however, need to be honest and appropriate. Notice also that "and" was used rather than "but" because people have a tendency to disregard anything that comes before a "but." In addition, asking for and obtaining verbal agreement is important at this stage. This lets the other person know what is expected of him or her and that he or she has agreed to do this. Later, if there is movement to a higher C, discussion of the verbal agreement re-enters the process. Here are some things to think about at this conferring stage:

– Was this done in private?
– Have I respectfully expressed my concern?
– Have I found out any new information?
– Did I use the "3+++wish?" strategy?
– Did I receive voluntary agreement?

Used in good faith and practiced in low level conflicts first as you get comfortable with this approach, it can enable most conflicts to end here. When there is more to be done, it will be necessary to move to a higher C.

Consult

Conferring uses the least amount of your assertive capacity. When it does not successfully resolve the issue, it is necessary to shift to a more formal level, the consultation stage, with emphasis on the other person. Starting again in private, the leader reminds the other person about the previous agreement and the fact that the agreement had not been honoured. The leader listens to what the other person may wish to say about the situation and serves as a consultant in offering suggestions regarding what the other person might need to do. In this role as consultant, leaders may clarify and monitor their own feelings, review expectations, ensure understanding, or consider reconceptualization of the issue, always, however, emphasizing the previous commitment to the agreement. The leader may wish to help the person keep the agreement and may invite brainstorming in this problem-solving mode. Individuals come into conflict usually through miscommunication and/or a strong and opposing

About Consulting

I was a principal in a secondary school where a group of veteran teachers actively and consistently undermined attempts to integrate students with special needs in their classes. Recognizing the negative impacts on students and the school culture, I met with the leader of the group to discuss his intentions. I began by highlighting his leadership skills, his positive contributions to the school, and his commitment to school success. I then voiced concern about his pattern of resistance and its impact on students and new teachers. Recognizing that I couldn't legislate his compliance, I invited him to assist in leading a school-wide committee to support mainstreaming. With mentoring and guidance, this teacher was able to play an important role in bringing other veteran teachers on board. Although this was before the construction of the Six Cs, it was done with the same doing-with spirit.

stance on a situation or an issue. When expressing concern and conferring on the issue do not resolve the conflict, consulting all parties is the next step toward resolution. This requires more direct guidance and intervention as those involved are consulted on what they can bring to the situation to help to solve it. While the first two stages are optimistic that this can be done earlier, the consult stage discusses what actions can be taken to come to a resolution and places responsibility squarely on the shoulders of all parties.

Returning to the situation where your colleague is coming late to meetings, even after agreeing to come on time, you may brainstorm and decide to move some of the meetings closer to his school. Again, you obtain his agreement to be on time and may choose to shake on it. Here are some things you may wish to think about at this stage:

- Have I gone over what was previously agreed to?
- Have I listened to determine if there was any new information that came up?
- Have I tried to help the other person meet the agreement?
- Have I examined the consequences of not resolving the conflict?
- Have I started keeping records about what is happening?

As good as you may be at problem-solving and working as a consultant, sometimes the conflict is still not resolved. If this happens, it is time to move to the next C.

Confront

The word "confront" comes from the Latin word *confrontare*, meaning to face and to challenge. To move from consulting to confronting is a move to face an ongoing challenge with a no-nonsense, straightforward attempt to resolve the concern. Sometimes leaders need to remind people of their professional, legal, and ethical obligations. Although still working from an inviting stance, a leader will indicate that the concern has been repeatedly addressed, with the other person agreeing to make the necessary changes, and yet the situation has not changed. This is not acceptable, so it is now necessary to state the consequences that will follow if the other person does not successfully live up to what had been previously and repeatedly agreed upon.

Returning to the colleague who still comes late to meetings, even though he specifically moved closer to his school, now is when you assert what will be done about his non-compliance. In this case, you might state that this will be reported in writing to his superior. Again, you can acknowledge that you really do not want to do this but, in order to honour the integrity of the work that is being done on the committee, you will do this if the situation does not change. Here are some things to think about so the situation can be handled at this level:

- Have I honestly tried to deal with the conflict at a lower level?
- Have I documented the previous efforts, beginning at the consulting stage?
- Do I have sufficient knowledge about what will happen next?
- Do I have adequate power to take the next step?
- Do I have ample will to follow through?

Having been intentional at the previous levels and feeling that the consequences are respectful, if the lateness continues then it is time to move to the next C.

Combat

As a noun, the word "combat" refers to a battle or warfare. That is not the part of speech we are referring to here. "Combat" as a verb means to contest or eliminate a situation, not a person. You are trying to follow up on a concern that has been repeatedly ignored and you are now providing the logical consequences of non-compliance. This is a critical stage and you need to use direct, immediate, and definite action to move on the previously stated consequences. This is an obviously important step and the emotional reaction to what happens may be volatile if your colleague feels overly threatened. When one considers the time and effort necessary to combat an escalating, explosive situation, then the need for careful thinking cannot be overestimated. Returning to your continually late-arriving and agreement-ignoring colleague, you now, regrettably, send a formal letter to his supervisor reporting the incidents. Some things to think about at this level:

- Is there room for any other solution?
- Have I discussed this issue with another colleague for a perceptual check?
- Am I following due process?
- Do I have support to combat the situation?
- Do I have the wherewithal (skills, power, and resources) to combat the situation?
- Can I ethically and publicly justify what I have done?

This is one of the real tests for an invitational leader. Committed to an inviting stance means that respectful treatment, as difficult as it may be at this combat stage, is still required. After the consequences have occurred, it is time to go to the next C.

Conciliate

This last C was added after reflecting on the result of ending in the combat mode. There may be much high tension and ill-feeling that needs to be dealt with. For an invitational leader, there is a need to return to a state of goodwill and trust. This means that the former participant and observers of the combative situation need time and opportunity to find ways to come to grips with what has happened. Three guiding rules are helpful at this stage. First, let the fire die down. Emotions do not dissolve at the exact moment a formal conflict has been concluded. Second, give you and others some space and time to reflect, act, and change. This is not the time for an in-your-face style of leadership. Third, trust the process. By sticking to the principles and practices that you have been using throughout the process you are demonstrating your personal and professional integrity. Returning one last time to your tardy colleague, imagine that he has been suspended for three days and then returns to your committee. What to do? Try to let bygones be bygones, use intermediaries to communicate key points, and if there is another conflict, try to begin at the first C. Some things to think about at this stage:

- Have I avoided rubbing it in?
- Have I given people time and space to work things out?
- Can I use some helpful intermediaries?
- Have I continued to act in a respectful manner?
- Will I return to the first C when a new concern occurs?

Conciliation, however, is not only the end of a conflict-management process; it can also be a reflective, uniting process that involves a deeper understanding of each of the previous five Cs. For example, an invitational leader has to come to terms with the personal distinction between a concern and a preference. Letting go of some concerns is a freeing of time and energy, a letting go of unnecessary baggage (First C). Learning to confer and say "Will you do this for me?" is a way to open oneself to more reciprocal ways of being with others. It is not always easy and it involves vulnerability; nevertheless, it is a way to engage in more personal relationships (Second C). Consulting, involves reminding someone that they have not lived up to a responsibility. This is something you may not like doing or really want to do, but it may have to be done (Third C). Coming to terms with confrontation means learning to deal with the frustra-

> ### *About Not Making It Personal*
>
> *I was a department chair, and realized I needed to remind or nudge colleagues to get things done. This task was much easier when I realized I could say, "I would be remiss in my responsibilities as chair if I did not...." Here I would insert what the issue was and let the person know that I took his or her responsibilities seriously and the issue was not personal (Third C). Most of the time, colleagues accepted the reminder and acted on their responsibilities.*

tion you may feel when you have been empathic and respectful and yet the conflict has grown deeper. This may not seem fair and it is easy to get angry or back-off from the conflict. However, seeing oneself as a caring and respectful person takes practice, especially when the sun is not shining and smiles may be concealing seething emotions (Fourth C). Conciliation with your combative self represents coming to terms with the necessity to take responsibility for following up with actions required by fairness. It is not easy, but to do otherwise would be inauthentic and letting people down (Fifth C).

The logic of the Six Cs enables conflict to be managed at lower emotional levels so that time and energy are saved, hostility is reduced, and learning can develop. That's a lot to offer. Is this a quick, easy, foolproof method? No. It takes time, effort, vulnerability, and persistence. Will it work every time? No. Humans are much more complicated than that. However, in the spirit of melioristic optimism, it can be a way to manage difficult conflict situations in ways congruent with the spirit of an inviting stance and make combative situations less volatile. This ameliorative way of thinking can carry over to dealing with larger, more philosophical differences.

MANAGING PHILOSOPHICAL DIFFERENCES

In a fast-paced, multicultural world, philosophical differences can occur with predicted regularity. Political candidates often avoid serious discussions by making glib comments or by distracting by using humorous anecdotes. Although humour may have its place, democratic conversation is corrupted when politicians are merely trying to win voters and influence the media rather than deal honestly with serious issues of mutual concern. Our philosophical beliefs go to the core of what we believe we are and want to become. To ignore serious discussion of them is to become encrusted in deep superficiality, moving deceptively on thin ice. On the other hand, to engage in abstract ideological squabbles in ways that generate more heat than light is to engender bottomless gridlock, and eventually a hostile silence. What's an invitational leader to do?

One way to avoid philosophical superficiality or disaster is to use an approach to conflict developed by one of the authors on a ski lift with his daughter. He was talking with his then 11 year-old daughter on a two-person ski lift (philosophical issues sometimes require privacy) about John Dewey's concepts of continuity and interaction. He explained that if you take seriously these ideas you realize that everything that has happened in the universe has led to this very moment and what we do now will carry on in the future. Waiting for a response, he was surprised by his usually articulate daughter's silence. Then a few seconds later she replied, "Perhaps" and was quiet again. A few seconds later, to his surprise, she added, "Upon reflection, we could get sucked into a black hole so it won't matter what we are doing now." Even more surprised, the author, in the spirit of the conversation said, "Perhaps, but it matters now and that should count for something." That conversation is still continuing.

This experience represented to the author the possibility of nurturing healthy and productive philosophical discussions. Using the framework of that conversation, an approach to the spirit of inviting reflection was developed that intends to do the following:

– Demonstrate sincere respect for an other's perspective;
– Show that you have seriously considered his or her ideas;
– Allow you to state your concerns through honest questions;
– Call forth the possibility for a deeper conversation and a richer understanding.

With these intentions and the experience of a rich and provocative conversation, the SPURT-Q approach was developed. Each of the letters stands for an important part of the five-step process:

1. **S**: *Silence.* To respond immediately to a deep philosophical concern of another person can imply that you have not really heard what they meant or that your response is rehearsed and does not require much thought on your part. Either of these responses serves to negate the value and depth of the other person's thoughts.
2. **P**: *Perhaps.* Used honestly, this might be the most important word in a philosophical conversation. When used honestly, "perhaps" means that you have a sense that there is something positive to what the person is saying but you also have your doubts.
3. **UR**: *Upon Reflection.* This phrase indicates that you wish to go below the surface and take the conversation beyond ideological certainties, both yours and the other person's.
4. **T**: *Tentative* agreement. You articulate what part of the other person's statement you agree with or, upon restatement, could agree with. This provides a common ground.
5. **Q**: *Question.* You put the ball back on the other person's side of the court by asking a question regarding what you have concerns about and what needs further conversation. You are not merely playing the devil's advocate but, because you have used an honest "perhaps," have a pressing question you would like addressed.

Let's now put this to work. Imagine a colleague continually says to you, "These kids today really have it a lot easier than we did, back in the day." You feel that this statement is often a code for criticizing an empathic approach to working with people and can be used to justify a more punitive disciplinary style. Realizing that reacting in a knee-jerk style will probably just entangle you in an endless battle, you decide to try the SPURT-Q approach rather than ignoring or seething about the remark. The conversation might go like this:

1. You remain silent for a few seconds to overcome your first unreflective tendency and see if you can find any other ways to look at what is being said.
2. Finding some other ways to make sense of what has been said, you sincerely say "Perhaps."
3. Showing that you have given the statement some deeper thought, you add, "Upon reflection."
4. You now back up your reflective phase with the thought, "I can agree that students have more conveniences to work with and more freedom to explore ways of being in the world. In many ways I am upset too by what they may take for granted."
5. You then raise your question and state, "Do you think, however, that they are living at a time that is filled with dangers and obstacles we never had to consider?"

Done this way, there is the possibility that a more extended conversation about the issues today's students face and what is needed to know to be able to approach them in an educationally meaningful way. Will this happen every time? Probably not. In discussing heated issues with real people, many complexities may come forward that cannot be known in advance. What the SPURT-Q approach does offer, however, is an attempt to turn two "no's" into a deeper "yes." Managing to do that deepens democratic discourse and is a key part of invitational leadership.

After moving through each stage of conflict and hoping for a resolution at each stage, conciliation can appear as the furthest thing from one's mind after the combat stage. By the time a conflict reaches combat, there is likely a lot of emotion and hard feelings surrounding the situation and relationship. A cooling off period may be required, whether it be formally or informally. It is, however, important to do so in order to restore relationships and contribute to an inviting school culture. Conciliation may not only be the most difficult of the Six Cs but is perhaps also the most important for an inviting leader and an inviting school.

As each of the Six Cs reveal, an inviting leader is intentionally hopeful, trusting, respectful, and caring. Each of these foundational values contributes to the conciliation of the relationship despite the combat that resulted. When each stage is explored faithfully and all parties are invited to contribute to the solution along the way, despite the combat, a respect for the process can provide the foundation for the future relationship. It is up to the leader to initiate, as the combat stage likely relied on the power and authority of the role to resolve the situation. When that is the case, that authority and hierarchy remains over the situation until conciliation is achieved. The first step may be the most difficult after the cooling off period, but the extension of the olive branch, whether accepted or not, sends a strong message of the priorities of the leader and supports the intentions stated in the first four stages of the conflict process: relationships are important and despite the disagreement and escalation, they are still valued and welcome members of the community.

Conciliation requires an invitation back to the table with a focus on moving forward. Throughout the conflict process multiple opportunities were provided to come to consensus and to collaborate and none were successful so the probability of being able to do so after the combat stage is poor. Revisiting the situation or trying to achieve what was not achievable in the initial stages of conflict after the fact is not the point of conciliation. What happened and the priorities and fortitude of all parties were revealed throughout each stage. Conciliation is about moving forward together. There may need to be a re-establishment of appropriate boundaries or guidelines for interaction or conflict resolution but the focus of conciliation is the future rather than a revisit of the past. Conciliation is a big step but one that sends a strong message of priorities and provides all involved with an example of living the professed values of invitational leadership.

MENTORING CONVERSATIONS

Q: This all sounds wonderful in a book. How does it connect with the reality of contemporary schools?
The reality of contemporary schools is that conflict is inevitable, we have chosen an emotionally charged vocation, and being mindful of a way to manage conflict

effectively and respectfully is good practice. Being dismissive of a way to approach conflict as being unconnected to reality unfortunately places a leader in the position of being on the defensive whenever conflict occurs. As a leader, you would not run a school by improvising, nor should you manage conflict on the fly. While each situation and context is unique, there is a universality to approaching conflict from a caring core (concern), being willing to collaborate (confer), partner (consult), have courageous conversations (confront), be prepared to stand firm when required (combat), and respect the dignity of all by reconciling (conciliate). Any situation can be thoughtfully managed with an eye toward solving at the lowest possible level. Approaching conflict through the Six Cs keeps the respect and dignity of all in mind at all times, and provides a thoughtful consideration of how to work toward a positive resolution. Conflict is reality. Understanding how to manage it effectively is as real as it gets for educational leaders.

Q: The Six Cs seem like a great approach when you have time, but what about when someone is in my face or in my office upset and ready to fight?
Managing emotions and responding appropriately is always important and especially so as an educational leader. When we are dealing with conflict that may involve people's children, or professionals, we are dealing with very sensitive emotions. Managing your own emotions, as a leader, is always important, and perhaps even more so when faced with direct confrontation and conflict. A leader should be able to self-regulate, respond appropriately and calmly, and redirect a volatile situation in a way that allows everyone to save face and maintain dignity. Sounds easy, right? In many situations, simply listening with a caring and empathetic ear can diffuse a situation and ease anxiety, as the first C (concern) asserts. Even when someone is visibly and obviously angry, a version of the Six Cs is helpful to manage your own emotions appropriately. A volatile situation needs time to play out before a positive resolution has any chance of success. As the leader, you cannot control who comes into your office or their moods. Your only control is over how you handle yourself and your reaction. Manage your emotions appropriately, don't take things personally, and move toward a solution when all parties are in the right frame of mind to do so.

Q: What happens if the parent is insistent that the situation needs to be addressed immediately?
Experience continues to reveal that there are very few situations that require dropping everything and attending to immediately. A leader needs to be able to discern the difference between a concern and a preference. Something that might make a parent or an educator angry might not be high on your priority list at the moment. You do not need to adopt the priority of others, no matter how angry they are. Part of your role as a leader is to constantly evaluate and prioritize. Discerning whether a situation requires immediate attention, attention in due time, or the attention of others in due time is an important skill to develop. If you take on others' priorities, you run the risk of losing sight of your own. What is important to someone else

97

should be acknowledged as such, but need not become your priority unless, upon thoughtful reflection, you recognized that it needs to be. Managing your emotions can involve managing others, how you deal with situations, and your priorities.

Q: What is the advantage of understanding the Six Cs?
The Six Cs provide a guide for thoughtful, reflective practice at each stage. The hope is that, despite the emotions that can accompany conflict situations, you do not go from 0 to 60, or confer to combat, without thoughtful reflection along the way.

CHAPTER 7

LEADING FOR VALUED KNOWLEDGE

A key part of educational leadership is to focus on what is learned in schools. With the goal of inviting educational lives, it is vital that students, staff, and community develop healthy self-concepts-as-learners in order to pursue mindful learning in creative and disciplined ways. Addressing concerns about the true, the beautiful, and the good and creating shared opportunities to define and redefine what this means from diverse perspectives provides a meaningful way to deepen an understanding and appreciation of the world of and for knowledge.

What is really important to learn?

Should taken-for-granted notions of what constitutes learning be challenged?

Is academic learning really that important?

What is necessary to see oneself as a lifelong learner?

Because of the sustained study necessary for deep and meaningful learning to take place, these are questions that need to be asked as educational leaders cultivate sustained growth in and through the teaching-learning process. This chapter will call into question your beliefs about what is learned in schools if you:

- Think philosophical deliberation is an abstract frill;
- Assume feeling is separate from thinking;
- Believe self-concept concerns are for touchy-feely types;
- Feel that education is really about getting good test scores.

This chapter will build on your beliefs if you:

- Think meaningful learning involves exploring issues in depth;
- Believe that feelings are fundamentally connected with thinking;
- Understand that learning you can learn is a vital concern for all educators;
- Feel that high stakes testing can be highly miseducative.

The word "invite" needs an object to complete its meaning if it is to be a useful educational concept. People are not merely invited; they are invited to something that is considered to be of worth. With the goal of educational living, people are invited to savour, understand, and better more of their individual and collective experiences. From a melioristic perspective, this has a better chance of happening if people feel reasonably comfortable with themselves as learners who can participate

99

in a community of inquirers. This chapter builds on inviting others professionally by showing what is involved in applying a healthy self-concept-as-learner to issues of meaningful and social depth.

PROMOTING A POSITIVE AND REALISTIC SELF-CONCEPT-AS-LEARNER

Underlying the inviting process is a valuing of deep learning and the promoting of democratic relationships. An emphasis on self-concept-as-learner can be a way to invite people to realize more of their positive potential to accomplish these goals because people who feel good about themselves as learners can inquire with others and learn even more important things.

In Chapter Two the component parts of the self-system were stressed (the "I," "me's," and evaluation). Although sensing some of the many "me's" of another person (e.g., athlete, reader, brother) can enable a leader to more meaningfully connect with a person, there are a staggering number of "me's" to work with. This can easily be overwhelming. Leaders who also possess a specific learning focus can be more effective for educative purposes. With that in mind, the Florida Key was developed (Finger, 1995; Harper & Purkey, 1993; Purkey, 2000; Purkey, Cage, & Graves, 1973) to give educators a more specific focus: self-concept-as-learner. Empirically validated, this instrument provides four key subcomponents: relating, asserting, investing, and coping. Attention to each of these areas gives leaders heuristic ways to work with all learners: staff, students, and themselves.

Relating

The first factor identified by the Florida Key is relating. Quite simply, persons who are good at relating have an advantage in learning because they can trust, appreciate, and identify with a variety of others in a school. People who relate well more often know and care about the lives of others around them. Others enjoy their presence. Not having to fight everyone around them enables good relaters to focus their energy on the learning opportunities that are taking place. An essential part of leadership is to help construct a larger sense of a learning community, a group of inquirers who take delight in successfully working and thinking together. Providing a variety of ways to meaningfully relate is essential to this process. Of particular importance for leaders is the inclusion of those who can easily be overlooked or ignored in professional settings. Ironically, some people work at being invisible, at being ignored. This may be due to personality and/ or social factors such as shyness or because of ongoing marginalizing experiences related factors such as gender, ethnicity, class, ability, and age. So leaders have to find non-threatening and unobtrusive ways to caringly connect with the often neglected people around them.

Going beyond psychological factors, in multicultural settings it is vital to remove what may be disinviting barriers to meaningful engagement and participation. For example, Ryan's (2006) work on exclusion in urban schools and communities illustrates consistent ways in which students' and parents' knowledge is devalued because their perceived cultural capital—that is, "the ability to talk, act, and think in particular ways" (p. 7)—do not conform to dominant white, middle class, heterosexual norms. The authors' research and practical experience in working with parents, students, and community members confirm that meaningful connections with others are achieved through respectful awareness of our diverse perspectives and backgrounds. How assumptions about valued knowledge, culture, and language are made can help or hinder authentic interactions with others. For example, it is important for teachers and administrators to talk about their work in non-jargonized ways. Using "edubabble" can easily create the division of people into two groups: an informed inner circle and a dependent group of marginalized others. Schools in which people are all in it together transform what can easily become polarized divisions into lively creations of vibrant diversity. Leaders who are seen as competent and caring in establishing and sustaining such schools make sure that students, teachers, staff, and community members get ample opportunities to relate and participate.

Asserting

Aristotle, often a very practical thinker who emphasized doing the right thing in the right way at the right time, noted that virtue frequently resides in the Golden Mean, the creative point between two extremes. For example, the virtuous contrast to cowardice is

> ### About Democratic Processes
>
> *I recognized that teachers and students were more comfortable with top-down management and deferring responsibility to others, so I worked with staff and students to institute grade level community meetings. These weekly gatherings were coordinated and led by rotating teams of students and teachers and provided a safe space and opportunities for the entire school community (irrespective of age, ability, or rank) to raise compliments and concerns in a democratic manner.*

not foolhardiness but bravery. Both the coward and the fool are overruled by emotions while the brave person is able to intelligently direct emotions in a beneficial way. Similarly, assertion can be differentiated from its contrasts: aggression and acquiescence. The aggressive person is essentially saying, "Only my needs matter." This being the case, others' needs are disregarded, trumped, or trampled. On the other hand, acquiescence is the disregard of one's own needs and the giving in to the purposes of the others. Both sides concur with the acceptance of doing violence to needs. Similar to the reasoning about bravery, assertion aims at a more complex cognitive and moral goal: meeting one's own needs while respecting the needs of others. Connecting this to learning tasks, assertion relates to the degree of control that a person has over a situation. Those who can

assert themselves do not think that they can control everything or that everything is out of control. In the process of asserting they are able to make learning
goals manageable and meaningful. Not suffering from learned helplessness or an
exaggerated ego, they exhibit a quiet confidence that enables them to engage in
extended inquiry regarding issues of worth. Assertive behaviour is promoted by
invitational leaders by encouraging democratic processes and moral reasoning.
By creating the conditions that enable people to develop the skills and dispositions necessary to manage themselves in socially appropriate ways, educational
leaders help bring to life the key invitational principle that people are valuable,
able, and responsible.

Investing

To invest is to devote one's time to
trying new things, to explore the
previously unexplored. This quality
involves enjoying looking at things in
different ways. In doing so, the joy of
exploration is its own reward. Echoing
similar sentiments, Daniel Pink (2009)
points out how people with high
investing characteristics exhibit what
he calls "drive": strong autonomy, a
desire for mastery, and a deep sense of
purpose. From this perspective, "car-
rot and stick" approaches are so last
millennium, and they were often dys-

> ### *About Investing*
> *One of the authors of this text recalls
> a time he was talking with a student
> in a classroom he was observing who
> knew the answers to a teacher's ques-
> tions but refused to answer because
> he said the teacher was not asking a
> real question if she already knew the
> answer. This student knew something
> very important about investing in
> authentic questions.*

functional then. So what's a leader to do to call forth investing behaviour? First, the
judicious use of open-ended questions can promote divergent thinking and extended
discussion. Leaders who wish to sustain authentic investing use brainstorming and
participation in real questioning. In doing so, learners can develop the satisfaction of
going below the surface and engage in meaningful inquiry.

Investing is crucial to the creative and sustained use of imagination. John Dewey
and Joseph Tufts (1932) pointed out the imagination is the chief instrument of the
good. By that they meant that investing imaginative effort into understanding the
possible consequences of actions enables more possibilities to be perceived, understood, and evaluated. This investing prowess is vital in a pluralistic democratic
society that seeks the means to extend moral imagination to the creative challenges
it faces. The specific solutions of the past may be of limited use when situations
change, and they may not have ever been good in the first place. Investing opens new
possibilities because the best way to have some good ideas is to have many ideas.
The ruts generated by certitude and rigidity are transcended by sustained habits of
imaginative investing.

Coping

Earlier in the book the concept of "flow" was introduced. Flow involves the ability not to be overwhelmed or underwhelmed by events. Similar to flow, coping is the ability to not be overwhelmed by expectations—that is, thriving rather than surviving. This is not so easy for serious students and educators who have expectations coming at them from the outside and inside. To pay heed to the often discordant complexities of a whole array of expectations is to guarantee the paralysis of analysis, to stop trying because there is so much to worry about. To overcome imagination used for the wrong purposes, inviting educational leadership involves assisting people with coping challenges by providing a manageable perspective on the past, clarity about the present, and hope for the future. Showing that they have given important matters serious thought and have found meaningful patterns, attainable goals, and a better future, invitational leaders demonstrate the ability to use ideals as meaningful guides, not as weighted baggage. In a culture of high-stakes testing, this involves being able to wisely use standards and test results as providing a perspective on what has, is, and will be done to promote meaningful learning. This approach is illustrated in the approach of former principal Barbara Whitney, who is credited for creating a culture of high expectations and success at Mary Wright Elementary School in South Carolina. When she inherited a "low performing" or "below average" school that was characterized by demoralization and hopelessness, she worked consistently with staff, students, and community to instill a sense of pride, a spirit of family, and a culture of high expectations and empowerment (Schramm-Pate et al., 2006). This approach is also illustrated in the approach of former principal William "Billy" Tate at Belvoir Park Primary School in East Belfast, Northern Ireland. Working within a traditionally loyalist, sectarian housing estate, Billy sought ways to invite the community into the school, bring the outside world in, and challenge the barriers to this process. He cultivated a culture that started to look beyond the community toward the wider world by inviting games, culture, and language instruction from beyond the community. For this to happen, a long-range perspective is needed, with missteps seen as important feedback. This is easier said than done, but it still needs to be said, and more importantly, it needs to be done with grace and persistence. Coping involves developing the savvy and determination to get up after you have been knocked down. Being knocked down is not as overwhelming if you are going to someplace important with people who matter.

As we have seen, self-concept-as-learner applies not only to students but to all involved in the educative process. People with a healthy self-concept-as-learner possess what Carol Dweck (2006) calls a growth mindset. They seek to cultivate their intelligence and demonstrate dedication and hard work to learning meaningful material. Artfully orchestrating relating, asserting, investing, and coping involves promoting this dedication to learning in a mindful way.

LEADING MINDFUL LEARNING

In John Dewey's (1938) short analysis of experience and education, any learning transaction involves continuity and interaction. Continuity describes the perceptions we bring to any encounter and interaction refers to the new perceptions that develop. Obviously both are necessary for learning to make an impression, to stick. If we hold on to our past perceptions too rigidly, we miss what is new in the present situation. If we come to a new situation with no previous perceptions (something we cannot actually do), we are so open-minded that nothing stays with us. The Golden Mean needed for the proper balance of continuity and interaction is mindful learning.

The concept of mindful learning involves using past perceptions as a springboard to more promising possibilities. Psychologist Ellen Langer (1989, 1997, 2009) has studied this concept for more than three decades, paying attention to how people often stick to excessively rigid and dysfunctional perceptions of what could be done. The mindful learning she describes involves creating new categories to understand something in fresh ways, an openness to new information, an awareness of a variety of ways to view something, and a persistence to stay in the present. Quite simply, she wants people to get out of the perceptual ruts they habitually dig for themselves. This has serious implications for the development of self-concept-as-learner.

In a similar vein, Richard Rorty (1989) talks about the importance of being ironists, people who are always looking for better ways to make sense of things, rather than metaphysicians, people who claim to know the final outcome of inquiry. Possessing the confidence to learn things that will disturb one's habitual perceptions requires a desire to grow, a desire to avoid a "hardening of the categories," a desire to go below the surface. Becoming a mindful learner is to take delight in replacing bad habits with more productive strategies. Looking at learning from Langer's perceptual expanding view involves challenging the half-truths which have become encrusted certainties. Among these half-truths are the following:

- *Practice makes perfect.* This may be true for learning mechanically repetitious ways of responding. However, most of life is not like this. Ignoring the importance of contexts for application shortchanges the learning necessary for more complex perceptions to develop.
- *Be still and focus only on the matter at hand.* Sometimes. However, sometimes by allowing one's mind to explore emerging questions, new ways of looking at matters at hand can develop. "Distractions" can be the basis for brainstorming and unpacking unwarranted assumptions.
- *Delayed gratification is important.* Implied in the notion of delaying gratification is the idea that the present is joyless. Being able to continually find satisfaction in the ongoing process of learning keeps inquiry alive. This takes imagination and positive self-talk.

- *Rote memory is to be emphasized.* Learning without personal meaning and deep understanding is, like Teflon, guaranteed not to stick. Rote becomes remote and of little note for reflective practice. The forest is missed because the trees have been memorized.
- *It is valuable to remember everything.* Too much of anything, even trivial- pursuit-winning total recall, is too much. Too many details can get in the way of a fresh vantage point needed to clarify and extend an emerging situation. Learning to chunk material into meaningful components allows new connections to be made.

Schools, as key institutions of education, are about enriching and expanding perceptual fields. Working through habitual blocks that restrict perceptual growth enables educational leaders to promote deeper dimensions of educational living. The savouring, understanding, and bettering of experience is more fully expanded as students and educators come to grips with subjects that matter and questions that underlie them.

VALUED KNOWLEDGE

Thus far we have emphasized the importance of educational leaders promoting a healthy self-concept-as-learner and mindful learning. Moving beyond the process of learning to the subject matter of what is worth learning, it can help to mindfully rearrange perceptions and think of subject matter as *subjects that matter*. That is, subjects that matter because they focus attention on the importance of confronting issues of "truth (falsity), beauty (ugliness), and goodness (evil) in full awareness of the problematic facets of these categories and the disagreements across cultures and subcultures" (Gardner, 1999, p. 35). The subjects that matter to Howard Gardner (1999, 2011) are related to the ongoing pursuit of truth, goodness, and beauty, especially in our ever-more fast-paced technological and value-ambiguous postmodern world. Gardner adds that the importance of the academic disciplines in this pursuit of matters of substance and moral purpose cannot be overemphasized.

If the goal of invitational leaders is to promote the savouring, understanding, and bettering of individual and collective experiences, this can be done intentionally by connecting these processes to disciplinary knowledge; that is, knowledge obtained through the serious self-correcting procedures used to pursue defensible perspectives. The success of disciplinary perspectives depends on the development of what Gardner (1999) calls educational virtues. A virtue refers to the pursuit of worthwhile goals in the face of temptations or obstacles. An earlier use of this way of thinking was pointed out by Schrag (1988) who argued that we get a better understanding of what is involved in critical thinking if we get beyond focusing on skills and instead reconceptualize critical thinking as the development of the virtue of thoughtfulness. This includes asking questions such as: critical thinking and knowledge for what purposes? To which ends? And for whose benefit or disadvantage? Thoughtfulness, then, is seen not as a technique to reach a narrow end, but the development of deep character in overcoming impulsivity and rigidity in thinking. Combining Gardner's valuing of the pursuit of the beautiful, the true, and the good with the three educational virtues promoted by inviting educational leaders shows the way to a deeper sense of savouring, understanding, and bettering perceptions.

Savouring More of Life

It is an interesting world we live in. It can be seen as a frenzied, digital postmodern chaos that overwhelms and breeds scepticism, or, on the other hand, as an amazing time to be alive, filled with opportunities and challenges. Perhaps it is both, and more, but as meliorists we have a better possibility to take advantage of the latter interpretation if we are able to overcome the sceptical frenzy of the former. It is here where developing the virtue of savouring plays an important role. To practice the virtue of savouring is to be able to take in and appreciate more of our encounters with the world. The temptations that need to be overcome are the tendencies to either numb ourselves to the overwhelming stimuli that envelop us or to run wild with extremes and seek the sensational. The ability to enjoy flow experiences, as mentioned earlier, involves the construction of challenging but not overwhelming mindful opportunities. Flow takes practice but can move us beyond the obsessive pursuit of flickering pleasures to the mindful enjoyment of meaningful activities that provide possibilities for growth. Dianne Ackerman (1990) in her compelling book, *A Natural History of the Senses*, shows how savouring can come from mindful engagement of smells, touches, tastes, sounds, and sights. After reading her book, one's sensing connection with the world, both within and without, expands. Earlier, operating on a similar sentiment, Aldous Huxley (1962/2010) in his classic book, *Island*, suggests that people can better show appreciation for a meal by holding the first bite in their mouth for a minute and allowing their taste buds to take in the subtleties that would ordinarily go unnoticed if they ate at their normal pace. Slowing down the habitually abnormal "normal" pace can open us up to more of the world around us. Adding to this, David Abram (1996), in his provocative book, *The Spell of the Sensuous*, shows how even breathing can be, well, a breathtaking experience. The point in mentioning these books is that they each point to ways in which experience can be enlivened, one of the goals of educational living.

Savouring can also be developed in encounters with great works of beauty from different cultures. Gardner (1999) goes into insightful detail about what is involved in appreciating

> ### *About Savouring More of Life*
>
> *It wasn't until I retired from school leadership that I recognized the little things that made my vocation such a joy. I missed the sounds of the children in the yard, doing group work in the classroom, sharing ideas, getting excited about projects. I was very focused on doing good things for the right reasons as a school principal, I just wish I had stopped to appreciate and reflect upon the everyday, everyday.*

Mozart. The aesthetic experiencing of Mozart goes beyond taking pleasure in his music to a deep sense of appreciation of the structure of his creation, how the parts fit together to produce a compelling experience. Similar to learning to like olives, savouring is an acquired habit that improves with time. The virtue to be acquired in this case is the ability to put ourselves in the position to be capable of appreciating an experience and then letting the encounter have its effects on us. John Dewey's *Art as Experience* (1934/1980) is a detailed explication of the work of art in aesthetic experiencing of the world, the doing and the undergoing necessary to have vibrant experiences. In Howard Gardner's (2011) more recent book, *Truth, Beauty, and Goodness Reframed*, he points out that there are objects that go beyond the traditional arts' emphasis on beauty, but these works of art have three antecedent features: "The object is interesting; its form is memorable; it invites further encounters" (p. 49). This is very different from many schooling experiences that are dull, forgettable, and that we want never to come into contact with as soon as the test is over. Whatever else a school should be, it should not be a place that deadens us to life's possibilities; it should not be the antithesis of a deepening connection to the world around us.

Disciplined Understanding

To understand something is to grasp how it works. To look more closely at the literal meaning, to understand is to stand under. If you stand under the lighting in a classroom and examine what is above, you should be able to find wires that will eventually connect you with electrical power sources. There is logic to understanding lighting and if you see the connections you have become enlightened in many different ways. A good educational experience turns lights on. It provides aha! experiences. This is very different from the experience of rote learning that is emphasized as students are preparing for high-stakes tests. Whatever else a school should be, it should not be a source of miseducative experiences; it should not be a place where understanding is denigrated and denied.

> ### *About Understanding*
>
> *I had the experience of visiting a high school where students were studying for the state tests. I spotted a student with an angry look on his face while he was glaring at a list of words. Going up to the student, I asked what he was doing. The student said he was memorizing these words and their definitions for his chemistry test. I asked the student if he understood what the definitions meant, and the student said no. The student then said that he tried understanding but he did not do as well as when he memorized a lot of facts. My heart dropped. The student had learned that understanding is not worth the effort. Is this what our testing is doing to students, providing them with miseducative experiences that enable success at the price of understanding?*

107

To fight the miseducative effects of schools, Kieran Egan (2008) asks us to reimagine our schools from the ground up. He then provides a provocative 50-year program of educational reforms. Not as earth-shaking, Howard Gardner (1999) maintains that educators should teach for substantive understanding by putting an emphasis on key disciplinary ideas and studying their implications in depth. He seeks to give students the "intellectual heart," the "experiential soul" of a disciplined way of understanding the world. Since, without proper teaching, children learn a variety of common sense misconceptions about the world, it is important that they learn how "science refutes common nonsense" (Gardner, 2011, p. 126). For invitational leaders this means giving serious thought to teaching less material but teaching it in much more depth. Knowing something well, knowing it in depth, enables a person to more easily know the structure and workings of other things well. Knowing things only superficially keeps a person, well, on the surface. Good pedagogy involves starting with what people know. The larger move is to take their present perceptions and artfully connect them to the logic and the methods developed by disciplinary experts. Education takes time and effort to get beyond what Gardner (1993) calls the unschooled mind, with its misconceptions, rote algorithms, and stereotypical reactions to people and situations. This requires educators who are leading educational lives themselves and who are intellectually interesting and interested in the pursuit of bettering the educative experiences of all involved.

Bettering Educative Experiences

In order to live in a human community, adults and children need to develop a sense of better or worse, right or wrong. Having done this as a natural part of living in a human community, we are able to enter into responsible discussions about good and evil and how to make a better world. As Dewey noted in 1916, schools have a responsibility to purify and enrich student experiences. Invitational leaders realize this and work to develop what Gardner (2011) calls the habits of neighbourly morality and role ethics. Neighborly morality is about "those interactions that exist between or among human beings by virtue of their common humanity, their mutual recognition of this fact, and their membership in some kind of a designated tribe, clan, or local community" (Gardner, 2011, p. 165). Role ethics refers to the more professional responsibilities involved in participating in complex positions (e.g., educator, writer, coach, citizen). Regarding neighbourly morality, students learn to be "less egocentric, more cognizant of the welfare of other members of the group, and more alert to the "common good" (Gardner, 2011, p. 177). Regarding role ethics, there is the challenge to be responsible, even when it is not to one's advantage. Gardner's point in making this differentiation is that the automatic and common sense notions of neighbourly morality do not automatically translate into the intricacies of role ethics, to our responsibilities as workers and citizens. For example, as workers and citizens, Gardner emphasizes the importance of developing the virtues of excellence (meets relevant standards), engagement (finds meaning in the work being done), and ethics (accepts responsibility for what is done). Educating for good work in the area of role ethics involves reflective thought, public discussion, and ongoing analysis. This is not easy work, but in a more complex society these are the types of issues that need to be brought to life in schools that promote educational living in the 21st century.

In bringing moral and ethical thinking to life, Gardner (1999) suggests having students study something that is clearly evil, like the holocaust, to better understand the complexity of human intentions and what has been called the "banality of evil" (Arendt, 1963). Extending Gardner's ideas, by critically studying meaningful issues with substantive content such as poverty, genocide, slavery, and sexism, students and teachers get to understand the depth of thought and feeling required to decide on complex issues. By directly connecting these issues to their own contexts, students can also see the relationship between local and global patterns of oppression, understand how and why well-meaning individuals unknowingly benefit from and are complicit in perpetuating "evil," and determine the types of everyday concerns that need to be faced in moral and ethical ways.

For invitational leaders, Gardner's work points out the importance of coming to terms with the world of and for knowledge. The world *of* knowledge represents that which has taken, in some cases, centuries to develop. These academic disciplines involve the structured, cumulative, and critical analysis of some, but certainly not all, key aspects of human experience. Developing the feel, sensitivity, and logic of the intellectual, aesthetic, and moral spirit of various disciplines takes students beyond their undisciplined minds and into issues of depth and importance. The world *for* knowledge stands for the everyday vital and perplexing world that is open for experience and needs to be examined before and when tensions develop. This is the world freshly encountered, the world that the book has not yet been written about. The art of leading for valued knowledge is to bring these two worlds together. Learning and interrogating key concepts of academic disciplines can provide a depth of ideas, feelings, and purposes. Experiencing and examining the everyday world in depth provides significance, insight, and an ongoing sense of connection for what is, what could be, and what should be.

Leading for valued knowledge moves all involved in the educative process to develop the virtues necessary for ongoing vitality and a depth of inquiry. Whatever else a school should be, it should be a place that calls forth deep, sustained learning. Invitational leaders lead with this in mind.

MENTORING CONVERSATIONS

Q: How can we invite leading for valued knowledge when the curriculum is rigid and prescriptive in terms of what needs to be covered?
Schools should be educational places where students want to be and want to learn. At our core, as educators, we strive to ignite the love of learning in our students. We are preparing students to contribute to a world we can only begin to imagine so we

need to be more imaginative about how we encourage students to embrace learning. Students who are curious, passionate, reflective, considerate, creative, and collaborative are developing educational living. Our role, as educational leaders, is to encourage, model, and support this process. The concept of "covering" the curriculum should be retired from our professional vocabulary. Coverage implies surface treatment of ideas, concepts, and knowledge. We should, as educators committed to living educational lives, go much deeper than coverage suggests. The curriculum can be regarded as a tool to teach deep and critical thinking, collaborative inquiry, and creative communication, rather than an expansive repertoire of concepts to be mentally filed. Ask anyone you know—teacher, bus driver, doctor, sales clerk, anyone—how much they remember about specific curriculum expectations. We suspect knowledge-based recollections will be slim. Students who develop a passion for living educationally while developing the aforementioned skills will be better equipped for a future we can only imagine. Covering standardized curriculum is not as important as teaching, encouraging, modeling, and supporting students. We should consider ourselves to be educators, which goes a lot deeper than the deliverers of standardized curricula.

Q: The curriculum is what it is. How do we lead for deep knowledge?
Developing a learning community in which curiosity, creativity, passion, and reflection encourages this process. Billy Tate introduced games and culture activities in East Belfast that had never been considered within the community before. He led with a genuine curiosity and that curiosity became infectious within the school and throughout the community. To lead for deep knowledge, start with yourself. Model educational passion, commitment, and care for learning. Live in a way that encourages others. Take courses. Teach courses. Attend conferences. Speak at conferences. Read papers and articles. Write papers and articles. Share your curiosity for how things work, how things are, and how things can be with others. You may find your educational enthusiasm is more infectious than you had ever imagined with teachers, students, parents, and community members.

Q: I struggle with small talk. How can I connect with people?
Connecting with people in meaningful ways is not about small talk. In fact, it is, in many ways, quite the opposite. Small talk involves the sharing of limited, surface-based information. Connecting with others in meaningful ways involves a deeper commitment to understanding others' likes, dislikes, passions, dreams, commitments, and pursuits. Connecting requires recognizing the similarities with yourself or ways in which commonalities and understandings can be cultivated. A leader need not be an expert on anything nor expect his or her passions to be embraced by others. Instead, finding a way to connect involves recognizing shared values, pursuits, and commitments and developing them in pursuit of strengthening connections. Inviting others requires an understanding of what others bring to the table in an organization and how their gifts and talents can contribute. If small talk is something you are uncomfortable with, you might be more interested in getting below the surface and

engaging in a deeper, richer connection sooner. Think of small talk as the knock at the door and the first interactions as being the awkwardness of standing outside until you are invited in. Once inside, relationships can develop and flourish. Connecting deeper recognizes that small talk introduces, breaks the ice, and allows a level of comfort to develop through which deeper relational understandings can develop.

Q: How is assertiveness congruent with an inviting perspective? How can I be assertive without being a bully and remain inviting?

Just like we wouldn't want you to confuse inviting leadership with being a pushover, don't confuse assertiveness with aggressiveness. Being assertive is not, or should not be, overpowering, intimidating, or singularly focused. Instead, think of assertiveness as being able to clearly articulate and/or demonstrate your ideas, opinions, or expectations. As leaders, especially within education, we consider ourselves as servants, leading from behind, enabling others to do good things in the classroom, and provide the appropriate circumstances for our students to be successful. As a school principal, one of the author's approach to leadership as a new leader was to say "What can I do for you? How can I support your growth/ideas/development?" These are all appropriate leadership questions to ask as we work toward supporting others to do great things. What the author learned, however, was that to add an important, assertive follow-up to any discussion. Now, when working with staff, he might say "What can I do to help/support/encourage you?" and follow that up with "This is what I need/expect from you." This inviting approach to assertiveness is a more clear articulation of expectations in order to achieve desired outcomes. Being assertive does not mean imposing. Instead, being invitationally assertive encourages the thoughtful consideration and articulation of expectations so that collectively, everyone has a clear understanding of the goals, the ways to get there, and individual responsibilities. Assertiveness, at times, is a companion to effective communication. Making sure your needs and expectations are known and understood creates a much better chance of success.

MANAGING EDUCATIONAL SENSIBILITIES

Although it is important for invitational leaders to care about thinking, it is also important that they think about caring. By managing from and reflecting on caring, core leaders are able to make invitational learning come alive, help call forth successful intelligence, and promote the development of ethical fitness.

What are leaders expected to model?

What are some guidelines for managing learning based on caring principles?

What is successful intelligence and how can it be promoted?

How can leaders learn to manage ethical conflicts?

Because of the care necessary to call forth and promote valued knowledge, these are questions that need to be addressed as educational leaders manage to maintain, protect, and enhance the sensibilities needed to educationally care for people, ideas, and priorities. This chapter will call your beliefs into question about the dynamics of caring and thinking if you:

– Do not think caring is a curriculum issue;
– Do not see thinking and learning as relational issues;
– Believe that learning is only about individual effort;
– Feel that ethical thinking is primarily about following rules.

This chapter will build on your beliefs if you:

– Feel that there is a deep connection between caring and meaningful learning;
– Think that real learning links individual and social meanings;
– Believe that thinking about the processes and outcomes of learning can improve both;
– Think that ethical sensibilities can be enhanced.

Managing educational sensibilities is about keeping the educational impulse alive in one's relationships with people, ideas, and adventures and possessing the competence to make it a vital part of deep learning. For, just as students are saying to teachers, "We don't care what you know until we know that you care," teachers are often saying to their colleagues and supervisors, "We won't show you more until we believe that you are coming from a caring core." Managing a caring core and connecting it with deep learning involves the blending of serious thought and demonstrable commitments.

CONSIDER CARING

Managing to consistently care about the pursuit of valued knowledge is something that is much easier to command from others than to demonstrate unwaveringly one-self. Talking the talk comes easier than walking the walk. However, to command caring sounds absurd. To act in contradiction to what we would like to see happen in others puts an even bigger divide between words and actions. Words become mere rhetoric and a source of discomfort, disbelief, and dissension when confirming action does not precede and follow. The leading and learning promoted in this book are person-focused, building on the dynamics of working from an inviting stance, a stance with caring at the core.

The challenges for invitational leaders that we have posed thus far are to live an educational life oneself, to work with others in doing with relationships, and to actively promote the pursuit of valued knowledge. This is a lot to manage to care about but, as Nel Noddings (1992) points out, we are living at a time when there is an acute caring deficiency suffered by medical patients, old people, "and children, especially adolescents" (p. xi) in schools. The inviting stance, with trust, intentionality, respect, and optimism centred around care, seems challenging in fragmented educational systems that present multiple demands. Today's educa-tors face conflicting policies, a top-town curriculum, a test-obsessed mania that wants numerical answers to deeper questions of understanding and meaning, and pervasive pressure from those outside the schools, along with demands to do more with fewer resources and less support. As publicly funded employees of the gov-ernment, educators consistently appear to be fair game for public harassment. Attacks telling teachers and administrators that "You are overpaid, underworked, and unproductive and we are going to make you change!" are demoralizing. They lead educators to believe that if they make things better, those who have castigated them will take the credit. This is not a political climate that calls forth caring edu-cational sensibilities. In spite of this challenging context, and as difficult as it is, education is still fundamentally a caring profession. It is hard to imagine parents wanting their children to go to schools where educators do not know their children and do not care about their children learning important things. Managing to care about deep learning is *sine qua non*, an essential condition for the sustained pursuit of this virtuous task.

If educational leaders are to care about the virtue of deep learning, they need to learn about the virtue of deep caring. In her original and continuing work on caring in education, Nel Noddings (1984, 1992, 2005) makes the point that ethical decision-making is more than thinking about consequences of actions or acting in principled ways; it is a way of encountering others that manifests receptivity, relat-edness, and engrossment (Noddings, 1992). In other words, caring educators take the time to establish focused, open relationships with others as people, students, and thinkers. These caring relationships are more apt to develop if educators consistently demonstrate these four characteristics:

- *Modeling.* In terms of caring, talk is cheap and relationships are deep. If we want students, colleagues, and staff to be thoughtful, in the sense of caring about thoughts and feelings, we have to demonstrate this consistently ourselves. One way to do this is to show people how and why we think about a complex issue that has mutual meaning. For invitational leaders, this means being able to articulate the educational reasons for why we do things a certain way and listening in a caring way for the meaning that lies in the responses made by others.
- *Dialogue.* It is not enough just to model caring efforts; it is also necessary to talk about the dynamics, commitments, and concerns of working from a caring core. This commitment to a caring core involves engaging in open-ended and ongoing conversations about what it means to care, what are the obstacles to sustaining caring, and how these might be overcome. Through meaningful dialogue members of a caring community see their work as a shared human endeavour rather than a lonely but heroic death march.
- *Practice.* In terms of valued learning, learning the value of working from a caring core needs to be put into action. Developing school projects around caring themes and tasks enables all who choose to be involved to deal with the nitty-gritty of developing caring relationships. Issues that develop from involvement in caring projects are the source for new ideas about what to do, how to do it, and why to do it. This deepens thinking about caring and caring about thinking. Deep thinking is put in the service of deep and sustained caring. The pursuit of social justice initiatives, which many schools undertake, should emanate from a caring core. A willingness to care for and about others is the motivation rather than a sense of obligation or collective guilt.
- *Confirmation.* The ethics of caring are based on relationships (Noddings, 2013). One does not care in isolation, it is not something merely done with one's thoughts and feelings. One cares for concrete others. It is important for those others to acknowledge that they are a part of a caring relationship. The confirmation of the carer is a way of calling forth a person's better self. This is done through imaginative acts of authentic connection that pick up on the better parts of what a person wants to learn and wants to be. The carer and the cared for appreciate the contribution of each other.

Managing to work from a caring core for meaningful learning and deep thinking is not a formulaic technique that educators can plug in when they come to school. Rather it is a virtue that a person embodies in her own thinking and feeling about what makes education a worthwhile endeavour. This pursuit of cognition and caring, as Rebore (2001, p. 28) points out, becomes a cultivated disposition, an integrated and growing part of a person's emotional and intellectual life. It can be better managed when it is merged with an invitational interpretation of some basic principles of learning.

DIALOGUE ON INVITATIONAL LEARNING

The goal of invitational leaders is simple, but not easy. It is simply to create and care for educational environments where people want to be and want to learn things that matter. Sounds good, but if it were easy, everybody would already be doing it all of the time. People would be simply learning abundant things that matter. This, however, needs some unpacking to be of use. For something to be a learning matter for invitational leaders, it should promote the cognitive, emotional, physical, moral, and social development of individuals who can make contributions to the democratic development of their community and the ever-more-connected global society. This challenging task becomes easier to manage if educators can discuss key principles about what should be learned, how it should be learned, and where it should be learned according to an invitational perspective. Ronald Brandt (1998), former executive director of the ASCD, in his summary of research on learning, provides 10 guidelines that can be examined from an inviting perspective. These guidelines, though written in 1998, are congruent with the current practices in contemporary schools. School boards, principals, and teachers are challenged to differentiate instruction, recognize that all students learn differently, set achievable but challenging goals, work collaboratively, and think about problems creatively and strategically, build upon prior knowledge, use appropriate strategies, and provide descriptive feedback for ongoing improvement and success. Leaders are similarly challenged. To be able to articulate the meaningfulness of each guideline from an inviting perspective enables an educational leader to better manage the learning of valued knowledge.

1. *People learn what is personally meaningful to them.* This corresponds with a core belief of the perceptual approach, the idea that people behave according to how a situation looks to them. Knowing a person as an educator means knowing what is important to him or her. Going back to self-concept theory, people pay more attention to those "me's" that are closest to the centre of their self. The "me's," the roles and attributes that are vital in a person's existence, provide the living connection to what is to be taught. To ignore the meaningfulness of a person's "me's" is to cut out their existential heart. Educators who care about this know their students and their lives and can work as translators who connect what students want to learn to what they have to teach. They work to connect what John Dewey called the psychology of the student to the logic of the subject matter (Westbrook, 1991), understanding that this goes well beyond and is even contradictory to the surface responses that are prized in high stakes tests. By acting as subject matter interpreters, the perceptual fields of both the student and the educator are deepened. Both can see themselves as learning something that matters.

2. *People learn when they accept challenging but achievable goals.* Adults and children alike live up or down to our expectations. Who would want to be continually overwhelmed or continually underwhelmed? Both take their toll. Overwhelmed people live in a state of high anxiety while underwhelmed people live in a state of perpetual boredom. Neither can have a positive effect on a person's positive self-concept-as-learner. Caring about students means having a

grasp of their personal whelm level and providing the coaching and personally significant material for them to be meaningfully engaged, with the goal of them learning to be able to do this for themselves. Learning to be an autotelic learner is developing the capacity and habit of learning to care about what you are doing, as you are doing it. This is the embodiment of being meaningfully engaged. Finding ways to do this is the embodiment of caring teaching. Leading with this in mind is the embodiment of invitational leadership.

3. *Learning is developmental.* The positive side of understanding the developmental nature of learning is understanding that different people can go through similar stages and face comparable needs for structure, content, and meaning. An understanding of development in general can be of great help as educators move to greater levels of complexity in the subject matter they use to encourage deep thinking. However, in caring for individual students, it is important not to get locked into seeing only their stage or assigned label and missing the person. This means that leaders remain open to the unique perceptions and sensibilities of the individuals they are working with. This understanding of both openness to the uniqueness of the individual and understanding the structure of development enables an educator to be flexible and fluent in dealing with the robust nature of the students and subject matter.

4. *People learn well when they can learn in their own way and have some degree of choice and control.* Respect for a person is an acknowledgment of their need for autonomy, which is also the essence of the democratic ethos in which everyone matters as a person. Each person is a unique individual with a distinct perceptual field from which comes personal meanings and insights that need to be taken in consideration in planning for learning. Understanding the psychologic of a person, their unique patterns and strategies of meaning making, is one of the means and ends of invitational learning. Providing a variety of opportunities for learning, including ways to create shared meanings, enables people to become enriching members of more meaningful groups. It is in such groups that uniqueness and deeper development of common goods grow.

5. *People learn well when they use what they already know as they construct new knowledge.* From the perceptual point of view learning is about making connections and we use the past to predict the future. Humans are not blank slates; even before birth the interaction with the environment is two-way (Pinker, 2002). The process of knowing involves using the perceptions available to construct working hypotheses of what might happen in the future. Each person, as George Kelly (1963) noted in his work on personal construct psychology, is a personal scientist who can develop the habit of imaginatively reframing perceptions to come up with richer and more functional hypotheses. Becoming a good personal scientist involves having a healthy self-concept-as-learner in that you have to go beyond what Kahneman (2011) calls System 1 thinking (fast and automatic intuitions) to System 2 thinking (slow and deliberate reflections). It takes thoughtful confidence to test and overrule your initial intuitions, but this is required for much deep learning.

6. *People learn well when they have opportunities for social interaction.* As Dewey (1916) noted, in the process of communicating we find ways to hold things in common and thus create communities. Working in groups where we are asked to clarify what we mean gets us beyond vague feelings to specific thoughts that can then be further examined and expanded. Realizing that it is not just enough to say "I believe" but to have to say "I have good reason to believe," and to then have to supply those good reasons and then to listen to the reactions, deepens the quality of the thought processes for people both professionally and personally. Internalizing the public group processes of deliberating can carry over into a person's internal self-dialogue and help remove distorted ways of reasoning.

7. *People learn well when they get helpful feedback.* It has often been said that leaders need two things: to be infallible and to learn from their mistakes. Since nobody really is infallible, it is better to concentrate on learning from mistakes. This is crucial in leadership. Feedback is the basis for self-correcting inquiry, the slow and deliberate processes of changing one's mind and the course we may be pursuing. Psychologically, the key word in the statement may be "helpful." Feedback which is communicated with an air of annoyance or superiority is a surefire way to produce defensiveness and avoidance of effort. A way to manage to give feedback in a caring way is provide specific information on what a person did well, what needs improvement, and how to go about making this improvement.

8. *People learn well when they acquire and use strategies.* In terms of everyday situations, strategies are not infallible solutions to complex problems. Rather, strategies provide logic for understanding and a start in resolving a difficulty. Understanding the logic of a strategy enables a person to say, "I can see why they go about it this way." Understanding the complexity of real-life situations enables educators to not let strategies become straightjackets or thoughtless algorithms. Strategies need to be adjusted to the subtleties of different contexts and situations. One size does not fit all. What disciplined understanding provides is a sustained examination of the logic and methods of complex inquiry. Strategies evolve and open up to us a more complex world that is potentially graspable in parts.

9. *People learn well when they experience a positive emotional climate.* On the one hand, high-stakes testing works against a positive emotional climate when it provides overwhelming pressure on students, teachers, and administrators. On the other hand, an unstructured, shallow curriculum provides an underwhelming and uninspiring emotional climate for all involved. A whelming environment, a safe and challenging setting, calls forth the possibilities to explore and expand perceptions because a person does not have to defend himself or herself from unnecessary threat or distraction. This is done in schools by having students, teachers, administrators, staff, and community members become part of a caring community of learners that explores what is involved in creating and

sustaining a positive emotional climate on an ongoing basis. Without a caring learning environment, the stakes of high-stakes testing are being driven into the educational heart of everyone in the school and beyond.

10. *People learn well when the learning environment supports the intended learning.* David Perkins (1992, 2010) takes seriously the idea that we can create what he calls "smart schools," places that can move from training memories to educating minds. Such schools do not happen by accident but are the result of working with people to intentionally orchestrate places, policies, programs, and processes that call forth sustained deep learning. Such intentionally inviting schools are the embodiment of educationally caring about learning. You can tell when you are in such an educationally stimulating environment because the school is filled with art work, charts, diagrams, and learning groups for a variety of purposes. You can feel the glow of active learning being directed at meaningful and deepening subject matter.

Brandt's 10 guidelines provide a vehicle for managing care about learning and learning about care and are closely connected to current pedagogical practices in contemporary schools. Teachers differentiate, create positive learning environments, scaffold learning by building on prior knowledge, facilitate social interactions for learning, co-create success criteria, provide ongoing descriptive feedback, and set realistic but challenging goals for success. By attending to and reflecting with all involved in a school on what is learned (that which is personally meaningful, challenging, and developmentally appropriate); how it is learned (building on choice, previous knowledge, interaction, feedback, and strengths); and where it is learned (in positive and supportive environments), educational leaders have a way to deepen educational sensibilities. The management of this effort is enriched when it is focused on the development of successful intelligence.

SUCCESSFUL INTELLIGENCE

Educational leaders want their students to do well inside and outside of schools. They want students who become more intelligent as a result of their schooling experience. But what kind of intelligence should be promoted and for what purposes? Robert Sternberg (1997) makes the claim that schools should teach for successful intelligence because "that will be the most valuable and rewarding in the real world after school—both in our work and our personal lives" (p. 269). He provides much research to support this assertion.

School leaders should be very aware of the power of modeling lifelong learning. Talking with staff, students, or parents about courses being taken, scheduling night classes, or working on term papers, whether in graduate classes or additional qualification courses, reveals an authenticity to the assertion that learning is a lifelong process. The fact that a designated leader, such as a principal, is still enjoying learning and actively engaged in education as an educator, leader, and student is a message educators should be proud to model for the community. It is one thing to claim that education is important and to profess it publicly, and another to model it by living educationally on an ongoing basis.

The successful intelligence promoted by Sternberg (1997) is about the qualities necessary in reaching important goals. This type of thinking is the joining together of creativity (finding new ways to look at things), analysis (breaking things down into component parts), and practicality (working in the real world). Each one of these brings something important to the success equation. The artful blending of these works occurs by finding a good problem to pursue along with good initial solutions to those problems and then making those good solutions even better. Sternberg's approach involves setting into motion the wondering rather than the worrying parts of our minds. Working to activate rather than sabotage our efforts is vital for successful intelligence. Managing for successful intelligence is a goal for schools and something that should be developed in invitational leaders. Here is how Sternberg points out that successfully intelligent people have learned to flourish:

- *They know how to make the most out of their abilities.* They try a range of things and find ways to build on what they do well and compensate for their limitations.
- *They translate thought into action.* Rather than getting stuck in the "paralysis of analysis," they see ideas as hypotheses that need to be ventured forth, tested, and if necessary, reconfigured. This is a key idea for school principals.
- *They are not afraid to risk failure.* Failure is only really negative if it gets a person to stop learning. Otherwise it is feedback that lets a person know what does not work. If you want to learn to juggle, you better expect to drop some balls.
- *They have the ability to concentrate on the big picture.* The big picture provides a sense of where you want to go. Having a sense of where it is worth going can help you manage your efforts on what is necessary to get the right problem solved.
- *They have a reasonable level of self-confidence.* In being realistic about solving a problem, a successfully intelligent person should see beyond the unreasonable self-talk of self-doubt and self-delusion. Realistically, chances are we are not the greatest or the worst at anything.

What makes Sternberg's research all the more interesting is his personal story. Sternberg was a poor test taker but used that limitation as a way to study the limitations of traditional testing. In the process he became a much respected academic and President of the American Psychological Association. His educational sensibility grew from learning from failure. Working from an ethic of care and reflecting on principles of learning and successful intelligence, an inviting educational leader can now apply this commitment to thinking to the development of ethical fitness.

MAKING TOUGH CHOICES

In the best-selling self-help classic, *How to Win Friends and Influence People*, Dale Carnegie (1936) advised people wanting to be successful that they should learn to dodge talking about religion or politics. Certainly, this can be prudent advice, but artful dodging comes at a price: missing out on the exploration of issues of mutual and significant importance. We agree that educators should be prudent and appropriate in their discussions of emotion-filled topics but we also think that it is essential that they manage to deal with issues of mutual and significant importance in their practice. These significant and important issues may not always be about religion or politics, but they certainly will be about conflicts between values, between what Rushworth Kidder (1996, 2005, 2010) calls ethical dilemmas. Ethical dilemmas, to Kidder, are not about right-versus-wrong choices. These are not dilemmas because if we know something is clearly wrong, we know what we should do: the right thing. Doing the right thing may not be easy, may certainly take courage in facing risks and hardships, but is not a moral quandary. Kidder provides guidelines for handling these in his book, *Moral Courage* (2005). Moral dilemmas, on the other hand, involve a tension between the following prototypes of competing rights (Kidder, 1996; Purkey et al., 2010, p. 33):

- Truth versus loyalty. You have to make a decision between being forthright about a problem in your school versus promoting your school's reputation.
- Individual versus community. You have to decide what to do with an unruly student, who would gain from being in a regular classroom, but is an impediment to other students' learning.
- Short term versus long term. You have to decide between teaching to the test or building on students' needs, concerns, and interests.
- Justice versus mercy. You have to decide between applying a zero-tolerance policy or taking mitigating circumstances into consideration.
- Privacy versus security. You have to decide between respecting the right to be left alone or searching everyone for safety purposes.

The choices above are complex. They are like a running automobile engine with two motors facing the opposite direction: using a lot of energy and going nowhere. Still, something has to be done and Kidder provides a strategy for developing the ethical fitness to handle these agonizing problems. This strategy involves being cognitively engaged in looking at real issues on a recurring basis and being committed to acting on your best judgment in each case. The ethical fitness strategy provided by Kidder (1996, pp. 183–186) involves the following nine steps:

1. Recognize that there is a moral issue. Is the tension in this issue a right-versus-wrong or a right-versus-right concern?
2. Determine the actor. To what extent and in what ways am I responsible for what is happening in the present and in the future?
3. Gathering the relevant facts. What details do I need to know to find out what is happening?
4. Test for the right-versus-wrong issues. Does this involve a fundamental lack of principle, terrible consequences, or a total lack of care?

5. Test for right-versus-right paradigms. Which two deeply held values are in conflict with one another?
6. Apply the resolution principles. How does being aware of my duties, the consequences of what is happening, and my desire to extend care in this situation influence what I think is possible and desirable?
7. Investigate the "trilemma" options. How can I go beyond either/or thinking and honour both/and possibilities?
8. Make the decision. How can I summon up the moral courage to act on what my reflected judgment has shown to be the right things to do?
9. Revisit and reflect on the decision. What have I learned in taking action on this decision? What would I do differently?

Developing an educational sensibility for ethical issues is not easy or without its costs. Time, effort, and agonizing are required to be an ethically growing human being. Obviously, the nine-step process is meant to be a heuristic provocation not an algorithm straightjacket. It offers invitational leaders logic for approaching difficult issues and suggests some steps to take. In times like this, where there are a myriad of complex and pressing issues that need to be faced, developing ethical fitness comes with the territory. Kidder (2010) is aware of this and suggests that we start early. The title of his book, *Good Kids, Tough Choices: How Parents Can Help Their Children Do the Right Thing*, gets right to the point.

MENTORING CONVERSATIONS

Q: Is everything in education an ethical issue? This can be overwhelming.
There shouldn't be anything intimidating or overwhelming about doing the right thing for the right reasons. Luckily, we are not faced with deep ethical dilemmas on a regular basis. Instead, what we are suggesting is an intentional alignment of our thinking so that it is through an ethical lens—an inviting lens. Just like most actionable situations, practice makes perfect. The more we align our thinking to be ethical, the less brainpower and decision making will be required to do the right thing at the right time. Perhaps thinking about it with these questions in mind will help to develop ethical thinking and practice which will, over time, become less cumbersome when making decisions: Is this decision good for kids? Does this support our teachers/parents/students? Does this decision align with our professed goals? Can I live with this decision over the long term? Am I comfortable defending this decision if asked to do so?

We recognize that there is a political element to leadership of any kind—including educational. Our political advice would be that the more ethically you act, the better your chances are politically. Our assertion would be that over time, a leader who consistently makes good ethical decisions and conducts himself in ethically defensible ways gains more respect and political currency. People who do the right thing for the right reasons at the right time tend to be highly regarded and widely respected. Reflect on the fact that it is a good thing to be known as a leader who consistently conducts himself or herself ethically.

Q: Can you care too much? Won't people burn out if they approach everything with this sense of deep caring?

Just like we suggest an appropriate level of "whelm"—neither overwhelmed or underwhelmed—a leader can and should care, and understand what is appropriate in terms of getting involved in the lives of others. A leader who might "care too much" might be someone who takes on everyone's problems and concerns personally. Caring does not mean carrying the weight of the world on your shoulders. You can care about others, support them and their goals, and do so appropriately as a leader. You cannot go home and parent for others, take care of their financial stressors, nor protect them from harm. Caring for others does not necessarily mean unreasonably bearing the burdens of others.

Q: The talk about risking failure sounds good until you really do fail. Aren't leaders supposed to hide their failures?

When administrators are first promoted, they can focus a lot of time and energy on trying to prove that they are worthy and capable of the position by trying to know everything, or at least appear that way. The role of the principal is one that expects competency from the first day. That can be a lot of pressure on a new principal. The worst thing new principals can do, however, is to pretend they know more than they do. Principals who have been in the role for a few years, have experience, or come to the role with a strong sense of themselves understand that failure is not only inevitable, but important. Tremendous learning happens from failure, something we teach our students, and failure makes us human, and better able to connect with others. Perfection is not possible and not relatable. The more you know, the more you realize how much more there is to learn. Modelling that as a leader not only makes you more relatable, but also encourages students to understand how much there is to learn and how failure is, in most cases, the prerequisite of success.

Q: Regarding ethical dilemmas, the more I think about them the harder they get. Isn't it best to just follow your first impulse? Can you overthink them?

Ethical dilemmas are never easy. That's why they are ethical dilemmas. First impulses may be valuable, but careful consideration, input from others, and reflection on experiences will lead to good decisions. "Going with your gut" can, at times, be a way to take a shortcut and shirk the responsibility of making thoughtful, measured decisions. There can be value in your first impulse, and there can be value in thoughtful consideration. Your first impulse can be validated through thoughtful consideration, reflection, and experience. Appropriate reflection and consideration should lead to a decision you are comfortable with. There is a point at which you probably know what the right decision is and it is at this point that you should make it comfortably and confidently. Ethical dilemmas and decision making need not be a binary exercise between gut reactions and debilitating deliberation. An appropriate consideration should take into account initial reactions, reflect on experiences, and consider the variety of angles. Once you have the appropriate information you can make a decision and see it through.

LEADING EDUCATIONAL COMMUNITIES

The thoughtful use of metaphorical language is an important way for inviting educational leaders to communicate and structure vision, and focus creative efforts. The contrasting images of a school as an inviting family or as an efficient factory provide very different perspectives on the values and aims of educational organizations. Using key characteristics of an inviting family school, leaders can structure and sustain co-operative and caring practices through the people, places, policies, programs, and processes of their organization.

Should schools be the most efficient place in town?

Should all inviting schools look alike?

Can schools be free of structure?

Can structures be liberating?

Because of the mutual care and support needed to make schools work in inviting ways, these are important questions for leaders to ask as they attempt to build educational communities. This chapter will call into question your beliefs about the organization of schools if you:

- Think efficiency is the chief ingredient of a good school;
- Believe that all good schools look alike in their best practices;
- Feel that structures are merely strictures;
- Think freedom is attained by merely eliminating constraints.

This chapter will build on your beliefs if you:

- Think that education is a co-operative, collaborative activity;
- Believe there are many defensible ways to be a good school;
- Feel that a sound structure can be the basis for more complex freedoms;
- Think that a good family provides the care needed for its members to grow in thoughtful ways.

This chapter builds on the previous chapters' focus on developing the personal, interpersonal, and curricular commitments of leaders and extends these commitments to deal with the structure and freedom needed to construct and sustain inviting educational communities.

CHAPTER 9

STRUCTURE, FREEDOM, AND COMPLEXITY

Discussions about the structure of organizations can often be abstract and vague ponderings on intangible and uninteresting issues with questionable relevance to the everyday realities of schools. Understandably, this is the sort of thing that tends not to excite educational leaders. When asked to explain structure to educational leaders, an image that comes to mind is that of trying to hold a bird. If you hold it too tight, you squeeze the life out of it. If you hold it too loose, it flies away. The point being that too much and too little structure both have their problems. The task for a leader is to find the dynamic balance. The reason this analogy is used is because it can talk about structure in a vivid and insightful way. It is a good use of figurative language that can get a challenging conversation started, something thoughtful leaders need to do. The difficulty with the bird-

> ### *About Structure and Creativity*
>
> *I wanted to take a creative writing course at university but wavered on whether or not to sign up for it because the reality of having to be creative on a deadline appeared counterintuitive to the creative process. How can a writer be creative when doing so to meet externally imposed deadlines? As it turned out, I discovered that the imposition of deadlines was perhaps the only way that anything creative was to be created by me. The structure of the course required creativity and content on a strict timeline. As the course progressed, I realized how important the structure was to the completion of assignments and the creativity that resulted.*

handling image is that it only touches the surface of a more complex issue that needs deeper exploration if it is to move leaders beyond articulating insightful but limited possibilities. Insight needs to point to sustained meaningful action. That is why Robert Pirsig's (1992) creative analysis of structure is more than insightful. It is abstract (and hence generalizable beyond specific settings), interesting (connects to varied interests in insightful ways), and informative (tells you things you may not have known).

An unusual question can spark interest. A provocative way to answer an unusual question can stir an educational imagination (Pink, 2013). Evidence based on the provocative answer can promote a program of inquiry. Robert Pirsig (1992) provides all of these, beginning with his surprising question, "How do atoms become chemistry professors?" His answer to this unusual question is far-ranging, in that he presents a way of thinking about how within the 13.7 billion year history of the universe the basic energy flow has worked through the physical, the biological, the social, and the intellectual realms by means of the processes of structure and freedom. From Pirsig's perspective, structure is what protects emerging processes (freedom) and gives them a chance to sustain and develop their newly formed complexities.

If you have structure without freedom, all you would have would be mere repetition of time-worn processes in which nothing new can come into being. For an

126

organization in rapidly changing times, this becomes catastrophic when it has not developed the inner capacity to handle the new reality. It is literally overwhelmed, lacking the means to do anything new. Structure without freedom is a problem, but so is freedom without structure. Without structure, new complex development is without protection and cannot sustain itself. It is a mere soap bubble, glittering here for an instant and then poof. This is the story of many educational innovations: interesting possibilities lacking the protection to develop.

The challenge of inviting leaders is to caringly bring structure and freedom together so that new qualities take hold that can enable their organization to use the energies within and outside of their school to deepen educational purposes. Returning to Pirsig's analysis of the transformation of energy, over eons and eons the balanced combination of structure and freedom has enabled energy to move from operating at the physical level (where there are only mechanical interactions based on the laws of nature), to the biological level (where life is following the law of the jungle in order to survive and reproduce), to the social level (where cultural life has encoded rules and its members have laws to follow), to the intellectual level (where humans in advanced institutions can develop complex and workable concepts and instruments for understanding the previous levels, and where chemistry professors can understand atoms). This last level, the intellectual, represents both a growth of complexity and a growth in understanding the possibilities of mindfully participating in this complexifying process.

Applied to organizations in general, the growth of complexity outside needs to be matched with the growth of complexity within by providing the structure and freedom so that ruts are avoided and deeper forms of interaction and thinking can be sustained. If this does not happen, chances are the organization will not survive. Inviting educational leaders certainly want their schools to survive but they also need to develop more caring structures that enable people to have the protection and freedom to develop more thoughtful forms of learning and relating. In terms of educational theory, Brent Davis and Dennis Sumara (2006) offer insights and concepts on how understanding complexity can move educational conceptualizations beyond linear and reductionist approaches to deepen the research processes necessary to understand how teaching, learning, and organizing work to form emerging structures that can creatively deal with new realities that are faced in schools.

Earlier it was stated that invitational leadership is about calling forth and sustaining imaginative acts of hope. That abstract call to action can be given more structure by providing two images to consider: the image of the school as an efficient factory and the school as an inviting family.

EDUCATIONAL METAPHORS (FACTORY VS. FAMILY)

Try to imagine a school without an organizational structure. This is very hard to do because even if a school does not follow an official set of principles and procedures, there will be informal policies and rules that develop. Structureless organizations do not really happen in the human realm because of the deep-seated need for some degree of predictability. Some would argue that the development of some form of bureaucracy is inevitable in any organization. Complex interactions, to be sustained, require some degree of structure. Now try to imagine a school with total freedom. You can do anything you want, any time, any place. You are likely imagining total chaos, a school that would not be able to sustain itself. Moving from these extremes, schools with rigid structures can prevent opportunities for innovative development to take hold. On the other hand, schools with unprotected freedom can almost guarantee that nothing of substance will stick. Everything is running in too many directions, and the school's institutional memory is over-whelmed by hyperactivity. The challenge is to construct a harmonious balance of structure and freedom so that defensible educational experiences are maintained, protected, and enhanced. So how might an educational leader even start thinking about this?

First, in recognizing that we live in a pluralistic society with democratic aspirations involves a commitment to use structure and freedom in humane ways. Schools need the freedom to do things in different ways because there are different people in each school and good grounded ideas come from being intelligently involved in unique contextual events. One size does not fit all. There is a need for ingenuity, diversity, and change to come from the ground up. On the other hand, schools need stable structures because scheduling, role differentiation, and evaluation, amongst other things, need the time and attention to be dealt with in a dependably caring way.

There is a needed safety in rigid structures and rules that new, inexperienced, or unconfident leaders can appreciate. However, external rules can be hidden behind and remove responsibilities. Understanding how to work within and around the system, as well as how and when to say "no," to deviate, push back, and change course is the role of the responsible leader. Inviting others helps this process. Understanding the potential of an underlying ideal metaphor can enable a leader to have leverage to move in educationally defensible ways, from factories to families.

Here are two models for structuring schools, the efficient factory and the inviting family. Our preference is obvious but the contrast enables the factory's and family's underlying rationale to be clearly perceived.

> ### *About Educational Metaphors*
>
> *I was teaching exchange students from China and asked them to discuss the concept of structure versus freedom. After a few moments, I invited their comments. One group brilliantly described the necessity of structure for freedom by describing a kite. In order to soar, it needs to be tethered to a string. Without the string, it will not maintain flight for long. I asked the group who was responsible for such an insight; their response was "We all are."*

SCHOOLS AS EFFICIENT FACTORIES

Factories can be diverse, ranging from sweatshops to high-tech robotic industrial units, but they all deal with making a product and most demonstrate a traditional form of organization. Unfortunately, this traditional form of organization based on making a product lives on in the rationale and practices of many schools. Because factories are in business to make money, they have to be efficient. They must get rid of waste and duplication. Ironically, too much emphasis on a narrow view of efficiency and elimination can make a business more vulnerable because minor glitches can become major roadblocks (Homer-Dixon, 2000). School boards regularly hire external consultants to examine the numbers and dollars and cents. They may make recommendations and decisions unconnected to educational priorities. The reality of funding in public school systems is the maintenance of balance between the budget and the educational priorities of the schools and the system. That being said, narrowly defining efficiency leads to the promotion of the following six characteristics: mass production; uniform production; cost effectiveness; technology, centralized control; and workers as functionaries (Novak & Purkey, 2001; Purkey & Novak, 1996). When this is applied to schools, these characteristics are manifested in the following ways:

- Mass production: In quantity there is strength. Having bigger schools with more and more students bussed in while, at the same time, imparting a narrowly prescribed curriculum in a lock-step way, is taken as the quick and easy way to raise test scores. Choice is a deviant distraction.
- Uniform product: In sameness there is strength. Making sure students possess the same test-taking skills and facts gives a significant number of students the expertise to meet or exceed performance indicators measured by standardized tests. Those students who are out-of-step with the program are considered shoddy and sent to what is the counterpart of a factory-outlet store to be put out to the world at a price below market value. The challenge is that some parents often seem to prefer this model because it provides a simple comparison measure which is a source of pride for those doing well or concern for those who are not.
- Cost effectiveness: In cheapness there is strength. Applying continual pressure to do more with less and attempting to get a bigger bang for the budgeted buck means aesthetic concerns are considered a frill and programs that do not provide instant and direct evidence of the investment of resources are eliminated. Issues such as school closures are a reality of cost effectiveness as smaller community schools are considered for closing in favour of mega-schools that can hold two to three times the number of students. Financially the mega-school makes sense as one principal, one custodian, one building to maintain is preferable to multiple smaller schools.
- Technology: In machines there is strength. Possessing the mindset that whoever has the most machines wins, the school is dominated by wireless wonders and electronic elaborations. Contact with real human beings in real time is seen as so last millennium. Much time and attention is spent in protecting the technology from theft and corruption.

- Centralized control: In hierarchy there is strength. Operating from central headquarters, mandates are delivered regarding what is to be done and how it is to be done and where it is to be done. Growing gaps develop between the mandaters and the mandatees. Hierarchical organizational structures emphasizing rigid and formal rules dominate.
- Workers as functionaries: In obedience there is strength. Everybody in the system is continually told what to do. The job of the principal is seen as getting teachers, staff, and students to do what the principal's superior told him or her to do. Teachers are seen as expendable and interchangeable and are always worried about keeping their jobs.

This is an exaggerated picture of what many schools were or are becoming. The vital educational questions—"Efficient for what? For whom? For taxpayers? For parents? For students?"—are not asked. Much of educational worth is ignored in this factory orientation including why people became educators in the first place and what sustains them in their vocation to work with people who matter to them. The quip, "If you do not feed the teachers, they will eat the students," seems all too real in such schools. To understand the limitations of the factory model, it is helpful to look at another way to structure schools, the inviting family school model.

SCHOOLS AS INVITING FAMILIES

Not many people are born in factories, and if they spend too much of their early years in an industrial unit it is rightfully seen as a breach of social justice. People are born into families and it is there that they are hopefully provided the care and experiences necessary to begin and sustain a flourishing life. If we wish students and educators to lead educational lives, we will have to see through and beyond the image of schools as factories. We will have to work with an image that hits closer to home, the inviting family model.

The inviting family model is not based on a one-size-fits-all formula of what families should look like. Inviting families come in a variety of shapes and sizes and go well beyond traditional relationships. People in such groups may or may not be biologically related. What makes them inviting families is that they are held together by a commitment to the care and development of each other. This way of being together is distinguished by the following six characteristics:

- Respect for individual uniqueness: In incomparability there is strength. Emphasizing the matchless and irreplaceable nature of each member of a family means that each person is seen as a distinctive part of an important group. As family members get older they are given more choices in how they make their contribution to family living.
- Co-operative spirit: In working together there is strength. Believing that "we are all in this together," family members care for and accept care from each other.

The caring impulse is called forth and nurtured through the growing relationships that develop in shared activities.

- Sense of belonging: In caring there is strength. Acting on the idea that the home is the base for connection and renewal, family members share a feeling of trustworthiness and warmth. This is what makes it "Our Family."
- Pleasing habitat: In vibrancy there is strength. Realizing that the home is a place where nurturing and co-operation abound, the residence is alive with plants, colour, and comfort. Common areas and private areas are treated with aesthetic and ethical respect.
- Positive expectations: In appreciation there is strength. Being grateful for being a part of a valued group, family members are celebrated in the present and are encouraged to develop unique talents and assume appropriate responsibilities.

> ### *About Schools as Inviting Families*
>
> *While I was the principal of a school, I wanted to create a new school crest. I articulated my goal, and encouraged others in the school—teachers, students, and parents—to contribute to the creation of a new school crest. I encouraged the consideration of the school's mission statement and foundational values and how they might influence the design as a visual representation of the school. Timelines were established for submissions, and logistics such as size, dimensions, and colours were established. These structures provided guidelines and parameters to assist with the creative process. From there, creative licence was given and encouraged. The submissions were wonderful celebrations of the creative spirit of the school and contributed to the creation of the new school crest.*

- Vital connections to the larger society: In reaching out there is strength. Sensing the necessity and importance of responsibilities outside of the home, family members take their interests and talents out to the world and bring back and deliberate what they encountered. They help create rich and varied interests within and outside the family.

This model of an inviting family can provide a rationale for structuring a school around an ethos of care and competence. The following checklist (Novak, 1999) is a concrete way for educational leaders to develop invitational audits of their schools and districts and to begin discussions regarding school practices and the metaphors underlying them:

1. **Respect for individual uniqueness**
   What is positive and unique about this school?
   In what way are evaluations done in a caring way?
   If students are having difficulties, how are they cared for?
   How are inimitability and diversity celebrated?

2. **Co-operative spirit**

   How is mutual support emphasized?
   In what ways do people take individual and collective responsibility?
   In what ways do teachers, staff, students, and parents have a say in making decisions?
   Is peer teaching encouraged?

3. **Sense of belonging**

   Who perceives the school as a caring place?
   Does each student have a core nurturing person?
   How are people treated before and after absences?
   How are shared social events developed?

4. **Pleasing habitat**

   Does the school look like a place where people care?
   How are people involved in taking care of the school?
   Are there living plants in the school?
   Does the school feel vibrant?

5. **Positive expectations**

   Do administrators say positive and specific things about teachers?
   Do teachers say positive and specific things about each of their students?
   Can students say positive things about their teachers and administrators?
   What imaginative acts of hope were demonstrated in the school?

6. **Vital connections to society**

   Can the school be seen in the outside community?
   Can the outside community be seen inside the school?
   Are volunteers visible in the school?
   Are global connections explored and deliberated at the school?

   One last question: Would you like to spend a year at the school?

These 25 questions are intended to start a conversation regarding to what extent a school is functioning as an inviting family. If they seem strange or unusual, educational leaders and their school communities may wish to discuss the underlying image that is structuring the culture of their school with the goal, we hope, of creating a more inviting school.

IMAGINING AN INVITING FAMILY SCHOOL

Inviting schools may embody imaginative acts of hope in the abstract but the schools are not imaginary or remote conceptualizations. They really exist. They are located around the world, in the United States, Canada, China (Hong Kong and Mainland), Northern Ireland, Mexico, and South Africa and more than 200 have received awards from the International Alliance for Invitational Education for creating and sustaining caring and competent qualities. We have been welcomed into schools in Hong Kong, throughout the United States, and Northern Ireland, and enjoy supporting and contributing to the development of inviting schools such as the Welcoming Schools Project in Northern Ireland. The book, *Creating Inviting Schools* (Novak et al., 2006) depicts the work of educational leaders in developing such welcoming places. Using our collective memories, here is an example of some of the practices you might initially see in an inviting family school (Purkey & Novak, 2008):

> Imagine that a family is moving to a new location in the summer. A key question on everyone's mind is, "What kind of schools do they have there?" Well, even before they get there they get the local paper and find out some very important things. The paper has a section titled, "What's Happening In Our Schools," where they discover that the schools have teachers and students who are a part of an international exchange program, teachers write articles on recent books they have read, and students are involved in more than 10,000 hours of volunteer work in the community. The article contains an up-to-date website that goes into more detail about the activities and upcoming events. Readers are aware that the schools have a strong academic purpose along with a variety of events that involves an abundant and enthusiastic number of students.

> When selecting where to live, the family comes in contact with a real estate agent who has an impressive knowledge of the schools because she recently participated in a breakfast reception for the town's realtors. She said she received a tour of the school and an informative packet of material. What stayed with her the most was the professionally relaxed atmosphere of the school personnel. People seemed really glad to be there and share good feelings about the school. During the process of moving into their new place, the family visits stores in the area, sees students' artwork on display and finds copies of the school system's newsletter. In some stores they see that the students are a part of a project collecting books to send to schools in another country. The schools are quite visible well outside their facilities. There is even mention of the schools' international relief project on television.

> When the parents phone the school to enrol their children the phone is answered without delay by a real person who gives a friendly greeting, the name of the school, and an offer of assistance. The greeter seems delighted that the family will be coming to the school. Driving into the parking lot the family sees that the school is clean and green, with sparkling windows and plants everywhere. The signs in the parking lot do not tell you what not to do but, politely, what is requested. Rather than "No Parking," signs say "Please Park in Designated Areas." There are also prominent parking spots for guests. Entering the school, there are clearly marked signs which not only give directions and information but also explanations. Rather than "Quiet in the Halls" the signs say "Please, no loud talking when class is in session." The school is filled with fresh smells,

shining floors, and colourful bright paint. Students have a place where they can display their work and it is filled with their paintings, drawings, and sculpture. The school communicates a contagious vibrancy.

In the main office, there is a comfortable room with a deinstitutionalized feel. The traditional counter is not there. There is a receptionist's desk and comfortable furniture, arranged with the intention of making people feel relaxed. It certainly does not feel like the school most people went to. Waiting for the new enrolees is a parent volunteer who knows everyone's name and where they are from. She then escorts the family to the "Welcome Centre" where there is an array of educational materials along with fresh flowers, fruit, and juices. The Welcome Centre is the headquarters where the official school tour begins. Led by a student volunteer, the family is guided by a knowledgeable and informative young representative of the school. The sixth-grade student takes the family to her room and talks about the co-operative activities and interesting things she has learned. She feels good about her school and asks questions about where her guests are from and what they enjoy doing. She listens well and is a good conversationalist. Everyone thus far has been an impressive ambassador for the school.

The school cafeteria also looks deinstitutionalized. There is a sign that says, "Dining Room" and the eating area for the start of the school year will focus on a book that everyone in the school will be reading and discussing. The school guide explains that music is played during lunchtime and everyone knows that if they cannot hear the music, they are talking too loud. Vending machines have healthy drinks and it is obvious that the school promotes an active wellness program. The student guide also takes the family into the faculty workroom, which is clean, filled with educational materials, and some humorous signs. There are up-to-date bulletin boards with notices about team-teaching meetings and faculty seminars. A sign outside the door is stated positively and says, "Teachers' Workroom. Please Knock Before Entering. Thank you." rather than "No Students Allowed." As the tour is finishing, family members use the school's restrooms that are clean and well-maintained with doors on the stalls and mirrors at every sink. There are posters reminding and explaining to students the importance of washing their hands.

At the end of the tour the family is escorted to the parking lot and given a bumper sticker that reads: "Our School: The Most Inviting Place in Town." The family judges this to be truth in advertising. Later that day the family reads the information packet and finds that the policies seem based on a high level of respect, the programs seem interesting and challenging, there is a school council that encourages everyone to have a say in the processes of the school. The next day, the family receives a phone call letting them know their visit was appreciated and asking them if there are any questions. The year is off to a good start.

Are all inviting schools like this? Of course not. One size does not fit all and schools have a variety of participants who have competing ideas and priorities. Schools like this do exist though. You may read the above and think "There is no way that could ever happen in my school." We would submit that you, as a leader, are absolutely right if you truly feel that way. Leadership has such an influence on the establishment of any program, policy, or process in the school as well as on the place and the people within the school. The ideas from the school above can be taken individually as ideas that can be appropriated in any school with an eye toward the establishment of an inviting school. Each school tries to take ownership for the underlying principles used to develop their unique and appropriate way of putting into practice their creation of their inviting family school. Is this all there is to being an inviting family school? Of course not, but it is a good beginning. It is also important to see how an inviting family school goes below the surface and invites the essentials.

THE ESSENTIAL FOCUS OF AN INVITING FAMILY SCHOOL

Structuring a school on the model of a family is something most people can easily identify with. The word "family" can be thrown around superficially to refer to loosely affiliated organizations. While factories are associated with being cold and impersonal, families can be idealized as warm and unique. Most people want to be a part of a warm and unique group. That's a good thing. Moving beyond this, Csikszentmihalyi (1990/2008) connects the family model to the long-term promotion of self-directed learners and notes these five underlying caring principles that promote the development of what we referred to earlier as autotelic learners:

- Clarity: Students are not directionless. They know what is expected of them and the general direction of where they should be heading.
- Centering: People are interested in what students are doing at present. They are not seen as future investments but are appreciated in their uniqueness.
- Choice: Learners are not locked into one way of doing something. They have a variety of possibilities to work with.
- Trust: Students feel unselfconscious in trying something new. They feel safe to explore with their freedom.
- Challenge: Parents provide life opportunities that encourage participation in the development of more complex abilities. Learners are encouraged to enjoy and grow.

Relating this to an inviting family, the warm and unique setting also provides challenges and the opportunity to grow in meaningful ways. Creating a caring and competent setting means that inviting family schools need to become autotelic institutions whose members demonstrate clarity, centering, choice, trust, and challenge in their own lives. Research by Reginald Green (2001, p. 65) found that in such schools:

- Teachers were knowledgeable about students' in-school and out-of-school lives.
- There existed a collective sense of caring and responsibility for student success.
- A sense of family existed and was shown in the collaboration among the professionals.

135

Such schools do exist and they are successful. Returning to Postman and Wein-gartner's (1973) conventional functions, inviting family schools structure their focus in these ways:

- Time structuring: There is flexibility in how time is used and students are encouraged to choose how to organize their time.
- Activity structuring: Students are actively engaged in shaping their learning within and outside of the school.
- Defining intelligence, worthwhile knowledge, good behaviour: Successful intelligence, the blending of creative, analytical, and practical thinking is directed to learning to savour, understand, and improve academic and everyday thinking and living.
- Evaluation: Students' strengths and areas of concern are illuminated so that achieving success can occur in meaningfully challenging ways, rather than being primarily test-driven.
- Supervision: Students are involved in formulating, implementing, and evaluating some of the school's key activities.
- Role differentiation: Everyone in the school is a potential educational leader and is encouraged to use his or her expertise to bring about deeper learning.
- Accountability to the public: Parental and community participation is encouraged and the school is willing to be accountable for what it can defend as its educational mandate.
- Accountability to the future: The school aims to develop flourishing leaders of educational lives.

Leading for caringly structured educational communities involves attention to big ideas (structuring for effective freedom) and important details (the caring policies put into practice). Considering structures and how they can support your priori-ties rather than regarding them as bureaucratic obstacles can mean the difference between merely getting by year-by-year and creating and sustaining an inviting school. Managing these diverse factors is achievable with a strategy for understand-ing and orchestrating people, places, policies, programs, and processes, which is where we go in the next chapter.

MENTORING CONVERSATIONS

Q: Schools as inviting families sound wonderful, but it must only work in par-ticular contexts. It would never work in mine, would it?
One of the authors was a school leader in a community with low student attend-ance, high poverty, single-parent families, poor academic results, and limited par-ent engagement for his first assignment, then transferred to a high socio-economic, high-achieving student, highly involved parent community. The individual contexts could not be more unique within the same school board/district. The common factor between the two was the leader. Creating an inviting school looked very different in

each community but the common leadership approach to care, trust, respect, meliorism, and intentionality had a tremendous impact on the creation of an inviting school in each. Contexts may differ, but a leader's approach to a creating an inviting family school can and should start from these foundational principles. Statements such as "that would never work in my context" or "that sounds great in theory, but would never work in practice" are the mantra of the maintenance of the status quo. The dismissal of ideas and ideals reduces practice to implementation and delivery. New ideas which are presented as fully formed can understandably be overwhelming. When considering new ideas and how they might work in individual contexts, choose something to focus on and try to live it in your practice. Small changes can make significant impacts.

Q: How can I lead an inviting family school when our system or standardized testing and curriculum encourage efficient factories?
Leadership need not be an either/or proposition. In fact, experience teaches leaders to become comfortable with grey areas and ambiguity. School leaders can encourage the creation of inviting family models within the structures of standardized testing and curriculum. We can respect the uniqueness of individual students and recognize how each learns differently and respect how they contribute to the class and school. We can foster a sense of belonging and co-operative spirit where we learn from one another, celebrate differences, and respect individual contributions. We can establish positive expectations within an environment where students want to be and want to learn and do so in a way that makes connections beyond the school yard and out into the community. We can utilize standardized testing to find out more about individual students' learning needs and program accordingly. Standardized testing may be widely used to measure, rank, and compare schools, but recognizing that they will continue to take place, we can use the information for so much more to do unique and creative things for individual students. Our assertion is that when you lead with this in mind, you create cultures of learning that will encourage student success and translate into academic success, even if the measure is merely standardized testing. A leader need not approach leadership by either buying into a rigid approach to learning or an inviting family model. Instead, lead from the perspective that all endeavours are enhanced from an inviting family model as students feel supported, safe, recognized, and encouraged. Good things will result in potentially unexpected ways.

Q: The structure and freedom bit seems much too philosophical for me. How can it help me in my thinking and work?
Understanding the balance between structure and freedom can help you to achieve and manage the appropriate degree of "whelm." Not overwhelmed, and not underwhelmed. New ideas, programs, and initiatives can seem overwhelming in their entirety. Structures can help to break things into manageable components in a step-by-step manner. When taking on a new task or trying to lead a new initiative or change, structuring can help to organize thoughts or ideas and provide a way forward. Within each manageable component or step, being open to creativity, flexibility, and

new ideas can lead to innovative approaches and encourage team building. Structure can also do the same for others in the organization as they can recognize how they fit into the big idea and contribute in meaningful ways. Artfully orchestrating freedom within the structure invites others to contribute their gifts and talents to the plan so they can participate in the process.

Q: Saying a school should be like a family sounds corny. Do you have any other metaphors?
The use of families as a metaphor is an important one because of the degree of responsibility, connection, and relationship that it infers. Families care, encourage, respect, stick together, and have mutually vested interest in success. The use of family as a metaphor attempts to challenge any barriers that might place parents, students, teachers, and leaders in mutually exclusive silos and instead recognizes the interconnectedness of each to one another. It may seem corny because there is an emotional element to families that those who want to keep others at a distance may not be comfortable with. As parents as well as educators, we want our children to be in schools where people care about them, connect with them, encourage, support, and challenge them. We want to send our children to places where we know they will be safe and we know they will be held accountable in loving and nurturing ways. When we want this for our own children, we recognize the responsibility we have to encourage educational leaders to foster this in their schools so that parents can send their children off each day confident and comfortable that their children will be part of a school family.

CHAPTER 10

MANAGING A STARFISH

Everything and everyone in a school either adds to or takes away from the success of each student and the quality of life of the educational community. This is perhaps most especially true of educational leaders. In the management of inviting schools, educational leaders work with people to promote and design places, policies, programs, and processes that intentionally communicate care and competence.

What factors come together to make a school work?

How can schools be invitationally designed?

How can change be approached in a co-operative manner?

Can schools become beacons for leadership?

Because of the continuity and coherence needed to align the various parts of a school community, these are important questions for invitational leaders to ask as they work to develop and sustain deeply educational settings. This chapter will call into question your beliefs if you:

– Think professional development is just a frill;
– Feel that a school can only follow society's lead;
– Believe that there is insurmountable resistance to change;
– Think you have to create a crisis for schools to change.

This chapter will build on your beliefs if you:

– Think that educators want to work in good schools;
– Believe that school buildings can be deinstitutionalized;
– Feel that good policy making is a collaborative effort;
– Think that a cohesive planning approach is a win-win situation.

This chapter is based on the premise that just as everything in a health care unit should promote positive health, everything and everyone in a school setting should encourage flourishing educational lives. This challenge can be better managed with a guiding analogy.

STARFISH POWER

Inviting schools do not just happen. It takes dedicated and thoughtful people working together to face challenges and resistance. It also takes a perspective that can face resistance with a strategic, ameliorative mindset, and a sense of humour. An important part of being a leader is to create situations in which people do not feel overwhelmed. One way to do this is to use an easy to understand analogy created by one of our colleagues, William Purkey (Purkey & Novak, 2008). His aquatic analogy puts thinking about planning and resistance in perspective. It goes like this:

> A starfish lives to eat oysters. To defend itself, the oyster has two stout shells that fit tightly together and are held in place by a powerful muscle. When a starfish locates an oyster, it places itself on the top shell. Then gradually, gently, and continuously, the starfish uses each of its five arms in turn to keep steady pressure on the one oyster muscle. While one arm of the starfish pulls, the others rest. The single oyster muscle, while incredibly powerful, gets no rest. Irresistibly and inevitably, the oyster shell opens. ... Steady and continuous pressure from a number of points can overcome the biggest muscles of oysters and, by analogy, the biggest challenges faced by any school. (pp. 19–20)

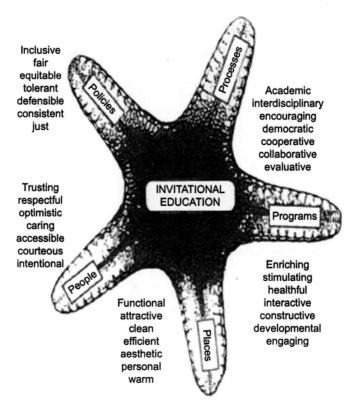

Figure 2. The starfish analogy.

This analogy is most appropriate for thinking about managing an inviting school because the inviting approach is not about one program, one place, one policy, or one process; it is about the transformation of the total culture of a school. School cultures can be very powerful structures, and, understandably, do not change easily. Many schools are "stuck" (Stoll & Fink, 1996) and when you go to these schools you start to believe you are hearing the warning of The Borg from *Star Trek*: "You will be assimilated. Resistance is futile." There appears to be one massive resistance muscle, and it seems overwhelming. Those who have tried to change the dysfunctional culture have often been assimilated or eliminated. Similar to the starfish, undaunted, well maybe a little daunted, the invitational leader uses a multifaceted strategy to change attitudes, behaviours, and cultures, because really, most people want to work in places that provide exciting, satisfying, and enriching experiences for everyone. Such places work by focusing on the development of the five basic areas addressed by invitational educators: people, places, policies, programs, and processes.

Five Potent Ps

The inviting approach to educational leadership has high aspirations, but in order for it to be more than aspirational, it needs to focus on down-to-earth details. Viewing the educational ecosystem as comprised of people, places, policies, programs, and processes enables leaders to celebrate successes in these areas and develop plans to apply steady and consistent pressure to that which needs improvement. Thinking of each of the Five Ps as a finger on a human hand, the first P to be considered is people, the thumb which enables grasping to take hold.

1. People-Centred Practices
People are key in an inviting approach. Everything begins and ends with people. People have to develop and sustain places, policies, programs, and processes. In addition, every person in the school is an emissary of the

About Contrived Congeniality

Leaders recognize that good people doing great things within any organization is the key to success. I've been inspired by one administrator who takes the time at the beginning of every school year to sit down with every staff member from the custodian to the teachers, secretaries to the lunch room supervisors. He connects with them about their families, what they leave every morning and go home to every night. They talk about passions and pursuits outside of the school and what can be contributed within. Through these conversations I have seen him develop an understanding of what each person can contribute to the school, when to ask for help and encourage participation, and when to back off and allow other situations to resolve. I admire how he values individuals, fosters in a way that contributes to the community as a whole, but understanding each person as a unique individual willing to invest in the school as a whole.

school. This includes the teachers, the students, the administrators, the staff, the librarians, the food service professionals, the custodians, the bus drivers, the parents, and the volunteers. They are all adding to or taking away from the quality of educational life of the school. If we look at people as thumbs, they are all either pointing up or down. They are not neutral because to be neutral is to be apathetic, to be running on an empty spirit. To be neutral is to have a thumb pointing sideways trying to hitch a ride out of the school.

By now it should be quite clear that the inviting approach gets its energy from people creating, sustaining, and, most importantly, enjoying positive relationships. It is very important that the civility of an inviting school is not based on what Hargreaves (1994) calls a contrived congeniality, filled with counterfeit countenances and insincere smiles. Such pretences run thin and barely conceal some deep-seated hostilities, which come out sooner and later, and in the time in between. A deep sense of civility is sustained by a commitment to collegiality, a commitment to see one's work partners as competent and well-intentioned (Sergiovanni, 1992). This is contrary to the tendency of people in organizations to see those with different opinions as either foolish or evil. This feeling of collegiality depends on a sense of acceptance, empathy, and pluralism mixed with honest conversations about what and why some practices call forth or shun educational flourishing. A concrete practice of such schools involves staff calling students and parents by name. The simple act of remembering someone's name sends the message that they are important, valuable members of the community. Jenny Edwards (2010) has shown more than 100 ways teachers can promote invitational learning through caring conversation starters. Taken to the administrative level, an elementary principal from South Carolina we know writes a birthday card for each student and staff member in her school. One school superintendent from Ohio sent a positive comment about a principal to the principal's parents. The principal said when he visited his parents he found the praiseworthy letter under a magnet on the refrigerator. He said he appreciated the imaginative act of hope and hoped it would not be repeated.

2. Places That Promote Caring

To state a truism, in all senses places are everywhere. They are the sights, sounds, smells, the tangible totality taken in by the senses. If you are totally surrounded by litter, peeling paint, putrid smells, dust, clutter, grime, and weeds, you may want to hide, but where will you go? Inviting educators do not excuse self-induced squalor in their schools and are acutely aware of the messages sent by the upkeep of their institutions. This point is emphasized by Malcolm Gladwell (2000), in his bestselling book, *The Tipping Point*, when he describes the "broken window theory of vandalism." Quite simply, when a window is broken and left unrepaired, a message is continually transmitted that in this neighbourhood no one is in charge and no one cares. This encourages more broken windows and more crime. A race to the bottom ensues. Inviting schools work to send the opposite message: This is our school. We all care. We all are in charge.

The good news is that places provide tangible opportunities for immediate improvement: Litter can be picked up and receptacles provided; rooms can be painted; fresh air can be circulated; halls can be dusted, offices can be made user-friendly, and the school's grounds can be appropriately and creatively landscaped. Donia Zhang (2009) has written about the positive effects of school gardens and ways attentive and creative landscaping brings life to a school. Anybody wanting to see wonderful educational places in action can go to the more than 200 schools throughout the world that have won the Inviting School Award given by the International Alliance for Invitational Education. The schools communicate a vibrancy that says "We care about where we learn and live."

A principal we know began her tenure at a school by arriving in August to find broken windows around the building and smashed fluorescent light bulbs at the front doors. She began the process of creating an inviting school by paying particular care to what she had the most control over—starting with the office—and then working throughout the school in the hallways, classes, and front and back garden. Over time, she would arrive at the school after the weekend and find one less window broken, then less, until there was no more vandalism over evenings and weekends. When she suggested making the entrance of the school more inviting by purchasing and decorating urns at the front doors, the custodian dismissed her plans by suggesting that the urns would quickly find their way through the front windows and there would be an even bigger mess to clean up. She considered the hesitation, and moved forward regardless. The urns became a welcome addition to the school, commented on by visiting guests and parents alike, and changed with each season. Five years and thousands of guests later, the urns have yet to be thrown through the window!

3. Policies With Educational Purposes

Officially, policies are written up in the school's mission statement, directive codes, and regulations. Unofficially, they are the unwritten rules that govern what happens in the school. The official and unofficial rules tell you about the rulers and how they rule. Inviting schools, being guided by the democratic ethos, want more and more people to be involved in formulating, implementing, and evaluating the official statements and unofficial rules of the school. Inviting schools prepare people to be active and knowledgeable citizens in a democracy. This image goes well beyond aiming to develop insatiable consumers or self-satisfied isolates. It involves, what Robert Westbrook (2005) has consistently emphasized, schools that "educate every student for the responsibilities and benefits of participating in public life" (p. 218). He adds, "One reasonable measure of the strength and prospects of a democracy is the degree to which its public schools successfully devote themselves to this task" (p. 218). That's a lot to ask of the principled policies of an inviting school. A way to verify if an inviting educative community is operating is to find out if those affected by the policies perceive them as fair, inclusive, democratic, and respectful.

Working to make policies inviting also means contesting those perceived as remote, out-of-touch, exclusive, and contradictory, those that forbid anyone to ever think about going "up the down staircase." Such messages communicate an oppressive, confused, and unrealistic way of operating. Paying attention to the processes and product of developing policies regarding attendance, grading, discipline, promotion, and professional developments is a key part of an inviting school. Such policies should be evaluated in terms of how well they convey the caring core of invitational education: trust, intentionality, meliorism, and respect. Policies may be dated and can be worth reconsidering at the school level. For example, though intended to maintain safety, zero tolerance policies often inadvertently hurt students who may bring penknives to school without criminal intent. Consequences such as suspensions and expulsions also deprive students of valuable educational opportunities. School districts may also have policies about the use of mobile phones in schools that are meant to protect privacy, limit distractions, and prevent academic dishonesty, among other reasons. All worthy endeavours in any school. However, the proliferation of smartphones and the equity of access to these devices present new and exciting access to information and tools for collaboration and discussion. Policies banning mobile phones entirely may cling rigidly to a way of doing things that is no longer congruent with contemporary tools and the reality of living and learning in our information-rich world. Enforcing bans of smartphones simply because of policy, rather than for educational purposes, surrenders educational authority. Finding creative ways to embrace, rather than hold in abeyance, can challenge policies to evolve and grow educationally.

Discussions about an attitude of "gaming the system," taking self-serving advantage of the letter of the law but disregarding the spirit of the law, are a key part of being in an active democracy. Inviting leaders do not hide behind policy or use it as an excuse for making a difficult decision. Leaders make decisions based on the foundational principles of care, trust, respect, optimism, and intentionality, not because a policy "says so." There can be times when the policy as written is incongruent with the complexities and uniqueness of a situation and needs to be considered and potentially modified in order to make the best decision possible grounded in the foundational principles. Educational leaders reveal themselves as inviting leaders when they can stand on their foundational principles rather than behind policies, and interpret policies in ways that support students.

4. Programs With Curricular Coherence

It matters what is stated as the official curriculum of a school. This is an affirmation of valued knowledge. It also matters what is actually taught in schools. This is what teachers emphasize in their classrooms as meaningful content worthy of attention and exploration. But, perhaps most importantly, it matters what students learn in schools. In the best of all possible worlds, there would be great overlap among the official, taught, and learned curricula. In a world of high-stakes testing, what is often learned is surface knowledge about both the world of knowledge and test taking. In this context, knowledge is about getting the right answer and test taking is an isolated activity that really does not go on anywhere outside of classrooms. Inviting leaders look for ways to work around and beyond this.

A way to start in examining curriculum is to begin with the basic idea that the school's programs are to meet the wide spectrum of needs of students facing an ever-growing, more complex world. With this in mind, programs should promote equity of access, with built-in opportunities for all students to succeed. Programs which should be promoted are those that encourage students to see themselves as autotelic and co-operative learners who are developing successful intelligence in coming to terms with the world of academic knowledge (the world of knowledge) and out-of-school learning (the world for knowledge). These two worlds can be successfully bridged by integrating curriculum components which allow students to engage in short-term and long-term placements (e.g., job shadowing, volunteering and co-operative education activities). In addition, inviting programs promote conflict resolution and group guidance activities that are useful in handling disagreements and encouraging students to work together (Purkey & Novak, 2008).

> ### *About Curricular Coherence*
>
> *I have been impressed by the ways my colleagues teach students to connect actions with consequences and local initiatives with global thinking, creative and collaborative partnerships. One principal I know of, in an effort to teach these 21st century learning skills, encouraged students, teachers, and parents to connect ideas and actions by serving others around the world by taking on local projects. Parents, teachers, and students joined together to work on ways to support the work of doctors and nurses at a children's hospital in Kenya. The program they collectively embraced under his leadership encouraged creative, critical thinking, collaboration, and local problem solving to meet global needs. As the principal of the school, his introduction of the program inspired the community and encouraged students to do things the principal would never have imagined.*

5. Processes That Promote Positive Possibilities

The final P, processes, is concerned with the intangibles: the tone, feel, and spirit of the way the other four Ps are undertaken. Positively, it manifests itself through a democratic ethos, co-operative procedures, and networking among teachers, students, parents, and community members. Perhaps it is best seen as the quality control element that orchestrates the vibrancy of the school culture. There is a problem with the processes in a school if bullying or harassment are a part of the way things are done at the school.

Earlier it was stated that "the process is the product in the making." As one of the Five Ps, processes entail not only what was done but how it was done. How something was done and the ways it lives on in the consequences of the actions that follow requires special attention to the underlying tone that is established in a school. Process-modeling, observing, and improving are subtle but vital parts of invitational leadership.

INVITING MEANINGFUL CHANGE

Thus far this book has presented rationales and strategies for creating and sustaining inviting schools. The inviting school movement has shown itself to be a trend, not a fad. It has been around for more than 35 years and is a part of a larger global movement to create more humane and caring institutions. It is time to look at a transformation process that fits the ethos and developmental nature of inviting change.

Inviting meaningful change is about the artful orchestration of the principles, practices, and insights of invitational theory to situations that involve a diverse group of people with varying degrees of knowledge and commitment to the inviting perspective. With all of this inviting in mind, the invitational helix (see Figure 3) was developed (Novak, 2002; Novak & Purkey, 2001; Purkey & Novak, 2008) for use by educational leaders in many different parts of the world.

The invitational helix is a strategy for principled change that accepts the fact that people and groups will have different degrees of knowledge and commitment

About Meaningful Change

I remember the first workshop I did on "Becoming a Change Agent." Still young and a little silly, I took a coin dispenser with me and asked the participants how many ways there were to allocate pennies, nickels, dimes, and quarters to make a dollar. (Yes, we had pennies!) The participants looked perplexed and they asked, "What are you up to?" I played with the audience and told them that I thought the workshop was for people who worked at a coin-operated commercial laundry facility who needed to become quicker at giving out change: becoming effective change agents. Again, the participants replied, "What are you up to?" and I responded that the concept of change, to be meaningful and moral, involves moving from something to something better. If it is the case that people want to make change, it is important that people have a good understanding of what they are changing, why they are changing, how they are changing, where they are changing, and when they are changing. The participants had a bit of a laugh but understood the danger of changing without thought can be like jumping on the educational bandwagon of the month riding again, and again, and again, going nowhere at debilitating speeds.

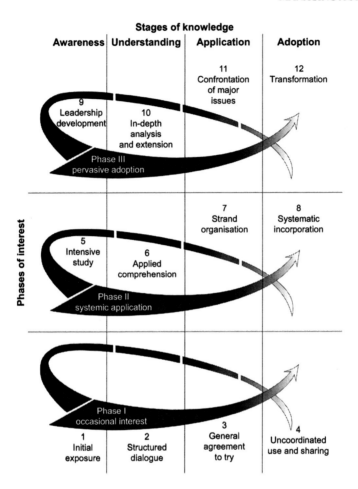

Figure 3. The invitational helix (source: Novak, 2002).

to an inviting perspective. Looking first at knowledge development, knowledge can move from people becoming aware (knowing about the approach), to understanding (knowing the important concepts and key ideas), to application (knowing how to proceed in a concrete manner), and finally to adoption (knowing how to sustain successful practices). Similarly, the intensity of commitment to an inviting perspective can spiral from occasional (enthusiastic renewal), to systematic (orderly treatment), to pervasive (extended leadership). These four stages of knowledge and three phases of commitment are put together as a 12-step process for inviting meaningful change. Of course deep educational change processes are more complex than this, but the helix gives educational leaders a structure to guide the process and prompt the development of artful orchestration of invitational transformation.

Occasional Interest (Phase I)

Inviting educational leadership is a meliorist approach to appreciating the good things educators are currently doing, along with pointing to areas that need particular attention. By giving recognition and praise to the variety of good practices already in place, inviting leaders help develop the structures to sustain these practices. The enthusiastic renewal begins with discussions about why people came into education initially and what makes it worth it now. Since it is difficult to teach with a broken spirit, renewal of the joy of teaching is a way to appreciate both the people engaged in, and the excellences embedded in, the vocation of teaching and educational leadership.

Initial Exposure (Step 1)   People need to know something exists before they can do something with it. Becoming acquainted with the inviting approach can happen in many ways: reading some introductory material; hearing a speaker; attending a conference; or visiting an inviting school. Orchestrating an initial meeting to present the inviting approach should build on the dignity and excitement of becoming a teacher and educational leader in the first place and point to the importance of getting back to what really matters in education.

Structured Dialogue (Step 2)   Following a presentation, meeting, or reading materials, an organized discussion deepens the understanding of what it means for something to be inviting. Talking about inviting practices already in place again gives appreciation of the good things that are already happening. Probing into why practices are inviting gives a better understanding of the underlying dynamics of the approach. It is here that participants talk about times they were personally disinvited and invited and reminded of the personal power and longevity of inviting and disinviting messages.

General Agreement to Try (Step 3)   Quite often people like to talk about inviting process in the abstract. This stage moves beyond the talk and moves to develop a consensus to try some new things, or extend previous practices, collectively and individually. Some small ways to begin involve changing the wording of signs, cleaning up a part of the school, or starting new clubs. It can help to call these activities "provisional," to take some of the pressure off trying something new. Members leave this first meeting with something they are going to put into practice.

Uncoordinated Use and Sharing (Step 4)   Since invitational leadership is based on a communicative approach to others, issues, and projects, new initiatives need to be shared to be understood, appreciated, and improved. It is at this step that people report what is working, what is challenging, and what is being abandoned. New practices such as changing the reception area of the school, modifying school signs, and having teachers in the halls recognizing students by name may be publicly affirmed and discussion about deeper commitments regarding the inviting approach may ensue.

Systematic Application (Phase II)

Following individual and group successes there can be movement to a more integrative phase. It is here where people work together for sustained periods of time, step outside their particular perspectives, and start thinking of the school as a whole. Making the whole school a shared concern is a prerequisite for a more structured approach to transformation.

Intensive Study (Step 5) The inviting approach is an integrated series of principles, concepts, insights, and strategies aimed at making schools places that intentionally invite flourishing educational lives. As a deeper awareness of the integrated components of the inviting approach is presented by a seasoned leader or invitational consultant, people are given a copy of the Invitational Theory Diagram (see Figure 4). The connection of the Foundations, Stance, Levels, Areas, and Five Ps are clarified and extended by a speaker who can model and provide examples of these concepts.

Applied Comprehension (Step 6) Comprehension of the systemic nature of the inviting approach means that those involved at this step are able to relate theoretical concepts to actual issues that are taking place in the school. For example, discussions about the model of the inviting family school as a criterion for judging current practices of the school can take place. It is here that the Five Ps are used to think about what is happening and what might be happening to make the school a more systematically inviting place. Those outside the school (e.g., parents and community partners) may be asked to share their perceptions.

Strand Organization (Step 7) Using a systematic method to brainstorm, evaluate, and implement new practices, teams of strands are organized whose members can include not only teachers and administrators but custodians, food service professionals, counsellors, librarians, students, and parents, among others. Individuals can be randomly assigned to one of five strands (People, Places, Policies, Programs, and Processes) and will participate in the 5-P Relay, created by William Purkey and found in Appendix A. Using a rotating procedure, each strand lists goals, specific procedures, obstacles and barriers, overcoming obstacles, action plan, and evaluation and refinement for each of the Ps. Each strand chooses a leader, a priority of goals, and reports back to the whole group. The 5-P relay is described in detail in Chapter 12.

Systematic Incorporation (Step 8) Each of the strands now has the chance to take on a life of its own by creating a name and a logo or mascot. Some schools have used names such as the "Blues Crews" or "Blues Brothers and Sisters." Strand members meet regularly and strand leaders meet together. Often the Processes Strand Chair serves as the coordinator for the Strand Leaders. Reports may be made to the school committee on a regular basis.

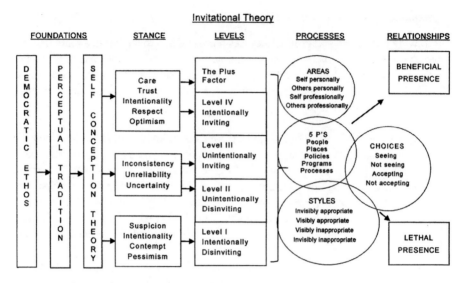

Figure 4. Invitational theory diagram.

Pervasive Adoption (Phase III)

This is the advanced stage of the helix where invitational leadership is manifested everywhere and becomes incorporated into the deep culture of the school. The school serves as a beacon for other schools which sent delegations to visit, observe, question, and learn. Leadership teams visit schools and make presentations and deepen their understanding by making contributions to the evolving theory of invitational practice.

Leadership Development (Step 9)   As leaders more deeply take on an inviting stance they develop a deeper awareness of not only know-how but also know-why and know-with. They can now provide principled reasons to justify the choices they made and the projects they have developed. Awareness now develops about using invitational leadership to explore deeper possibilities and larger projects. New ways of thinking about teaching, learning, and leading are tried out informally.

Depth Analysis and Extension (Step 10)   To really understand something is to be able to make distinctions that really make a difference in theory and in practice. At this step inviting educational leaders critically examine the inviting approach and compare and contrast it with other programmes and educational movements. New initiatives are analyzed from an inviting perspective to see if there is a focus on a person's perspective; an emphasis on self-concept-as-learner; an evaluation of humane effectiveness; an action orientation; and an encouragement of democratic deliberation in the pursuit of educational living (Purkey & Novak, 1996, p. 142).

Confrontation of Major Issues (Step 11)   At this step, the application of the principles of invitational leadership takes place not only within but also outside the school. Members of the inviting school family address key issues that have an influence on both the school and the larger community. Groups outside the school come to address issues of racism, sexism, heterosexism, and privilege and a deeper sense of the personal and social meanings of what it means to be committed to leading educational lives.

Transformation (Step 12)   In this final step, invitational leadership permeates the school. The school works from an inviting family model and has become a beacon school attracting visitors locally and globally. Members of the school make presentations about their work at conferences and are invited to other schools and districts on a regular basis. Celebrations of success, diversity, and creative engagement with real live issues are manifested throughout the school. The school is a vibrant centre where people want to be and want to learn.

Although what is sketched here is aspirational, it is also possible; it is also really happening. For example, Georgetown, Kentucky, under the leadership of Dallas Blankenship, and Hong Kong, China, under the leadership of Peter Wong and Clio Chan, have worked with hundreds of educators who have helped create schools that exemplify Step 12. They have also collaborated with each other and established an exchange program that has brought educators and students from rural Kentucky into deep and committed relationships with educators from ultra-urban Hong Kong. It has been an amazing process to watch. Many wonderful things can happen as leaders learn to manage the starfish.

MENTORING CONVERSATIONS

Q: You say that managing an inviting school is not about one program, policy, or process, but about the transformation of the total culture of a school. That seems overwhelming. How can a new school leader be expected to approach such a daunting task?

While it is important to keep the big picture in mind, focusing on the end result can make the process seem daunting. Change takes time, perseverance, and resilience and usually comes as a result of small, reasonable steps. While changing the culture of the organization might seem daunting on day one, opening your office door is a small and reasonable step in an inviting direction. Sitting down with individuals to find out about them is not only possible, but usually fascinating and encouraging. Considering the setup of your office, or the welcome area in the main office is a reasonable place to start. Getting to know the names of the students in the school can be step one. Without sounding too "zen" in our response, every journey begins with a single step. Instead of being overwhelmed by the end result, start to think about the simple, straightforward, first step that can become the foundation for your inviting leadership.

Q: What does "place" look like in practice? Schools are what they are, aren't they? What can a principal do to influence place that doesn't involve re-decoration and placing silk flowers and tablecloths throughout the building?

Being intentional about "place" need not be a big project such as the front garden. It can involve the reconsideration of the signs in the hallways or at the front doors. It could mean couches and chairs that people actually want to sit in when entering the office. It could mean rethinking the setup of your office. You could push your desk up against the wall to facilitate conversation and eliminate a power structure of sitting behind a desk. It could be the prominent displaying of student work in your office as a reminder of the priority of your work. It could mean the creation of an inviting meeting space or circular table in the office to welcome people and conduct meetings. Place is not about making spaces pretty, but about making them more inviting for people to enjoy, connect, and develop relationships in. Just as we noted above, each journey starts with a single step. One of the authors, when he first became principal, removed the principal's reserved parking sign and parking space from the front of the building and began parking in the space furthest from the school in order to free up as many spaces close to the front doors as possible for guests. He invited staff to do the same. The simple removal of the reserved sign rippled through the community and sent an inviting message out immediately, even before the first day of school.

Q: Policies are created, mandated, and governed centrally through the board or district. How can I make them inviting?

Policies can seem remote, and you may not have direct influence over policies at the board, system, provincial, or state level, but you do over what happens in your school. Inviting leaders don't perpetuate uninviting behaviour by hiding behind remote policies, and they consider how to do things in the school in ways that invite others into the process. If the process is the product in the making, the way things are done, how projects are conducted and led, have as much of a contribution to the culture and climate of the school as the final results. Inviting leaders don't dismiss uninviting behaviour by suggesting that it will be all worth it in the end. The consideration of how things are done is as important if not more important than the final result. As a leader, you have a tremendous amount of control over this.

Q: You mention inviting leadership as being part of a larger global movement. I'm not much of a joiner and am inherently suspicious of groups/organizations, membership, etc. Can I still be inviting?

The purpose of this book, and others written from an inviting perspective, is to get educational leaders to think about leadership differently and reconsider the existing leadership norms and challenge them by living and leading in an inviting way. This does not require the joining of an organization. If your first step on your journey toward becoming an inviting leader is remembering everyone's name in your organization, then wonderful. If you will now reconsider the setup of your office or the messages being sent by the front entrance of your school or where you decide to park your car daily, then that is a great first step. We would encourage you to continue to reflect and refine along the way. The global inviting movement is meant to provide support and encouragement to others around the world. There is strength in numbers, and knowing that others are living and leading invitationally across the globe hopefully not only provides you with inspiration, but also reveals inviting leadership as a living, breathing theory of practice that influences leadership in a variety of cultures. The global inviting movement connects inviting schools in Hong Kong with others in Northern Ireland, Ontario, and West Virginia. Connections with other educational leaders allows for the sharing of ideas and strategies in a variety of unique contexts. While this global resource can be a powerful support network, your leadership is your own. If you want to jump in with both feet, go ahead—there are numerous principals around the world to support you. The purpose of this book is to reconsider how things have always been done and see how you can do them better. That doesn't require a global movement. It only requires you. How's that for responsibility? Now do good things.

LEADING WITHIN AND BEYOND SCHOOLS

Invitational leaders are not to be charismatic advocates of the status quo but rather consistent and persistent campaigners for educational living both within and beyond their schools. This means not only caringly dealing with current community forces but conscientiously working to move attention and energy to deeper educational causes. Ethically addressing larger social issues deepens educational commitments inside and outside of schools.

To what extent can schools isolate themselves from outside forces?

In what ways can a school be an educational force in the community?

What are acceptable ways for the community to be in the school?

What are a school's responsibilities to the future?

Because of the persistence, resourcefulness, and courage necessary to take the school outside and bring the community inside, these are important questions for invitational leaders to ask as they aim to make a deeper educational impact. This chapter will call into question your beliefs if you:

– Think school and society are two separate realms;
– Feel that any contact with outside agencies will make schools worse;
– Feel that any contact with outside agencies will make schools better;
– Think the future will have to take care of itself.

This chapter will build on your beliefs if you:

– Think there is a vital connection between schools and the global society;
– Feel that educational relationships can be established with the world outside the school;
– Think that educators play an important role in the future;
– Feel that the present lives on in the future.

This chapter extends the LIVES model to look at an educational leader's relation-ship with the larger local and global society. Agreeing with John Dewey's (1897) observation made at the end of the 19th century that schools and society are vitally connected, and are getting more so, responsible leaders for educational living give serious thought to how they extend their schools beyond their physical boundaries and how they bring in and integrate the outside world. Schools, like individuals, are not neutral in promoting educational ends for a local and global society. This has important educational implications for the type of savouring, understanding, and bettering experiences educational leaders are encouraging and for the type of world they are trying to build.

SAVOURING REALITY IN A COMPLEX WORLD

Martin Luther King noted that "Our lives begin to end the day we become silent about things that matter" (as cited in Ury, 2007, p. 14). Since educational living by its very nature is about extending not ending lives, it is important that educational leaders have a sense of real issues that matter beyond the here and now in their schools. It is important the educational leaders come to grips with reality, which philosophers describe as that annoying stuff which does not vanish when we stop thinking about it. Savouring the real world is dependent on appreciating the relationships we have with each other and the planet that sustains us.

First the good news: This is a good time to be alive. There is strong evidence that human beings are getting less violent. Steven Pinker (2011), of Harvard University, has written an extensively researched and compellingly argued book, *The Better Angels of Our Nature: Why Violence Has Declined,* that claims that the world we live in now is proportionately less brutal, sadistic, and vicious than it has ever been, and since 1945 we are currently living in an era called "The Long Peace." It is Pinker's contention that this movement in a peaceful direction with less murders, tortures, wars, and cruelty per capita exists because of these five developments:

- The Leviathan: The historical movement which has given the state a monopoly on the use of force to protect its citizens from each other imposes heavy costs on aggressors. Individuals and groups have thus cultivated the habit of self-control, so violent impulses are curbed.
- Gentle Commerce: Trade which involves the exchange of mutual benefits allows both sides to be satisfied. There is less incentive to start a war when there are so many advantages to working together. Learning a customer's perspective encourages respect.
- Feminization: The cultural and political empowerment of female-inspired values has cut down on the emphasis on aggression and violent competition. Societies with large groups of young, unattached males are disproportionally more violent.
- The Expanding Circle: As an understanding of, and sympathy towards, larger and larger numbers of people grow, a world where everyone matters seems more possible. With larger numbers of people reading and coming in contact with others from around the world, people are no longer seen as abstract distant others but as fellow humans, just like you and me.
- The Escalator of Reason: Because of great increases in literacy, cosmopolitanism, and education, people are able to consider their own interests and others' interests as equivalent. "If I want to live a good life, I can imagine you want to also." This ability to step back and look more closely at logical relationships and empirical facts limits the leverage of outlandish beliefs.

Each of these points provides much to consider for educational leaders. For example: How can schools participate in the development and maintenance of good government? What ethical business practices can schools support? What types of co-operative strategies can be introduced into the school culture? Can online international networks be established? How can scientific literacy be encouraged in more parts of life? This is a lot, but there is more, and it gets complex.

Now the bad news: It's not all good news; there are other things to consider. These positive points of Pinker also need to be seen in light of the ecological, social justice critical perspective of Edmund O'Sullivan (1999), among others, who consistently and provocatively argue that there is a deep and serious problem concerning the survival of life itself in our present state of globalization. Contrary to Pinker, O'Sullivan is severely critical of where our modern, industrial, competitive marketplace way of life is taking the world. From his analysis, we are on an increasingly destructive path, using more and more irreplaceable resources and putting more and more toxic pollutants into the world. For O'Sullivan, schools can be either part of the problem or part of the solution. Again, there is a lot to consider here. It is easy to feel overwhelmed. What's an educational leader to do?

For O'Sullivan, there are three options:

1. Business as Usual: Educators can act as if these problems do not exist and schools are somehow immune from, or not in any way a part of, what is happening in the outside world. The essential job of the school is to prepare people for the high-stakes tests and do not let anything get in the way of that.
2. Tinkering Adjustments: Educators can add a course or a unit here and there, or bring in a speaker on a one-time basis to inform the students. This is a slight concession to the environmentalists and social justice advocates, but the basic structure of the school stays the same.
3. Radical Reform: Educators can transform the ideal of what education and schools are supposed to be about so people can democratically move in a more life-affirming direction. This can be a lot of positive rhetoric that needs to be unpacked if actionable proposals are to be developed.

To be an inviting educational leader is to care about the human prospect during this time of positive possibilities and paralyzing peril. The leadership task is to develop a reasoned, caring, and actionable educational perspective on the relationship between schools and global issues. On the one hand, to avoid thinking and discussing such issues is intellectually and ethically irresponsible. It is similar to having structure without freedom, things go on as normal and nothing new emerges within an institution. On the other hand, to think that schools can immediately attack all environmental and social justice issues at once is unrealistic and unfocused. It is like having freedom without structure; anything new that is tried cannot sustain itself in the bureaucratic and complex jungle of schools. A structured and freeing perspective is necessary for educators to begin to approach vital and complex issues. Such an approach can begin with a school ethical council that can examine global implications of school practices. Working with this council (it can be built around the policy strand of the 5-P Relay) to develop a set of ethical principles for school practices can begin by studying what other organizations have done. In an attempt to ignite a global ethical spark in business relationships, the Citizens Bank of Canada (2000) provides the following areas of concern that can elicit these types of educational questions:

- Human Rights: Does our school do business with companies that have poor human rights records or profit from child labour? What guarantee do we have that the companies that we are dealing with support international standards of human rights?
- Employee Relations: Does our school do business with companies that have poor records of employee health, safety, labour practices, or employment equity? How can we tell if a company is a fair employer?
- Weapons: Does our school do business with companies involved with the manufacture of weapons of torture or mass destruction? How can we tell if a company is so involved?
- Environment: Does our school do business with companies that have poor environmental records? How do we decide if a company has an acceptable environmental record?
- Treatment of Animals: Does our school do business with companies that conduct tests on animals in the development of cosmetics, personal care, or household products? How do we decide what is acceptable research with animals?
- Sustainable Energy: Does our school do business with companies that are involved in the production of nuclear energy? How do we decide what is wise energy production and conservation?
- Tobacco: Does our school do business with companies that manufacture tobacco products? How do we decide if a company derives significant revenue from tobacco-related products?
- Business Conduct: Does our school do business in an ethical way? How do we decide what ethical standards we should follow?

About Ethics

I was a beginning teacher on an LTO when I was asked to sit with the principal and secretary to make a decision. The challenge: What company would we deal with for the pizza lunch orders this year? One possible vendor offered a small discount to the school, the other offered a substantial discount if the school paid cash—under the table. To my surprise the cash deal was immediately the front runner—it was better for the school. I shared my belief that schools needed to model ethical choices—not to mention the fact that schools and our salaries were based on tax dollars. The decision stayed—the principal really could not see the point of my comment.

The above list is suggestive, not final. We do not have an answer to these questions and any educator should be suspicious of pre-packaged ethical kits based on the idea that "one size fits all." Inquiring into these questions can be a means for school leaders and members of the school ethical council to come to grips with the responsibilities of school–business partnerships. If the school ethical council wishes to pursue the issue on a more global level, they can explore the plan presented in the book, *2048: Humanity's Agreement to Live Together* (Boyd, 2010) which is an international movement for the development of enforceable human rights. By doing so, a school will be in contact with people around the world who are developing a plan to ensure that freedoms of speech, of religion, from want, for the environment, and from fear are available to all. If democracy means that everyone matters, learning about making these rights a reality is an important part of everyone's education. Savouring the complex reality of our present age means appreciating the long peace that has been developing, along with working to protect the planet on which it is taking place.

These considerations are perhaps highlighted when schools engage in fundraising activities whether for the school itself or for external charities. Helping students make the connection between their participation in a school project or fundraiser and the people they are supporting is important to connect within and beyond schools. This is where the concept of establishing and fostering relationships is so important. If a school picks a random charity each year and raises money by collectively holding a skip-a-thon or dance-a-thon, it might be difficult for students to consistently make the connection between their actions (skipping or dancing for an extended period of time) and the results (money raised for the Heart and Stroke Foundation or a hospital in Africa).

We know a principal who introduced his school community to the work of a children's hospital in Kenya. He started from a caring core, introducing students to the children at the hospital and the doctors, nurses, and staff who were caring for them and providing surgeries. He didn't introduce a project or dance-a-thon nor did he ask students to sell anything to raise money. Instead, he challenged them to live their lives in a way that would reveal their care for others, and to sacrifice in order to raise funds to support the hospital. He talked about the hospital, introduced the community to the work being done there, and asked the students to come up with their own ways to support it. He trusted everyone to do their part by not prescribing or imposing ideas, he respected their talents and creativity to come up with their own ways to live and act in order to raise funds, and he was optimistic about the results and talked about it with regularity over the announcements and at assemblies. The results were astounding year after year as students, staff, and parents continued to come up with creative and unique ways to utilize their gifts and talents or to sacrifice in order to support the work at the hospital. The ongoing relationship further allowed for deep investment in their work as the fruits of their commitment were revealed year after year.

Our experiences as educational leaders tell us that students will do amazing things when appropriately challenged. Parents and staff will similarly do so when

159

the students lead the way. Finding the appropriate way for students to connect their work with the results—whether globally or locally—is important for students to understand how they make a connection with others and develop and foster relationships. They will be less likely to consider themselves fundraisers and more likely to regard themselves as global citizens as a result.

UNDERSTANDING THE COMPLEXITY OF THE PRESENT

As we have just shown, savouring our present reality is not for the faint of thought. It takes a serious commitment to intellectual and ethical inquiry to work through complex issues which are fraught with ambiguous concepts and emotional land mines.

However, if the pursuit of deeper understanding is an authentic core educational value, this serious examination of important issues needs to be undertaken. Related to this pursuit, there is good news and other news.

First the good news: There is serious evidence that humans are getting smarter (Pinker, 2011) not only in information in hand and concepts understood, but also in abstract reasoning. According to a variety of test scores from around the world, people are reasoning better and improving in analytical skills.

Now the other news: The issues we have to deal with are getting more complex and we have less margin for error in dealing with them. Thomas Homer-Dixon (2000), in his award-winning book, *The Ingenuity Gap*, makes a powerful case for the idea that the requirements for ingenuity in our present world are increasing because of the "greater complexity, unpredictability, and pace of our world, and our rising demands on the human-made natural systems around us" (p. 314). His point is that it is foolhardy and dangerous to think that people can automatically develop the capabilities to solve all new problems and it is

> ### *About Complexity of the Present*
>
> *Exploring educational opportunities outside of my district has opened my eyes to educational possibilities and introduced me to inspirational educational leaders. Our school district might be doing great things, but they don't have the market cornered. I met another principal at a conference who was from Nigeria. The more we talked, the more we recognized the similarities of our approaches to educational leadership. We not only connected, but our classes have begun to connect regularly as well. Children are children everywhere. Making connections requires looking to the larger world for meaningful ways to do so. The realities of life in rural Nigeria may look different from the United States, but the aspirations and inclinations of the children in each class are remarkably similar. Opportunities to expand your world view will not likely land on your desk. Intentionality means exploring different ways to connect, lead, and share around the country and the world.*

160

naive and escapist to think that complex social and environmental issues will vanish if people develop more positive feelings for each other and a sense of solidarity. The error of both of these ways of thinking is that each perspective assumes it is merely up to us. Both erroneous ways of thinking leave out a serious acknowledgement of the complexity of the environment in which we live, which is often non-linear and filled with things that cannot be known in advance. Human beings possess brains, markets, scientific institutions, and communication technologies, all of which can do impressive things, but not everything. Within the "humbitious" yearnings of the position that Homer-Dixon is criticizing, there is hyperactive ambition but limited humility. We pursue this path at our own peril.

Homer-Dixon's point is that there is an ingenuity gap developing

> ### *More About Complexity*
> *Students at a high school were being taught about corporate decision making and ethical business practices in an upper year ethics class. Perhaps as a testament to the effectiveness of the teacher, they began to research the manufacturing practices of the school uniform supplier. The results of their research revealed the use of child labour and sub-standard wages at production facilities in a third world country. The students raised the concerns within the school, then throughout the community. While the media stories lauded the excellent work of the students, it provided a source of embarrassment for the district.*

between the growing human capacity to solve problems and the environments' ability to present viable solutions to these increasing complex problems. On the supply side for ingenuity, humans can work to develop the creativity and courage to deal with situations that are not perceived as hopeless or clear-cut. On the demand side, educational leaders need to examine the impact human consumption is making on the environment and on our socio-economic systems. Near the end of his book, Homer-Dixon observes that "What we value as wealth and as the 'good life' has enormous effect on our need for ingenuity" (2000, p. 398). Educational leaders working with their ethical school councils can raise some of the following questions:

– What is the carbon footprint of our school?
  Questions here can deal with the way in which such information is formulated and what is included and left out of the equation.
– What are we doing to reduce the carbon footprint?
  Questions here can deal with identifying realistic reductions as well as pipe-dreams.
– Does living an educational life mean low-impact consumption?
  Questions here can re-examine what is involved in learning to savour, understand, and better basic experiences.

– What are educational alternatives to high-consumption products?
Questions here can focus on the strength and weaknesses of new products, and the necessity of such products.
– How can a school call attention to problems associated with high consumption living?
Questions here can deal with the authority necessary to challenge job-producing ways of life that are adding to consumption.
– What obstacles are there to reducing the carbon footprint of the school?
Questions here can deal with what sorts of resistance can be expected as schools pursue these issues and how this resistance can be handled.

The educational good life focuses on learning to savour, understand, and better more of life's daily experiences. This way of life is committed to questioning a hyperactive consumerism that is degrading the conditions necessary to sustain a wide variety of forms of life (Sandel, 2012; Skidelsky & Skidelsky, 2012). In learning to appreciate more of a person's daily experiences, educational living is grounded in a responsibility to understand more about the world that supports this life. The larger global ethical project is for educational leaders to be a part of the movement to make this the preferred way of living. This project to help develop more educational lives will involve a deeper way of dealing with conflict.

BETTERING CONFLICTING POSSIBILITIES

If a leader is going to be an advocate who studies and calls attention to hyperactive consumerism, environmental degradation, and social justice he or she can expect some conflicting opinions to come forth. Earlier in this book we offered a way to handle interpersonal conflicts using the Six C process. This structured approach works well in key person-to-person parts of a leader's work. That's a good thing. However, when moving into larger social and philosophical arenas of contention, other strategies will need to emerge. Certainly the SPURT-Q Method is a good default position. In philosophical conflicts, learning to be attentively silent, sincerely using "perhaps" and "upon reflection," reaching tentative agreements, and asking honest probing questions to extend the conversation are useful in many situations. However, learning the power of a positive "no" and developing "third side" thinking can increase the educational depth of these encounters.

William Ury, the director of the Global Negotiation Project at Harvard University, has mediated conflicts around the world. Using ideas from his work as a negotiator in some very tense situations, he has written the very influential *Getting to YES* (1981/1991, with Roger Fisher) and *Getting Past No* (1993), two related and very positive books. A newer book, *The Power of a Positive No: How to Say No and Still Get to Yes* (2007), is not intended as a sequel to these books, but as a prequel. Ury felt that in his pursuit of the positive he did not do justice to the importance of the negative. Paying attention to an honest "no" is vital to realizing a real "yes." Educational leaders leading the school outside can expect disagreement. In encountering an issue, if a person ignores a deep feeling of "no," then chances are the discussion will only be polite accommodation or superficial chit-chat. Invitational leaders need to get below the surface if they are to engage in authentic educational deliberations.

According to Ury, a "positive no" is actually a "Yes! No. Yes?" in which people learn to express their interests, assert their power, and further their relationships (p. 17). Unpacking this, Ury is saying that when a "no" is being felt, it needs to be understood in terms of a larger interest that is being challenged (Yes!) and an ongoing relationship that needs to be furthered (Yes?). This process respects what is important to a person and the relationship with others. Stated another way, a "positive no" is a way to stand on your feet without stepping on another's toes. In discussions regarding social and philosophical issues, this is necessary if good and lasting agreements are to be reached. It is an important step in what Ury (1999) calls in another book, *Getting to Peace*.

Similar to, but not exactly like his Harvard colleague, Steven Pinker (2011), Ury thinks that we can use more of what we know to prevent, resolve, and contain destructive conflict, violence, and war. He bases his perspective on the idea that the "Knowledge Revolution offers us the most promising opportunity in ten thousand years to create a co-culture of coexistence, co-operation, and constructive conflict" (1999, p. 109). This promising possibility is made a reality if people learn and work to think in terms of the "third side," "the surrounding community which serves as a *container* for any escalating conflict" (1999, p. 7).

Third-side thinking moves beyond the perspectives of the two contesting parties to think in terms of the role of the larger community. Ury conceptualizes community to be "*people* – using a certain kind of *power* – the power of peers – from a certain *perspective* – of common ground – supporting a certain – *process* – of dialogue and nonviolence – and aiming for a certain *product* – a triple win" (p. 14). Moving beyond the mutual propensity to begin words with the same letter, an examination of these five dimensions can provide cogent concepts for those committed to using an inviting approach to educational leadership in addressing social and philosophical issues.

- People: Saying no to abstract hierarchical power structures, but not to individuals representing the ethical will of the community trying to contain harmful conflicts. In an inviting school, this could include all people who could speak to the conflicting parties from the perspective of what the harmful intensification of their dispute is doing to the type of culture they are trying to develop.
- Power: Saying no to the power of force, but not to the force of persuasion that aims to have the conflicting parties see their interests in relationship to the group norms. In an inviting school culture this could mean employing a third party to use the Six-C Process, or the SPURT-Q Method, or the Power of a Positive No to go back to a productive level of tension.

- Perspective: Saying no to the power of one side over the other, but not to the desire to appreciate the meaningfulness of each side's concern. In an inviting school culture there is an emphasis on a perceptual orientation which works to have each person's perspective understood and become a contributing part of an enriched larger shared perspective.
- Process: Saying no to the separation of process and outcome, but not to the dialogical process as the preferred mode of working together. In an inviting school culture every effort is made to have people involved in non-zero sum (win-win) rather than zero-sum (win-lose) situations. When this is not possible, the rationale for decisions is made transparent.
- Product: Saying no to one side losing everything, but not to the meeting of needs of each side and the community. In an inviting school, this means when a "no" needs to be said, there is a sincere effort to seek a "yes" that can also be affirmed in which people can invite themselves and others, personally and professionally.

The third-side approach works best if it catches a conflict before it becomes intensified and destructive. The inviting approach is by its very nature proactive, that is, forward looking and purposeful. Working to create an inviting ethos in a school carries over to the connections with the local community and larger society. The quality of this connection is enhanced through a deeper savouring, understanding, and bettering of the democratic ethos.

DEEPENING EDUCATIONAL DEMOCRACY

Earlier in the book we described the democratic ethos as a vital foundation for invitational leadership. This is based on the idea that democracy is an educative way of living and working together that allows people many opportunities and various ways to express, learn, and contribute to a vibrant social order. As such, a commitment to democracy is a commitment to a participative way of life that is a critical component for leading educational lives. Deepening an appreciation of this democratic commitment involves a recognition of democracy as an ideal involving cognitive and moral virtues, and a faith in the process of inquiry (Stuhr, 1993). Each of these requires elaboration from the perspective of invitational leadership.

- Ideal: As mentioned in Chapter 1, not something detached from reality or something that already exists, but that which, when united with imagination, seeks to express itself in action. In other words, the imaginative union of the actual and the socially desirable. For invitational leaders, this is the actionable vision of making schools places that call forth and sustain educational lives, even in these most difficult times.
- Cognitive and Moral Virtues: The development of the disposition to put into practice civic virtues in one's private and public life. This includes, as noted

by George Wood (1992, p. 81) in his book *Schools That Work*, the commitment to learn from but not be blinded by the past; the ability to enter public debate caringly and intelligently; the commitment to social justice; and a willingness to try new things. For invitational educators, this means teaching, leading, and living with and for these virtues

– Faith: The belief that people have the cognitive and moral capacity to inquire meaningfully into their individual and shared experiences with the possibility of making them better. The goal here is to have people become "hopeful meliorists [who] ... would act together to secure the goods of experience" (Westbrook, 1991, p. 362). For educational leaders, this is not meant to be an enticement to become foolish romantics, but rather an invitation to become seasoned meliorists who believe in what they are doing and learn from their experiences.

A deepened understanding of democracy is also a more intense understanding of the foundations of invitational leadership. With depth comes substance, strength, and subtlety; qualities needed to deal with leading within and beyond schools. In the next chapter we will show how this can be managed.

MENTORING CONVERSATIONS

Q: How can a school be an educational force in the community? Our responsibility is for the students within our building, how can it extend beyond the schoolyard?
Schools with positive reputations garner positive support and increased enrolment numbers while schools with poor reputations may suffer from low enrolment or poor regard within the community. It might be important for school leaders to keep this at the forefront of their minds as they consider how the greatest ambassadors for the school, the students, conduct themselves not only through their behaviour, but through their commitments, projects, and interests.

Schools that recognize the importance of connecting with the community and beyond put in place programs, processes, and policies that welcome community members and encourage students, staff, and parents to actively work toward improvement. This can involve connections with the local hospital, food bank, or community organization, or can mean commitments to global social justice and philanthropic organizations. A school can develop a reputation for developing globally responsible and ethical citizens (not a bad reputation for schools to develop!) by learning from community members and educating the community on not only what is happening locally and globally, but also suggesting ways to get involved. The eyes of the society are always fixed on the educational system as are the eyes of the community on the local school. This can be an awesome responsibility, and we would also say an awesome opportunity to educate outside the walls of the school as students go out into the world and influence it for the better.

165

Q: As a school leader, I feel constantly inundated with seemingly worthy organizations, initiatives, fundraisers, and events for our school to be involved in. It is overwhelming and I, at times, feel like schools are increasingly seen as fundraising machines for philanthropic organizations. Help!

Having a clear focus on a project helps to bring a community together and go deeper into an issue rather than spread widely. Intentionally developing a relationship with a philanthropic organization that lasts over many years rather than picking a new charity each year can help foster a sense of relationship and responsibility within the community. This will involve saying no to many worthy groups, but you can do so knowing that the work you have committed to is making an impact on your community and elsewhere. From a practical perspective, we have found it useful to maintain focus when engaging in projects, especially when there is fundraising involved. One school we know states clearly at the beginning of each school year that they will only ask for money *three times* throughout the year (beyond the normal field trips or pizza days). The first is focused on school improvement in the fall, so that all money raised is spent in that school year. The second is focused on the community and takes places over the Christmas holidays. The third is focused on global justice and takes place in the late winter, early spring. Students, parents, and staff have a clear understanding of what money is being raised for and how often they will be asked. The local community and global projects remain consistent yearly so that relationships are established and fostered over time, and everyone involved can see how their commitments are making a difference. Saying no to worthy projects and organizations may not be easy, but it is important to lead in a focused, intentional way in order to make connections, establish relationships, and simplify projects for the school community.

Q: The considerations for school councils on ethical business practices seem beyond the purview of most councils. These decisions are made at the board and/or district level. How can our school influence decisions at that level?

If we are going to lead schools that teach students to conduct themselves ethically and morally at all times, then it is incumbent on us to engage in practices that are congruent with those values. If we don't ask these questions, we run the risk of telling our students to think and act one way, while we think and act in another. These incongruencies will surface eventually and not only become a source of embarrassment, but potentially undermine the foundation of the institution. What we continue to find is that students are asking these questions already, sometimes long before we are. If we are doing our job right, we are encouraging students to think critically, reflectively, and to question ethical practices of institutions and organizations.

Schools can and should be asking these questions in order to "walk the walk" when it comes to ethical business practices. Not only how they conduct business but who they do it with further reveals the depths of convictions. When a school professes a commitment to ethical business, they do so from a stronger perspective when they are overt about who they will work with and under what conditions. As a school leader, you are more than an implementer of decisions made at the district level. You are a discerning educator who has not only the ability, but the authority to decide with whom you are going to conduct business. Your credibility will thank you for it!

Q: Asking schools to check on the human rights records of businesses they are dealing with seems to be politicizing things that are being taken care of by policies that are beyond the school. Where do educational leaders get the expertise and information to do such things?

The very process of asking appropriate questions about ethical practices models the reflective, critical behaviour we are trying to promote. No one expects the leader of a school to visit the factory where school uniforms are being made, but asking appropriate questions to any business is a simple, reasonable step to take. Inviting students, teachers, and parents to be involved in this process is a valuable learning experience for all and a model of collective, democratic decision making. The parent council and school council's involvement in posing questions regarding ethical practices provides a model for ethical decision making. Any business should be able to provide details on how their products are made, where, and what their business practices are. If they can't, or won't, it is well within your rights as the leader of the school to reconsider doing business with them. Asking questions is simple, appropriate, and a great way to let the community know the due diligence you commit to in order to intentionally see ideals in practice.

MANAGING SCHOOLS FOR A MORE
INCLUSIVE WORLD

A vital task for inviting educational leaders is to develop a school culture that can maintain, protect, and enhance an active democratic way of life. This means moving the school out into the community, inviting the community into the school, and becoming a living laboratory of democratic practice. Working together to look at and discuss the school's inviting qualities is a way to get everyone involved.

How can you make the school visible in the community and the community visible in schools?

How inclusive can a school be?

Are different and differing groups capable of developing a common vision?

Is it possible for invitational leaders to have time for a life outside of schools?

Because managing inviting schools requires people to work on a shared vision and an acceptable way to proceed, these are questions that educational leaders need to ask as they work to include others in the school community. This chapter will call into question your beliefs if you:

– Think schools should be islands of isolation;
– Feel that deliberation always ends up in gridlock;
– Think teachers and principals have all the answers;
– Feel that democracy is really only about voting.

This chapter will build on your beliefs if you:

– Think that inviting people to come into a school can make it more vibrant;
– Feel that learning to deliberate is fundamental to getting a good education;
– Think that differing perspectives can find common ground;
– Feel that learning to function in a democracy can make everyone smarter.

Working to construct democratic schools gets harder and harder because so many people want different things from their schools and for their society. This chapter looks at some practical things that educational leaders can do to take their educational message outside the school and caringly manage the quantity and quality of demands put upon their schools. To this end, the Inviting School Survey II (ISS-II) will be presented for getting those within and outside of schools to work together.

CHAPTER 12

Since good leaders manage well by using resources available to them, this chapter will show how some of the ideas presented earlier can be of special use both within and outside of school.

MANAGING TO TAKE THE SCHOOL OUTSIDE

In Chapter 9, an imaginative visit to an inviting school was portrayed. The school was intentional, vibrant, and connected to the outside world. We know of a project in Northern Ireland called "Welcoming Schools" which is working with school leaders to establish and sustain welcoming, inviting schools throughout Northern Ireland, particularly in traditionally divided, sectarian communities. In a country with lingering scars of violence and long memories, this project is inviting schools to open their doors to other communities and embrace an inviting global perspective. Progress has been measured but steady, as more principals commit to the creation of inviting communities. The ideal in each school may look different from the next, and may not resemble the school we described in Chapter 9. Though coming to terms with an ideally presented school can seem pie-in-the-sky-ish, the out-of-this world depiction can be unpacked with these 10 inviting practices that are manageable in the real world whether in your school or a Welcoming School in Northern Ireland or an Inviting School in Hong Kong or West Virginia. Here are some concrete things faculty and staff can do to get the ball rolling:

— Establish a communication committee that writes articles on a regular basis for the local newspaper, neighbourhood newsletter, or school district blog.
— Have a website committee develop and maintain a colourful, informative, and up-to-date website.
— Invite individuals and representatives from feeder schools and local community organizations, (e.g., real estate agents, district and state officials, business partners) to the school for breakfast or lunch and have a presentation that explains the school's programs and unique activities.
— Ask local stores, banks, and public buildings to display students' work and copies of the school's newsletter.
— Make sure that the school's telephones are answered courteously by providing a salutation, the name of the school, and an offer of assistance.
— Arrange to have the signs on the school positively worded and use "please" and "thank you," along with providing an educational rationale.
— Organize a "Green and Clean" committee that will make sure the school grounds are sparkling and flowers are abundant.
— Promote connections with local agencies so that schools can provide volunteers for community projects.
— Send invitations to community members to come to school fairs and other school performances.
— Develop skits and presentations that can be used on local television, radio, or YouTube.

These 10 practical suggestions are ways to signal that your school is energetic, welcoming, and intentional. A school can also get outside of itself and work with other schools to get mutual renewal projects going.

WORKING WITH OTHER SCHOOLS

No school is an island. By establishing lifelines with other schools, mutual growth and support can develop. One of the finest displays of schools supporting schools was developed by Dr. Peter Wong of the Education Department in Hong Kong. More than a decade ago, he brought together teams of five educators from eight schools to explore inviting practices. The teams included administrators, counsellors, and teachers who participated in an interactive workshop and developed an action plan to get things going. The project was so successful that more than 200 schools in Hong Kong have participated in similar workshops and the project has been taken to mainland China. This process is described in the doctoral dissertation *A Case Study on Introducing Invitational Education (IE) (a School Development Initiative) to a Secondary School and to Evaluate and Understand the Change Process, Effectiveness and Implications for Future School Development Work* (Wong, 2007). Another project called "Dissolving Borders" connected students from traditionally loyalist, Protestant communities in Northern Ireland with similarly aged students from traditionally republican, Catholic communities in both the Republic of Ireland and Northern Ireland. Students connected regularly over the computer at first, then through arranged events. The idea of Dissolving Borders was to challenge long-held assumptions about other communities, and to work at establishing relationships across traditionally accepted divides.

An activity called "Swap & Shop" developed by one of the authors was a successful way of getting educators from different schools to exchange ideas and initiatives and support each other. The activity involves the following seven steps:

1. Have members from each school fill in a 5X4 chart (similar to that shown in Figure 5), with the Five Ps (People, Places, Policies, Programs, and Processes) in five columns and Keep (something inviting already going on in the school); Remove (something that needs to be looked at); Add (something new you will try); Don't Add (something that is going on in other places but you will not try it

	People	Places	Policies	Programs	Processes
Keep					
Remove					
Add					
Don't Add					

Figure 5. Preparing for the 5-P Relay.

171

in your school) on four lines. Each school group has time to fill in as many of the squares as they want. For example, what is an inviting evaluation policy that you want to keep or what is an after-school program that needs further examination? The important thing is that the members of the school team discuss what they put there and why they put it there.

2. Each school then selects a spokesperson who stays at the home base while the other members of the team go visit other home bases to listen to presentations from the other spokespersons about their charts and schools.

3. The school members who visited other home bases return to their home base and discuss what they learned from each school. This has been especially important because many schools have found that they were not the only school that was having a particular challenge and that some schools had developed creative ways to work through difficulties and develop innovative practices.

4. With these new insights and examples of creative practice, each team now enhances its 5X4 Swap & Shop with new practices and strategies.

5. The enhanced Swap & Shop charts are now presented to the other schools and questions are raised and suggestions are offered from members of other schools.

6. The different schools establish a visitation schedule so that members of their teams can see how things are progressing at the other schools.

7. At the end of the year a celebration is planned to honour the efforts of all the schools.

This activity involves trust, co-operation, and a willingness to work with, and learn from, each other. It has worked and it can be an igniter in other school districts around the world.

WORKING FROM HOME

Even if a school sends a delegation to work with other schools, there is important work to be done when the delegation returns to their home school. In Chapter 9 we briefly described the 5-P Relay as a strategy to start the development of strands. Here is the specific plan for a half-day workshop developed by our colleague, William Purkey. The 5-P Relay has been used with educators around the world and participants have included administrators, teachers, students, counsellors, staff members, parents, and community members. A group of 15 is about the minimum number of people needed to make this work and we have seen it be very successful with a group of about 100. It will be helpful if people have read material, watched a DVD, or listened to a presentation on the inviting approach. A 3-hour time period is usually scheduled for the relay and is divided accordingly, including suggested time allotments [adapted from Purkey (1991)]:

1. During an orientation period this description is distributed to all participants and read aloud as everyone follows along. Questions are answered until everyone understands the purpose of the activity and their role. (Duration: 15 minutes)

2. Teams are formed randomly by having everyone count off by fives. After everyone has counted off, they are assigned to the five stations. "All the number ones please go to the station marked People. All the number twos please go to the station marked Places. All the number threes please go to the station marked Policies. All the number fours please go to the station marked Programs, and all the number fives please go to the station marked Processes." After these five teams are formed, everything is ready for the activity. (Duration: 15 minutes)

3. Instruct each team to brainstorm at least three doable goals for their particular P. They should write these goals on newsprint with their heading (People, Places, Policies, Programs, or Processes). The goals they choose should enable the institution to become a more personally and professionally inviting place. It is important that the goals they list be specific and measurable. Once each team has written the goals for their P, it prioritizes its goals, with 1 being most important, 2 the next, and so forth. The groups mark these priorities next to each goal they have written. At the end of this 15-minute activity a bell rings (any sound system will do, and timekeepers should be creative in the ways they keep people moving). (Duration: 15 minutes)

4. At the sound of the bell, each team immediately leaves its station, leaving its list of goals, and moves to the next station (that is, the People team moves to the Policies Station, Policies team moves to the Processes Station, Processes moves to the Programs Station, Programs moves to the Places Station, and Places moves to the People Station). After this move each team should be at a new station looking at a set of goals, written by a previous team. (Duration: 5 minutes)

5. Each team reviews the list of goals at their table and writes procedures to accomplish each of the goals starting with the highest priority. On a piece of newsprint, the group writes the heading "Here's How to Do It," and proceeds to list ways to accomplish each goal. At the end of this period, the bell rings. (Duration: 15 minutes)

6. Each team leaves its table and moves to the next station in the same order as before. (5 minutes)

7. Each team studies the goals and procedures at its new station left by the two previous groups, and makes a list of obstacles (barriers) that might prevent these goals from being accomplished or these procedures from being established. At the end of this period, the bell rings. (Duration: 15 minutes)

8. Each team leaves its lists and table, and moves to the next station. (Duration: 5 minutes)

9. The teams study the set of goals, procedures, and obstacles and makes a list of ways to overcome the obstacles. At the end of this period, the bell rings. (Duration: 15 minutes)

10. Each team leaves its table and moves to the next station. (Duration: 5 minutes)

11. Each team now reviews the goals, procedures, obstacles, and ways to overcome obstacles left by previous teams. Now they make a list of suggestions on ways

to evaluate whether or not the goals have been accomplished. "How will we know when each goal is achieved?" Teams will list methods to use in measuring outcomes and results. At the end of this period, the bell rings. (Duration: 15 minutes)

12. Each team leaves its table and moves to the next station. At this point each team should be back at the home station, where they first started the relay. Every participant has had an opportunity to be involved in each of the stations, as illustrated in Figure 6. (Duration: 5 minutes)

13. Each team studies its lists of goals, procedures, obstacles, ways to overcome obstacles, and methods of evaluation and prepares an action plan. This plan should include clear time lines, assignments and responsibilities for staff members, and an evaluation process. At the end of this period, the bell rings. (Duration: 15 minutes)

14. All participants come together in a large group and each team places its action plan on the wall where everyone can see it. A spokesperson for each team gives a brief report to the entire group. After the meeting these plans are typed, signed by team members, duplicated, and distributed to all the participants. (Duration: 35 minutes)

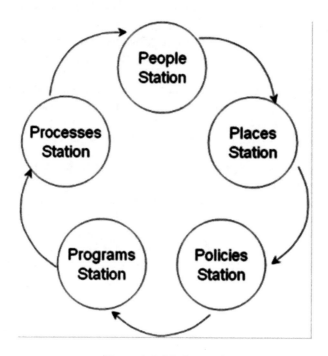

Figure 6. 5-P Relay rotation.

INVITATIONAL GOVERNANCE

One of the key charges of invitational schools is to prepare students to participate in their self-governance, that is, to take part in helping to make, enforce, and modify the rules which guide their collective lives. Invitational learning involves much more than merely hearing about democracy in the abstract; it is about seeing it in action, and, even more significant, being an active participant in governing processes. In addition, a vibrant democratically oriented school sends an invitation to the community to witness and participate in the goals and governance of the school. What is needed for this to develop in an inviting way?

The work on site-based school governance provides a guiding structure for exploring core values, developing plans, and monitoring processes by focusing on the development of a covenant, charter, and critical study process (Glickman, 1993). Using the thinking of Phase III of the Invitational Helix (Pervasive Adoption), the covenant, charter, and critical study process can be seen in the light of an actionable inviting perspective.

Covenant

A covenant represents a community's defining core values, the ideas that have been effectively communicated and deliberated so that they are held in common. It represents what a group of people are essentially about and the principles they work with. The basic principles of the inviting perspective provide a starting point for deliberation.

- People are able, valuable, and responsible and should be treated accordingly. (Do people agree with this? Do they understand the implications of this? What happens if this is violated?)
- Educating should be a co-operative and collaborative activity. (In what ways should we be co-operative? Is there room for people to work by themselves? Are there disadvantages in doing this?)
- The process is the product in the making. (How does this fit with an outcome-based emphasis in many schools? How does this help with the ever-increasing pressure for high test scores? How do we decide what are less than useful processes?)
- People possess untapped potential in all areas of worthwhile development. (Are there limitations on human development? What counts as worthwhile development? What areas of development can be focused on in our school?)
- This potential can best be realized by places, policies, programs, and processes specifically designed to invite development and by people who are intentionally inviting with themselves and others, personally and professionally. (Is potential controlled by genes and thus out of the hands of educators? Do we have to do all of this? Do I really owe it to my students to be good to myself?)

This set of principles is not uncontentious and not in its final form. It has, however, been used by schools throughout the world in establishing their covenants, mission statements, and operating principles. The next step deals with a plan for putting these into action.

Charter

As seasoned educators know, many mission statements are gathering dust in the archives and basements at central headquarters. They were never put into action because there was no second step, a plan to think with and implement these core beliefs. A charter is a plan for making core beliefs actionable. Since the core beliefs of the inviting perspective focus on putting into practice Five Ps (People, Places, Policies, Programs, and Processes) there is need to coordinate the alignment of these strand efforts. Dr. Kent Mann, who has served as Principal at Grand Island Senior High School in Grand Island, Nebraska uses a Building Leadership Teams (BLT) concept that is comprised of the following:

– Two co-chairs with a 1- and 2-year rotation. (This allows both continuity and freshness of perspective.)
– A steering committee of one person from each of the P strands with a 1-year rotation. (This allows for both diversity and good communication about what is being undertaken in the school.)
– A voluntary faculty committee with a 1-year commitment. (This allows for the infectious use of the energy of those who want to be involved.)

One other point, the rotation of members of the committee starts in midyear, so there is no disruption of activities at the beginning of the school year. Kent Mann (personal communication) has said that the BLT is so successful that it can run without the principal. This charter has been internalized and has become a key operating part of the school culture.

Critical Study Process

In schools, action initiatives really operate in a "Ready! Fire! Aim!" sequence. With this being the case, any successful learning community needs breadth, depth, and self-correcting feedback to understand where they are in terms of other possibilities. The invitational helix can provide a roadmap for looking at what is presently happening in a school

About Critical Study

When I transitioned into a school as principal I was told by the outgoing principal about the things that were to be kept from the School Council and the community at large, which were not ethical and legal matters of confidentiality. I knew I couldn't and shouldn't run a school that way. It took some time to bring this information to the surface and to establish open and transparent relationships, but it was worth it in the end.

and what might be happening next in terms of teaching, learning, school environment, and community involvement. Through a variety of groupings of job-similar (people teaching or working with the same grade or same subject) and job diverse (people working in different areas) educators can examine what is happening in their schools, explore creative practices in other schools around the world, and examine current research. The International Alliance for Invitational Education provides these possibilities for educators around the world and many strong links and partnerships have been made among schools from Hong Kong to Kentucky. Returning to the Building Leadership Teams at Grand Island Secondary School, during one school year they examined student/staff safety, teacher morale, and personalization of learning, among other things. They were excited and felt that they had only just begun to make more good things happen at their school.

INVITING COMMUNITY

Moving towards a more participative inviting school gains greater depth and diversity as more of the community get involved in the critical study process. Community members can be a part of a team that includes teachers, staff, administrators, parents, and people from local agencies who use the Inviting School Survey–Revised (ISS-R) to discuss what is happening in the school. This instrument has been developed by Ken Smith (2012) from The Catholic University of Australia and has been a key part of the Inviting School Award Process that has lead to the recognition and networking of more than 200 schools from around the world.

The Inviting School Survey–Revised (ISS-R) is a 50-item instrument that looks at the Five Ps of a school. As stated earlier, the inviting approach centres around people so this item occurs 16 times, with places next (12), then processes (8) followed by programs (7), and policies (7). The ISS-R is a summative instrument that gives participants a sense of the social, emotional, and academic climate of a school. As a basis for discussion, it encourages conversation along these dimensions:

- People: To what extent are the school personnel seen as trusting, intentional, and courteous?
- Places: Is the school pleasant, clean, and people-centred?
- Processes: Are people accessible, co-operative, and working together?
- Programs: Are programs inclusive, enriching, and enjoyed?
- Policies: To what extent are people involved in formulating and evaluating rules?

The ISS-R is meant to be heuristic, a discussion generator, and an idea stimulator. Each of the items can generate other possibilities for the school. Inviting educational leadership moves towards a more inclusive ethos. As a covenant, it is a contract. As with any contract, the truth is in the details. The details, however, are to be seen in light of calling forth educational life in all involved in the school. Done well, everyone involved should be able to savour, understand, and improve what is done and how it is done in the school and beyond. The 50-item ISS-R can be found in Appendix B.

MENTORING CONVERSATIONS

Q: The "Swap & Shop" activity you suggest involves a lot of trust. What do you have to do to get this trust to develop?

Often faculty and staff may be reluctant to share ideas or put themselves out there because they are fearful of the criticism that comes with not being perceived to be doing things "right." Encourage staff, as we would our students, to try new things, to learn from mistakes, and to not stress about perceived failures. This is the first step to getting people to open their doors, share ideas, and not feel intimidated by others. We know a number of schools and school districts that are actively engaged in processes like this, encouraging and facilitating moderation of ideas across schools. Teachers come together with grade partners from different schools to share best practices and strategies, and to plan together. What these session tend to reveal is increasing confidence and competency in staff as they recognize that their fears are shared by others, and that they are doing good things that are worth being shared and discussed. Most of this collaboration is happening within school districts, but not with other districts, or private or charter schools. We are, however, encouraged by the trusting approach to collaboration and professional learning that is happening in contemporary schools. The first step might be partnering within the school—for example, opening classroom doors, scheduling opportunities for collaborative planning and assessment, visiting each other's classes, sharing students, team teaching, and increasing flexibility. The next would be to move this to a wider, perhaps divisional level, then throughout the school. These and other initiatives can increase the connections within the educational community and effectively share new ideas with others.

Q: The covenant you describe sounds like warmed-over mission statements. Didn't these die out?

The covenant is simply a way to think about defining your core values and beliefs in a way that can be articulated and understood by everyone in the organization. We're not sure about the death of mission statements, but what we are sure about is the importance of having clearly articulated, congruent values amongst those working in the school. Sharing common beliefs that are core to invitational education—such as: people are able, valuable, and responsible and should be treated accordingly; educating should be a co-operative and collaborative activity; the process is the product in the making; and people possess untapped potential in all areas of worthwhile development that are tangibly realized—provides not only clarity of values and beliefs, but a clear direction regarding how to monitor and evaluate through the Five Ps. As seasoned educational leaders, we recognize the importance of collaboration and shared vision. We also recognize that in democratic schools, a variety of opinions and approaches co-exist. This fosters complexity, richness, and growth within communities. Core values and beliefs, however, should be aligned and collectively embraced in an inviting school.

Q: Isn't doing a critical study going to publicly air our "dirty linen"? Do you think that's wise?

Schools are public institutions accountable to the people in the community, whether through site-based or central office faculty and staff, central office administrators, school councils, and locally appointed or elected officials. Our experiences confirm that there will always be personal situations that require discretion, such as family matters or sensitive issues. However, leaders should avoid "dirty secrets" that they are unwilling to expose in their schools. Financial reporting should be transparent, decision making democratic and open, and leaders should be approachable and committed to partnering with the community. There will always be things we are great at, and things we need to work on. There should be no shame in that. Going through the critical process might be difficult the first time, but it sets a precedent of thoughtful, critical reflection which will become the norm. When it comes to the operation of the school, a judicious combination of open communication, care, trust, respect, and meliorsim can lead to positive and constructive relationships.

Q: After all this philosophical talk, how can you suggest that we use the ISS-R, a quantitative measuring instrument?

We hope that this book provides enough of the big ideas to stimulate reflection and consideration, as well as examples of the ways in which these ideas manifest themselves in schools around the globe. Our big idea for writing this book was that ideas and ideals matter, that philosophy informs practice, and that they can be revealed in practice in a variety of contexts and situations. As school leaders, you are both big-picture thinkers and detail oriented. You are not simply implementers of policy; you play a vital role in the success of the students, staff, and parents in your community. As such, you have an obligation to think about how to make things better. If you are committing to living educationally and inviting others to do the same, understanding how and why it is working is important in order to improve. The personal reflection process is important, as is a quantifiable means of reviewing successes. You may find that not everyone on your staff will be as enlightened as you and committed to living in this ideal. They might want facts, numbers, or proof that this inviting approach to educational living actually makes a difference. Use it as an additional tool to assess and reflect on your approach to invitational leadership and to plan for the future.

PART 3

DARE TO LEAD FOR EDUCATION

CHAPTER 13

HOPE FOR EDUCATIONAL LEADERSHIP

Putting into artful practice the LIVES model requires persistence, resourcefulness, and courage. It is not for the weak of heart, thought, or action because when you are working with five living systems there are always new dynamics developing. Looking at educational leadership from the perspective of expressing oneself through a language rather than achieving a final outcome, pursuing the LIVES model can be a creative quest for an educational life well lived.

How can one person do all that is required to be an inviting educational leader?

What type of questions might people ask about the inviting approach?

How can the key ideas of the inviting approach be succinctly stated?

What does it mean to speak the language of inviting?

Because inviting educational leadership aims to connect feelings, thoughts, and actions in creative and sustained acts of hope, these are important questions for leaders to ask if they are in education for the long run. This chapter will call into question your beliefs if you:

– Think that leading for educational lives is very easy or impossibly hard;
– Do not want to answer questions about important beliefs;
– Feel that core ideas cannot be adequately put into words;
– Dislike learning challenging ways to look at things.

This chapter will build on your beliefs if you:

– Like the challenge of leading for educational lives;
– Have some unanswered questions about the inviting approach;
– Enjoy getting to the heart of an idea;
– Think that learning new ways to look at things opens up larger horizons.

We have come a long way in this book as we have explored educational leadership from the point of view of an inviting theory of practice. In this last chapter we will revisit key intentions of the Educational LIVES model, show how to get to the gist of a dozen core inviting concepts, and look at the inviting approach as a creative new way of thinking to explore.

GETTING TO THE EDUCATIONAL HEART OF LIVES

From the point of view of the LIVES model, educational leadership is about the quality of the relationships in which people engage. Looked at in terms of positive possibilities, these relationships either call forth or shun human potential to live flourishing lives. Flourishing lives are more likely to occur if educational leaders take to heart the following themes underlying the relationships of the LIVES model:

- Leader within: Care to live! This is the belief that because life is not a dress rehearsal for something else, it is important to live everyday life well. Wishing to always be someplace else is to miss the wonders of the present and to live at best a half life.
- Individuals: Share to grow! Learning to live beyond the preoccupation with one's self enables a person to find the means to co-create shared experiences and vital relationships which take both parties to richer ways of being in the world.
- Values and knowledge: Compare to understand! Coming to terms in disciplined, co-operative, and creative ways with the world of ideas and the world that can be made into ideas enables new alternatives to be seen and more informed judgments to be made.
- Educational communities: Prepare to participate! The life-work of educational leaders is not to be spectators to an already written play, but playwrights in the human experiment to construct more just and beautiful ways to work and create together.
- Society and beyond: Dare to lead! Learning to find the *Yes!* beneath the *No!* and creating the means for it to be a part of an enriched life for all involves digging in with an inviting stance and finding ways to make solid connections with key social issues. This means being willing and able to speak up for what goes on in the name of education.

SPEAKING UP FOR EDUCATION

Early in the book it was stated that leadership involved developing a vision that paid attention to a variety of voices; being able to articulate that vision in an artful way; and enrolling participants who can enjoy the process. The vision expressed here was that the goal of living an educational life, a life of learning to savour, understand, and improve more individual and collective experiences, was a worthy pursuit, more justifiable than the goal of being a hyperactive consumer or an unquestioning ideo-logue. Articulating an inviting vision in an artful way depends on a leader demonstrating what Mortimer Adler (1991) calls logos, ethos, and pathos. Each of these can be placed in the light of invitational theory.

Logos

The logical order and cohesiveness of the ideas presented. The basic rationale of the inviting approach is made clear in progressing through its three foundations, the stance, the four levels, and the four areas and can be summarized in the following six-word statements. Six words were chosen for the sake of succinct clarity needed to move with others on issues of mutual importance (Pink, 2013):

1. Democratic ethos: Extend the ideal that everyone matters.
2. Perceptual tradition: Interpret behaviour from the inside out.
3. Self-concept theory: Don't motivate; work with internal energies.
4. Inviting stance: Connecting in respectful ways demonstrates care.
5. Intentionally disinviting: Fight cruelty, verbally, nonverbally, formally, informally.
6. Unintentionally disinviting: Not meaning to hurt, still can.
7. Unintentionally inviting: Being unreflective can lead to retrogression.
8. Intentionally inviting: Mean what you say and do.
9. Inviting oneself personally: Treat your only lifelong companion well.
10. Inviting others personally: Support the support group supporting you.
11. Inviting oneself professionally: Stay alive in your unique vocation.
12. Inviting others professionally: Focus on self-concept-as-learner early and often.

Let's now make explicit the logos of inviting leadership for educational lives. Inviting educational leadership is about constructing, sustaining, and extending imaginative acts of hope. In doing this, democracy as an ideal leads to an emphasis on the person and his or her hope for leading a flourishing educational life. Using an inviting stance centred around care, the aim is to make an educational connection with others that is based on trust, respect, meliorism, and intentionality. Being intentional means doing things on purpose, for purposes one can defend. If this approach makes sense and is good enough to use with others, personally and professionally, it should be good enough to use with oneself, personally and professionally. As an evolving theory of educational practice based on an ethic of caring relationships, the inviting approach focuses on what is taught and learned as leaders relate to themselves, others, valued knowledge, educational communities, and the larger global society and beyond. Its goal is to provide the conditions so that greater numbers of people can savour, understand, and better more of life's experiences. In doing so, it reconnects with the democratic educational ideal and the cycle begins again in an expanded form with the goal being to have everyone in the school become an inviting educational leader.

Ethos

The credibility and trustworthiness a leader is perceived to possess. An audience needs to know that a leader knows what he or she is talking about and is worth listening to. By showing that the knowledge, insights, and suggestions come from both professional and personal experience with an inviting perspective, a leader lets the audience know that what is discussed is not merely something taken from a textbook but rather that which has been thought about, studied, tried out, and consistently lived and deepened. Sharing professional and personal stories that enable people to look at things from new perspectives and broaden their horizons is an invitation to an educational experience.

Pathos

The degree of passion, commitment, and care a leader is able to communicate to an audience inspires imagination, and possibilities. An audience wants to know the extent to which a leader believes what he or she is saying about the inviting approach. They want to know why you care about this; what it has added to your life; and why they should care about this. They want to see that you can strike a deep human chord that makes life more vibrant and worthwhile. Pathos is perceived when an audience knows that you care about the inviting approach and want them to consider caring about it also. Pathos is developed not with gimmicks but through a sincere desire to communicate something of worth.

Meeting the requirement of logos, ethos, and pathos, a leader should next prepare to respond to some of the main reasons people give for not wanting to be involved with the inviting perspective. In their research more than a decade ago, Susan Brown and William Purkey (n.d.) found that administrators and teachers provided these hesitations (the basis for a reply based on the SPURT-Q Method is suggested):

– We are already inviting. Reply: "Perhaps. …Upon reflection, I can see that good things are happening in your school. These certainly should be celebrated. Do you think that possessing a systematic and growing language to explain and extend these practices and being in contact with a kindred group of educators from around the world could make this school even better?"
– It is just another bandwagon. Reply: "Perhaps. …Upon reflection, I can see that educators are weary and wary of having top-down initiatives laid on them any time there is a change of regimes. Caution and careful examination are certainly in order. Do you think that an approach that is a part of a larger ethical project and that has evolved over the last 35 years can get a school beyond superficial add-ons?"
– It involves more work than what we are presently doing. Reply: "Perhaps. …Upon reflection, if you do everything else you are presently doing and add on a bunch of inviting activities, you will certainly be doing more. Do you think that if an inviting approach can enable you to rethink what you are presently doing and reset priorities so that better working relationships and shared practices can be established it would make it easier to do what you came into education to do? Do you know that there is research (Purkey & Novak, 1996) to show that when a school adopts an inviting perspective there are improvements in discipline and morale?"
– It is an attempt to force change. Reply: "Perhaps. …Upon reflection, I can see where it is disturbing to have someone who is not in the classroom with you all day telling you what new things you ought to be doing. Do you think the inviting approach is something that teachers can own and work with to make their work more fulfilling?"

- It is too limited. Reply: "Perhaps. …Upon reflection, I can see that if the inviting perspective is interpreted as merely being nice, it would certainly be limited. Nice is nice but it is not enough. Do you think that the inviting perspective can provide guiding principles and strategies for people to develop more vibrant and caring places, polices, programs, and processes?"
- It is too "feel good." Reply: "Perhaps. … Upon reflection, I can see that trying some new things is not as easy as it sounds. Significant change does not always feel good. There will be some highs and lows. Do you think, though, that people tend to eventually feel better when they learn important things and are engaged in meaningful projects? Do you think that an approach that aims to have everyone able to savour, understand, and better more of their individual and collective experiences requires deep and serious thought along with celebrations and playfulness?"

Taking the effort to understand and answer these concerns along with the most difficult questions you can ask yourself deepens your logos, ethos, and pathos along with helping the deepening of the inviting theory of practice. Over the years, one of the authors has watched the change as people queried him with the same words: "What is invitational education?" In the beginning the question was often asked with a dismissive sneer. Years later it is asked often with a desire to understand. For those involved in evidence-based decision making, this constitutes an improvement. Perhaps someday the question will not have to be asked.

Developing a Seventh Sense

The job of invitational leaders is to be sources of life in a land of untapped potential. For this to happen, there is a need to develop the seventh sense, the ability to speak and act so that educational lives can flourish.

Moving beyond the negative and the unfocused, the practice of speaking requires developing a language of appreciation and transformation to call forth and sustain imaginative acts of hope. Aspects of this language have been encouraged earlier in this book in terms of inviting oneself and others, personally and professionally. A brief but more detailed look at the subtleties, nuances, and possibilities of this language can be made available if it is seen as parts of speech. Let's call this the inviting mood and look at the following eight parts of speech:

- Prepositions: Work to develop "doing with" and refrain from "doing to" or "doing in" relationships. Prepositions are about connections and the types of relationships that develop. Inviting educational lives pivot around the delicate and precious relationships that are necessary to connect oneself and others: to flourishing life-aspirations; to individual caring relationships; to understanding, probing, and extending values and knowledge; to commitment to work with an educational community; and to social responsibility for the world we are helping to construct. Intentionally working to make a doing-with connection enables educators to affirm a caring stance in what can often be too easily perceived to be an indifferent world.

– Nouns: Put people first when working to improve places, programs, processes, and policies but do not forget the importance of ideals, ideas, and adventures. Inviting educational leadership is a person-centred approach that begins and ends with people sending, receiving, and interpreting messages. The other four Ps leave a communicative residue that influences the perceptions, dispositions, and values of those who come into contact with them. Handled with an ethical imagination, ideals are projections of desirable present goods that promote moving the actual towards the better. Since education is about bringing the transmission and transformation of ideas to life, invitational leaders are deeply involved in the cultivation of an appreciative and growth mindset. Adventures come about naturally in the lively work of calling forth and sustaining imaginative acts of hope and are to be entered into with a spirit of hope.

– Verbs: Strive to use the active voice and remember that "invite" is a transitive verb that needs an object, something that is being invited, to complete its meaning. The active voice represents a proactive stance, a commitment to being a do-er rather than a done-to-er or a done-in-er. Invitational leaders are to be models and active voices in that which they are inviting: the savouring, understanding, and bettering of more human experiences. The self, rather than being viewed as a noun, a thing, can be seen as a way of being in the world, articulated in Buckminster Fuller's statement, "I seem to be a verb." Invitational leaders are not passive responders but active shapers and movers of flourishing ways of being in the world.

– Pronouns: Employ inclusive words to stand for people by thinking in terms of "we" rather than "they," and work to relate to a person as a "thou" rather than an "it." In ethics, the "we intention" is an inclusive move to include more and more people, and eventually everyone, in the circle of humanity. It develops in deeply felt ways as the common humanity of others is viscerally sensed. The reduction of violence and the using the "third side" in social conflicts is a manifestation of the possibilities of realizing this inclusiveness. Another expression of this inclusiveness is to work to participate in what Martin Buber (1970) calls "I-thou" rather than "I-it" relationships. In an I-thou relationship the other is seen as a centre of a life with meanings seeking to be deepened. In an I-it relationship the other is treated as an object to be used for one's own purposes. The "I" is always in relationship, and its more expansive ethical qualities are developed in "I-thou" relationships.

– Adjectives: Be very careful with superlatives, understanding their paralyzing potential. In particular, this means giving "best" a rest and finding ways to promote creative "betters." For example, taken literally, the command to "do one's best" can freeze a literally minded person who can be trapped in mental machinations of what this could possibly mean along with the horror and the humiliation of one's best not being good enough. By thinking of cultivating the creative better, the next step that can improve what is actually happening; positive movement rather than pervasive procrastination can be the default disposition that develops flow experiences and successful intelligence.

- Adverbs: Seek to give the proper tone to verbs by using them in the light of "caringly," "trustingly," "intentionally," "respectfully," and "melioristically." These words provide depth and focus to actions and enable an educational leader to dig in with an inviting stance and stand for something of educational substance rather than falling for the next cotton-candy panacea.
- Interjections: Celebrate the "Wow!" and take a "Gulp!" to be an invitation to inquire and grow. Surprises, deeper understandings, and new feelings of competence are the natural excitements of educational living. "Gulp!" represents an invitation from a real-life encounter to step back and try new things. By seeing the limitations of old ways of structuring a situation, new freedoms for more complex development can occur. Without gulps we would all still be cognitively undeveloped.
- Conjunctions: Focus on "and" and try to avoid "but"; work to use "if" to help generate imaginative possibilities. The word "and" is an attempt to link ideas together while "but" can be a way to exclude creative connections. When "but" is used at the conferring stage of conflict resolution, sincere acknowledgements and affirmations are disregarded. "If," a mere two-lettered word, can be seen as the basis for creativity. It is a button to turn on imagination and see alternative ways to make sense of what is going on and what should happen next.

Becoming fluent in using the language of inviting with oneself and others, personally and professionally, takes persistence, resourcefulness, and courage. Like any language, it helps to use this language where others are using it too. In such places the language can take on a life of its own and imaginative acts of hope can thrive. We have seen it happen close to home and around the world. This book is an attempt to use inviting educational leadership to help create and sustain such educationally flourishing lives.

We speak with words,
But they are not merely uttered,
They can be chosen.

We use a language,
But it is not merely words,
It is a way of being in the world.

We share this way of being with others,
But they are not mere recipients,
They open to us their hearts, minds, and hopes.

STRAND REPORT FORM

Team Leader: _____   **Team Member:**

Team Recorder: _____   _____

Team Energizer: _____   _____

Team Researcher: _____   _____

_____

_____

_____

_____

_____

_____

_____

Team focus: **people, places, policies, programs, processes** (please circle one)

Specific Activities and Goals	Person(s) Responsible	Time Frame Begin/End	Evaluation Success Measure

INVITING SCHOOL SURVEY – REVISED (ISS-R)

Thank you for your participation in this activity. It is very much appreciated!

We are interested in your opinions on a range of issues regarding your school.

Individual responses will be <u>strictly</u> confidential as aggregated data is only being analyzed.

1. Name of your school: _____

2. Are you: _____Male   _____Female

3. Are you a: ____Student ____Teacher ____Administrator ____Parent ____Counselor ____Other

4. If you are a student how old are you: _____

DIRECTIONS

The purpose of this survey is to determine what you think about your school. Following are a series of 50 statements concerning your school. Please use the five-point response scale and select how much you agree or disagree for each item. It should take approximately 15-20 minutes to complete

SA=*Strongly Agree* **A**=*Agree* **U**=*Undecided* **D**=*Disagree* **SD**=*Strongly Disagree*

Select 'N/A' only if the question does not apply to your school

APPENDIX B

Statements	SA	A	U	D	SD	N/A
1. Student discipline is approached from a positive standpoint.						
2. Everyone is encouraged to participate in athletic (sports) programs.						
3. The Principal involves everyone in the decision-making process.						
4. Furniture is pleasant and comfortable.						
5. Teachers are willing to help students who have special problems.						
6. Teachers in this school show respect for students.						
7. Grades are assigned by means of fair and comprehensive assessment of work and effort.						
8. The air smells fresh in this school.						
9. Teachers are easy to talk with.						
10. There is a wellness (health) program in this school.						
11. Students have the opportunity to talk to one another during class activities.						
12. Teachers take the time to talk with students about students' out-of-class activities.						
13. The school grounds are clean and well maintained.						
14. All telephone calls to this school are answered promptly and politely.						
15. Teachers are generally prepared for class.						
16. The restrooms in this school are clean and properly maintained.						
17. School programs involve out of school experience.						
18. Teachers exhibit a sense of humor						
19. School policy encourages freedom of expression by everyone						
20. The Principal's office is attractive.						
21. People in this school are polite to one another.						
22. Everyone arrives on time for school.						
23. Good health practices are encouraged in this school.						
24. Teachers work to encourage students' self-confidence.						
25. Bulletin boards are attractive and up-to-date.						

194

Statements	SA	A	U	D	SD	N/A
26. The messages and notes sent home are positive.						
27. The Principal treats people as though they are responsible.						
28. Space is available for student independent study.						
29. People often feel welcome when they enter the school.						
30. Students work cooperatively with each other.						
31. Interruptions to classroom academic activities are kept to a minimum.						
32. Fire alarm instructions are well posted and seem reasonable.						
33. People in this school want to be here.						
34. A high percentage of students pass in this school.						
35. Many people in this school are involved in making decisions.						
36. People in this school try to stop vandalism when they see it happening.						
37. Classrooms offer a variety of furniture arrangements.						
38. The school sponsors extracurricular activities apart from sports.						
39. Teachers appear to enjoy life.						
40. Clocks and water fountains are in good repair.						
41. School buses wait for late students.						
42. School pride is evident among students.						
43. Daily attendance by students and staff is high.						
44. There are comfortable chairs for visitors.						
45. Teachers share out-of-class experiences with students.						
46. Mini courses are available to students.						
47. The grading practices in this school are fair.						
48. Teachers spend time after school with those who need extra help.						
49. The lighting in this school is more than adequate.						
50. Classes get started quickly.						

REFERENCES

Abram, D. (1996). *The spell of the sensuous: Perception and language in a more-than-human world*. New York, NY: Vintage.

Ackerman, D. (1990). *A natural history of the senses*. New York, NY: Random House.

Adler, M. (1991). *How to speak, how to listen*. New York, NY: Simon & Schuster.

Anderson, W. (1990). *Reality isn't what it used to be: Theatrical politics, ready-to-wear-religion, global myths, primitive chic, and other wonders of the postmodern world*. San Francisco, CA: HarperCollins.

Ardell, D. (1986). *High level wellness: An alternative to doctors, drugs and disease*. Berkeley, CA: Ten Speed Press.

Arendt, H. (1963). *Eichmann in Jerusalem: A report on the banality of evil*. London, UK: Faber and Faber.

Armstrong, D. (2009). *Administrative passages: Navigating the transition from teacher to assistant principal*. New York, NY: Springer.

Bennis, W. (1989). *On becoming a leader*. Reading, MA: Addison-Wesley.

Berger, P., & Luckmann, T. (1966). *The social construction of reality. A treatise in the sociology of knowledge*. Garden City, NY: Anchor Books.

Berliner, D. (1986). In pursuit of the expert pedagogue. *Educational Researcher, 15*(7), 5–13. doi:10.3102/0013189X015007007

Bernstein, R. (2010). *The pragmatic turn*. Malden, MA: Polity Press.

Borg, M. J. (2010). *Putting away childish things: A tale of modern faith*. New York, NY: Harper One.

Boyd, J. K. (2010). *2048: Humanity's agreement to live together*. San Francisco, CA: Berrett-Koehler.

Brandt, R. (1998). *Powerful learning*. Alexandria, VA: ASCD.

Branson, C. (2009). *Leadership for an age of wisdom*. New York, NY: Springer.

Brown, D. H., & Purkey, W. W. (n.d.). *Why educators choose not to become involved with invitational education: Reasons and realities*. Retrieved from http://iaie.webs.com/ie/reason_realities.htm

Buber, M. (1970). *I and thou*. New York, NY: Scribner's.

Carnegie, D. (1936). *How to win friends and influence people*. New York, NY: Simon & Schuster.

Clance, P. R., & Imes, S. (1978). The imposter phenomenon in high achieving women: Dynamics and therapeutic intervention. *Psychotherapy: Theory, Research, and Practice, 15*(3), 241–247. doi:10.1037/h0086006

Combs, A. (1982). *A personal approach to teaching: Beliefs that make a difference*. Boston, MA: Allyn & Bacon.

Combs, A. (2006). *Being and becoming: A field approach to psychology*. New York, NY: Springer.

Combs, A., Avila, D., & Purkey, W. (1978). *Helping relationships: Basic concepts for the helping profession* (2nd ed.). Boston, MA: Allyn & Bacon.

Combs, A., Blume, R., Newman, A., & Wass, H. (1974). *The professional education of teachers: A humanistic approach to teacher preparation* (2nd ed.). Boston, MA: Allyn & Bacon.

Combs, A., & Gonzalez, D. (1997). *Helping relationships: Basic concepts for the helping professional* (4th ed.). Boston, MA: Allyn & Bacon.

Combs, A., Miser, A., & Whitaker, K. (1999). *On becoming a school leader: A person-centered challenge*. Alexandria, VA: ASCD.

Combs, A., Richards, A., & Richards, F. (1976). *Perpetual psychology: A humanistic approach to the study of persons*. New York, NY: Harper & Row.

Combs, A., & Snygg, D. (1959). *Individual behavior: A perceptual approach to behavior* (2nd ed.). New York, NY: Harper & Row.

Csikszentmihalyi, M. (1993). *The evolving self: A psychology for the third millennium*. New York, NY: HarperCollins.

Csikszentmihalyi, M. (1997). *Finding flow: The psychology of engagement with everyday life*. New York, NY: HarperCollins.

REFERENCES

Csikszentmihalyi, M. (2004). *Good business: Leadership, flow, and the making of meaning*. New York, NY: Penguin.

Csikszentmihalyi, M. (2008). *Flow: The psychology of optimal experience*. New York, NY: HarperCollins. (Original work published 1990)

Davis, B., & Sumara, D. (2006). *Complexity and education: Inquiries into learning, teaching, and research*. Mahwah, NJ: Erlbaum.

Dewey, J. (1897, January). My pedagogic creed. *School Journal, 54*, 77–80.

Dewey, J. (1916). *Democracy and education: An introduction to the philosophy of education*. New York, NY: Macmillan.

Dewey, J. (1922). *Human nature and conduct*. New York, NY: Henry Holt.

Dewey, J. (1938). *Experience and education*. New York, NY: Macmillan.

Dewey, J. (1980). *Art as experience*. New York, NY: Penguin Putnam. (Original work published 1934)

Dewey, J. (1997). *Experience and education* (2nd ed.). New York, NY: Touchstone.

Dewey, J., & Tufts, J. (1932). *Ethics* (2nd ed.). New York, NY: Holt.

DiPetta, T., Novak, J., & Marini, Z. (2002). *Inviting online education*. Bloomington, IN: Phi Delta Kappa.

Dweck, C. (2006). *Mindset: The new psychology of success*. New York, NY: Random House.

Edwards, J. (2010). *Inviting students to learn: 100 Tips for talking effectively with your students*. Alexandria, VA: ASCD.

Egan, K. (2008). *The future of education: Re-imagining our schools from the ground up*. New Haven, CT: Yale University Press.

Erikson, E. (1980). *Identity and the life cycle*. New York, NY: Norton.

Evans, R. (2001). *The human side of school change: Reform, resistance, and the real-life problems of innovation*. San Francisco, CA: Jossey-Bass.

Fairfield, P. (2012). *Education after Dewey*. New York, NY: Bloomsbury.

Ferrari, J. R., & Thompson, T. (2006). Impostor fears: Links with self-presentational concerns and self-handicapping behaviours. *Personality and Individual Differences, 4*(2), 341–352. doi:10.1016/J.Paid.2005.07.012

Finger, J. (1995). *A study of professed and inferred self-concept-as-learner of African American and Causcasian middle grade students* (Unpublished doctoral dissertation). University of North Carolina, Greensboro, NC.

Fisher, R., & Ury, W. L. (1981/1991). *Getting to yes: Negotiating without giving in*. New York, NY: Penguin.

Furman, G. C., & Shields, C. M. (2005). How can educational leaders promote and support social justice and democratic community in schools? In W. A. Firestone & C. Riehl. (Eds.), *A new agenda for research in educational leadership* (pp. 119–137). New York, NY: Teachers College Press.

Gardner, H. (1993). *The unschooled mind: How children think and how schools should teach*. New York, NY: Basic Books.

Gardner, H. (1995). *Leading minds: An anatomy of leadership*. New York, NY: Basic Books.

Gardner, H. (1999). *The disciplined mind: What all students should understand*. New York, NY: Simon & Schuster.

Gardner, H. (2011). *Truth, beauty, and goodness reframed*. Philadelphia, PA: Basic Books.

Gladwell, M. (2000). *The tipping point: How little things can make a big difference*. Boston, MA: Little, Brown and Company.

Glickman, C. (1993). *Renewing America's schools: A guide for school-based action*. San Francisco, CA: Jossey-Bass.

Goleman, D. (2010). *Ecological intelligence: The hidden impacts of what we buy*. New York, NY: Broadway Books.

Green, R. (2001). *Practicing the art of leadership: A problem-based approach to implementing the ISLLC standards*. Upper Saddle River, JN: Merrill Prentice Hall.

Habermas, J. (1981). *The theory of communicative action. Volume 1: Reason and the rationalization of society*. Cambridge, MA: Polity Press.

Hardy, T. (1965). *Tess of the D'Urbervilles*. New York, NY: Norton. (Original work published 1891).

Hargreaves, A. (1994). *Changing teachers, changing times: Teachers' work and culture in the postmodern age*. New York, NY: Teachers College Press.

Hargreaves, A., & Fullan, M. (2012). *Professional capital: Transforming teaching in every school*. New York, NY: Teachers College Press.

Harper, K., & Purkey, W. (1993). Self-concept-as-learner of middle level students. *Research in Middle Level Education, 17*(1), 80–89.

Homer-Dixon. T. (2000). *The ingenuity gap*. New York, NY: Alfred A. Knopf.

Huxley, A. (2010). *Island*. New York, NY: HarperCollins. (Original work published 1962)

Kahneman, D. (2011). *Thinking, fast and slow*. New York, NY: Macmillan.

Kelly, G. A., (1963). *A theory of personality: The psychology of personal constructs*. New York, NY: Norton.

Kidder, R. (1996). *How good people make tough choices: Resolving the dilemmas of ethical living*. New York, NY: Fireside.

Kidder, R. (2005). *Moral courage*. New York, NY: HarperCollins.

Kidder, R. (2010). *Good kids, tough choices: How parents can help their children do the right thing*. San Francisco, CA: Jossey-Bass.

Kouzes, J., & Posner. B. (2010). *The truth about leadership: The no-fads, heart-of-the-matter facts you need to know*. San Francisco, CA: Jossey-Bass.

Kumar, S., & Jagacinkski, C. (2006). Imposters have goals too: The imposter phenomenon and its relation to achievement goal theory. *Personality and Individual Differences, 40*(1), 147–157. doi:10.1016/j. paid.2005.05.014

Kymlicka, W. (1998). *Finding our way: Rethinking ethnocultural relations in Canada*. Don Mills, ON: Oxford University Press.

Langer, E. (1989). *Mindfulness*. New York, NY: Perseus.

Langer, E. (1997). *The power of mindful learning*. New York: Perseus.

Langer, E. (2009). *Counter clockwise: Mindful health and the power of possibility*. New York, NY: Ballantine Books.

Lee, G., Lifeson, A., & Peart, N. (1980). Freewill [Recorded by Rush]. On *Permanent Waves* [Vinyl record]. Morin Heights, QC: Mercury Records. (Recorded 1979)

MacIntyre, A. (1981). *After virtue: A study in moral theory*. Notre Dame, IN: University of Notre Dame Press.

Maslow, A. (1968). *Toward a psychology of being* (2nd ed.). New York, NY: Van Nostrand.

McMahon, B., & Armstrong, D. (2010). Unraveling the knots and strengthening the ties: Countering democratic racism. *International Journal of Urban Educational Leadership, 4*(1), 160–172.

Noddings, N. (1984). *Caring: A feminine approach to ethics and moral education*. Berkeley, CA: University of California Press.

Noddings, N. (1992). *The challenge to care in schools: An alternative approach to education*. New York, NY: Teachers College Press.

Noddings, N. (2005). *The challenge to care in schools: An alternative approach to education* (2nd ed.). New York, NY: Teachers College Press.

Noddings, N. (2013). *Education and democracy in the 21st century*. New York, NY: Teachers College Press.

Norris, T. (2011). *Consuming schools: Commercialism and the end of politics*. Toronto, ON: University of Toronto Press.

Novak, J. (1999). Inviting criteria for democracy's schools, *Thresholds in Education, 25*(1), 4–6.

Novak, J. (2002). *Inviting educational leadership: Fulfilling potential and applying an ethical perspective to the educational process*. London, UK: Pearson.

Novak, J. (2009a). Inviting passionate educational leadership. In B. Davies & T. Brighthouse (Eds.), *Passionate leadership in education* (pp. 35–56). Los Angeles, CA: Sage.

Novak, J. (2009b). Invitational leadership. In B. Davies (Ed.), *Essentials of school leadership* (2nd ed., pp. 44–60). London, UK: Paul Chapman.

Novak, J. M., & Purkey, W. W. (2001). *Invitational education*. Bloomington, IN: Phi Delta Kappa.

Novak, J., Rocca, W., & DiBiase, A. (2006). *Creating inviting schools*. San Francisco, CA: Caddo Gap.

Nozick, R. (1989). *The examined life: Philosophical meditations*. New York, NY: Simon & Schuster.

O'Sullivan, E. (1999). *Transformative learning: Educational vision for the 21st century*. London, UK: Zed Books.

REFERENCES

Palestini, R. (2010). *Practical leadership strategies: Lessons from the world of professional baseball.* Lanham, MD: Touchstone.

Perkins, D. (1992). *Smart schools: From training memories to educating minds.* New York, NY: Free Press.

Perkins, D. (2010) *Making learning whole: How seven principles of teaching can transform education.* San Francisco, CA: Jossey-Bass.

Pink, D. (2009). *Drive: The surprising truth about what motivates us.* New York, NY: Penguin.

Pink, D. (2013). *To sell is human: The surprising truth about moving others.* New York, NY: Riverhead.

Pinker, S. (2002). *The blank slate: The modern denial of human nature.* New York, NY: Penguin.

Pinker, S. (2011). *The better angels of our nature: Why violence has declined.* New York, NY: Penguin.

Pirsig, R. (1992). *Lila: An inquiry into morals.* New York, NY: Bantam.

Postman, N. (1996). *The end of education: Refining the value of school.* New York, NY: Vintage.

Postman. N., & Weingartner, C. (1973). *The school book.* New York, NY: Delacorte Press.

Purkey, W. (1970). *Self-concept and school achievement.* Englewood Cliffs, NJ: Prentice Hall.

Purkey, W. (1978). *Inviting school success: A self-concept approach to teaching and learning.* Belmont, CA: Wadsworth.

Purkey, W. (1991). *5-P relay.* Retrieved from http://www.invitationaleducation.net/ie/PDFs/5-P%20 Relay.pdf

Purkey, W. (2000). *What students say to themselves: Internal dialogue and school success.* Thousand Oaks, CA: Corwin Press.

Purkey,W., Cage, B., & Graves, W. (1973). The Florida key: A scale to infer learner self-concept. *Education and Psychological Measurement, 33*(4), 979–984. doi:10.1177/001316447303300436

Purkey, W., & Novak, J. (1984). *Inviting school success: A self-concept approach to teaching and learning* (2nd ed.). Belmont, CA: Wadsworth.

Purkey, W., & Novak, J. (1996). *Inviting school success: A self-concept approach to teaching, learning, and democratic practice* (3rd ed.). Belmont, CA: Wadsworth.

Purkey, W., & Novak, J. M. (2008). *Fundamentals of invitational education.* Kennesaw, GA: Alliance for Invitational Education.

Purkey, W., Schmidt, J., & Novak, J. (2010). *From conflict to conciliation: How to diffuse difficult situations.* Thousand Oaks, CA: Corwin.

Purkey, W., & Strahan, D. (2002). *Inviting positive classroom discipline.* Westerfield, OH: National Middle School Association.

Rebore, R. (2001). *The ethics of educational leadership.* Upper Saddle River, NJ: Merrill Prentice Hall.

Rogers, C. (1961). *On becoming a person: A therapist's view of psychotherapy.* London, UK: Constable.

Rogers, C. (1980). *A way of being.* Boston, MA: Houghton Mifflin.

Rorty, R. (1989). *Contingency, irony, and solidarity.* New York, NY: Cambridge University Press.

Ryan, J. (2006). Exclusion in urban schools and communities. In D. Armstrong & B. McMahon (Eds.), *Inclusion in urban educational environments: Addressing issues of diversity, equity and social justice* (pp. 3–30). Greenwich, CT: Information Age.

Sandel, M. (2012). *What money can't buy.* New York, NY: Farrar, Straus and Giroux.

Schmidt, J. (2013). *Counseling in the schools: Comprehensive programs of responsive services for all students* (6th ed.). Upper Saddle River, NJ: Pearson.

Schon, D. (1983). *The reflective practitioner: How professionals think in action.* New York, NY: Basic Books.

Schrag, F. (1988). *Thinking in school and society.* New York, NY: Routledge.

Schramm-Pate, S., Jeffries, R., & D'Amico, L. (2006). Reflecting on Mary H. Wright Elementary: Ideologies of high expectations in a "re-segregated" school. In D. Armstrong & B. McMahon (Eds.), *Inclusion in urban educational environments: Addressing issues of diversity, equity and social justice.* (pp. 45–70). Greenwich, CT: Information Age.

Schwartz, B., & Sharpe, K. (2010). *Practical wisdom: The right way to do the right thing.* New York, NY: Riverhead Books.

Sellars, W. (1997). *Empiricism and the philosophy of mind.* Harvard, CT: Harvard University Press.

Sergiovanni, T. (1992). *Moral leadership: Getting to the heart of school improvement.* San Francisco, CA: Jossey-Bass.

Seyle, H. (1974). *Stress without distress*. Toronto, ON: HarperCollins Canada.

Shade, P. (2001). *Habits of hope: A pragmatic theory*. Nashville, TN: Vanderbilt University Press.

Skidelsky, R., & Skidelsky, E. (2012). *How much is enough? The case for money and the case for the good life*. London, UK: Allen Lane.

Smith, K. (2012). *Manual for the inviting school survey—Revised (ISS-R): A survey for measuring the invitational qualities of the total school climate*. Retrieved from http://www.invitationaleducation.net

Snygg, D., & Combs, A. (1949). *Individual behavior: A new frame of reference for psychology*. New York, NY: Harper & Row.

Stanley, P. H. (1992). Inviting things to do in the privacy of your own mind. In J. M. Novak (Ed.), *Advancing invitational thinking* (pp. 231–239). San Francisco, CA: Caddo Gap Press.

Starratt, R. (2004). *Ethical leadership*. San Francisco, CA: Jossey-Bass.

Sternberg, R. J. (1997). *Successful intelligence*. New York, NY: Plume.

Stoll, L., & Fink, D. (1996). *Changing our schools*. Philadelphia, PA: Open University Press.

Stuhr, J. (1993). Democracy as a way of life. In J. J. Stuhr, (Ed.), *Philosophy and the reconstruction of culture: Pragmatic essays after Dewey* (pp. 37–58). Albany, NY: State University of New York Press.

Ury, W. (1993). *Getting past no: Negotiating in difficult situations*. New York, NY: Bantam.

Ury, W. (1999). *Getting to peace: Transforming conflict at home, at work, and in the world*. New York, NY: Viking.

Ury, W. (2007). *The power of a positive no: How to say no and still get to yes*. New York, NY: Bantam.

Wasicsko, M. (1977). *The effects of training and perceptual orientation on the reliability of perceptual inference from selecting effective teachers* (Unpublished doctoral dissertation). University of Florida, Gainesville, FL.

Wasicsko, M. (2005). Hiring for the fourth factor. *The Chronicle of Higher Education, 51*, C2.

Westbrook, R. (1991). *John Dewey and American democracy*. Ithaca, NY: Cornell University Press.

Westbrook, R. (2005) *Democratic hope: Pragmatism and the politics of truth*. Ithaca, NY; Cornell University Press.

Wong, P. (2007). *A case study on introducing invitational education (IE) (a school development initiative) to a secondary school and to evaluate and understand the change process, effectiveness and implications for future school development work* (Unpublished doctoral dissertation). University of Bristol, UK.

Wood, G. (1992). *Schools that work: America's most innovative public education programs*. New York, NY: Dutton.

Zhang, D. (2009). *Schoolyard gardening as multinaturalism: Theory, practice, and product*. Sanbrucken, Germany: VDM Verlag.

201

INDEX

Abram, D, 65, 106
Accountability, 17, 136
Ackerman, D, 106
activating ideal, 3
all or none thinking, 60
application, 55, 104, 147, 149, 151
Ardell, B, 65
areas of inviting, 32
artfully orchestrating, 4, 103, 138
asserting, 12, 86, 101, 103
assumptions, 19, 20, 22, 28, 101, 104, 171
authenticity, 40, 73, 79, 119
awareness, 46–48, 54, 55, 57–59, 65,
      101, 104, 147, 149, 150

Bennis, W, 41
Berger, P & Luckman, T, 42
Berliner, D, 49
Bernstein, R, 43
bettering (see meliorism)
Brandt, R, 116, 119
broken window theory, 142

care
  working from a caring core, 115
Carnegie, D, 120
Choices, 5, 39, 53, 54, 65, 66, 120, 130,
     150, 158
Collegiality, 31, 142
Combat, 87, 92, 96–98
Communication, 22, 70, 73, 78, 79, 83,
     87, 110, 111, 161, 170, 176, 179
community
  bringing into school, 103, 139, 165,
     166, 177
  taking school into, 137, 159, 165,
     166, 169, 179
comparisons, 11

complexity
  complexity of the present, 160
concern, 23, 35, 76, 78, 87, 89–95, 97,
     99, 101, 109, 115, 121, 123, 129,
     136, 145, 149, 157, 158, 161,
     164, 187
conciliation, 93, 96
conferring, 89–91
conflict (bettering), 162
conflict management, 85, 93
confrontation, 93, 97, 147, 151
connections to society, 132
consumership, 12
contemporary schools, 15, 43, 96, 119,
     178, 207
Combs, A, 72
Combs, A, Misner, A, &
     Whitaker, K., 41
conventions
  ideals, 10, 11
  inviting family school, 136
co-operation, 76, 131, 163, 172
coping, 100, 103
core values, 175, 178
Csikszentmihalyi, M, 42, 43, 56, 57, 58,
     62, 135
curricular coherence, 144, 145
curriculum programs, 22, 24, 28, 44,
     54, 110, 114, 118, 125, 129, 137

daily life, 53, 55, 56, 65
democracy, 23, 24, 143, 144, 159, 164,
     169, 175, 185
democratic ethos, 22, 23, 34, 36, 47, 74,
     78, 117, 143, 145, 164, 185
desirable directions, 4
Dewey, J, 6–8, 13, 21, 23, 56, 70, 102,
     108, 116, 207

dialogical relationships, 69
disciplined understanding, 107, 118
dissonance, 44–46, 50
doing-with, 71, 74, 90, 187
distinctions, 9, 42, 150

economic utility, 12
educational communities
  leading, 39, 125, 184, 185
  managing, 39, 125, 184, 185
educational democracy, 164
educational leadership, 3, 5, 15, 20, 35,
    43, 49, 64, 66, 69, 72, 82, 99,
    141, 148, 160, 163, 177, 183
Educational LIVES, 183
educational living, 42, 49, 53, 54, 56,
    65, 81, 89, 99, 105, 106, 10, 151,
    155, 156, 162, 179, 189
educational metaphors, 127, 128
educational perspective, 7, 9, 157
Edwards, J, 142
efficiency , 5, 70, 73, 125, 129
efficient factory school, 125, 127, 128
ethic of care, 120
emotional climate, 118
Erikson, E, 17
ethically defensible, 4, 5, 15, 18, 19, 35,
    63, 70, 122
ethos, 22, 23, 34, 36, 143, 145, 146,
    164, 177, 184, 185
expectations, positive, 131, 132, 137
experience, 42, 45, 48, 49, 54–59, 62,
    66, 75, 81, 94, 97, 104, 107,
    109, 118, 119, 123, 137, 165,
    167, 185

factory model schools, 125
feedback, 33, 57, 103, 116,
    118–120, 176
feelings, 10, 18, 40, 47, 50, 72, 75, 77,
    88, 90, 96, 99, 109, 115, 118,
    133, 161, 183, 189

Five Ps
  People, 141
  Places, 142
  programs, 144
  policies, 143
  processes, 145
Florida Key, 100
Flow, 6, 53, 57, 58, 62, 65, 103, 106,
    126, 188
following through, 75, 80
foundations, 22, 23, 149, 165, 184
freedom and structure, 125, 126, 128,
    137, 157

Gardner, H
  the good, the true, and the
    beautiful, 107
Gladwell, M, 142
global society, 116, 155, 185
goals, 5, 21, 28, 31, 32, 36, 40, 57, 59,
    64, 72, 87, 100, 102, 103, 105,
    111, 116, 120, 149, 173, 175

habitat, pleasing, 131, 132
Hardy, T, 79
Hargreaves, A, 73, 142
Homer-Dixon, T, 160, 161
hope
  imaginative acts of, 19, 31, 34, 62,
    77, 127, 132, 185, 188, 189
  meliorism, 73, 137, 144, 185
human potential, 15, 19, 20–22, 26, 184
human relations leadership, 5
human interaction, 118
Huxley, A, 106

Ideas, 16, 20, 22, 28, 31, 33, 34, 43, 51,
    62, 64, 66, 82, 83, 94, 102, 106,
    108–111, 113, 115, 120, 128,
    135–138, 145, 147, 153, 159,
    162, 170, 171, 175, 178, 183,
    184, 188, 189, 207

ideals
  and conventions, 10
  educational living, 11, 14
  institutions, 8
  democracy, 23, 164, 185
imaginative act of hope, 3, 4,
    9, 42
inclusive education
  managing, 169
  inclusive world, 169
individuals
  conflict management, 85, 93
inner conversations, 59
institutions
  constraints, 9
integrity, 4, 17, 30–32, 35, 39–41, 55,
    69, 73, 87, 91, 92
intelligence, 10, 55, 103, 113, 119, 136,
    145, 188
intentionality, 32, 53, 73–75, 114, 137,
    144, 160, 185
intentionally disinviting, 26–28, 185
intentionally inviting, 19, 26, 30, 32,
    35, 42, 69, 119, 175, 185
interaction, 57, 70, 94, 96, 104,
    117–119, 127
invitational governance, 175
interpersonal tensions
  conflict, 86
investing, 72, 100, 102
invitational education
  assumptions, 101
  foundational values, 131
invitational helix, 147
invitational leadership, 40, 47, 53,
    55, 73, 85, 87, 89, 96, 117, 127,
    146, 148, 150, 151, 164, 165,
    179, 207
invitations, 22, 25, 33, 73, 76, 79,
    81, 170
inviting
  areas of, 32

inviting community, 177
inviting family school model, 130
inviting meaningful change
  occasional interest, 147, 148
  systemic application, 147, 149
  pervasive adoption, 147, 150, 175
  inviting oneself personally, 32, 185
inviting oneself professionally, 32, 185
inviting others personally, 19, 32, 33,
    34, 65, 164, 175, 185, 187, 189
inviting others professionally, 19, 32,
    33, 34, 100, 118, 164, 175, 185,
    187, 189
Inviting School Success (ISS) Survey
  Smith, K, 177
inviting stance, 69, 73–76, 82,83,
    86, 91, 92, 94, 114, 150,
    184, 185, 189

Kidder, R, 121, 122
knowledge
  stages in invitational helix, 147
  values and knowledge, 14, 15,
    39, 184
Kouzes, J & Posner, B, 4, 40,

Langer, E, 104
Language, 27, 44, 71, 77, 101, 103,
    125, 126, 183

leader
  managing educational live, 113
  personal leadership, 41
leadership
  educational, 3, 5, 15, 20, 35, 43, 49,
    64–66, 69, 72, 82, 99, 103, 141,
    148, 160, 163, 177, 183
  educational communities, 39, 125,
    184, 185
  personal, 41
  values, knowledge and, 105
leadership development, 147, 150

learning
  invitational, 113, 115, 117, 142, 175
  mindful, 99, 104, 105
  self-concept as learner, 100, 103, 104,
    105, 116, 117, 150, 185
  self-directed, 58, 135
LIVES model, 34, 39, 155,
    183, 184
long term, 65, 72–74, 121,
    135, 145
luck, 74

management
  conflict, 85, 93,
  educational communities, 39, 125,
    184, 185
  educational life, 34, 53, 55, 161, 177,
    183, 184
  school and society, 155
  thoughtfulness, 105
Maslow, A, 25
McIntyre, A, 20
McLuhan, M, 13
meaning, structure, 126
meliorism, 73, 75, 137, 144, 185
mentoring
  mentorship conversations, 6, 76
messages, 17, 22, 26, 27, 29, 30, 34, 35,
    60, 66, 70, 71, 73, 74, 76, 77, 79,
    83, 89, 142, 144, 148, 153, 188
mindful learning, 99, 104, 105
modelling, 40, 41, 123

Noddings, N, 114, 115
NOPE (naïve optimism pessimistic
    entrenchment), 75
Nouns, 7, 92, 188
Novak, J., 131, 133, 146, 147
Nozick, R, 11, 42

Optimism, 53, 55, 64, 75, 94,
    114, 144
organizing ideals and conventions, 10

others
  inviting others personally, 19,
    32, 33, 34, 65, 164, 175, 185,
    187, 189
  inviting others professionally, 19, 32,
    33, 34, 100, 118, 164, 175, 185,
    187, 189
O'Sullivan, E, 157
Overwhelming, 10, 11, 14, 57, 65, 74,
    83, 100, 103, 106, 118, 122, 137,
    141, 151, 166

Palistini, R, 5
Pathos, 184, 186
People, 141
Perceptions, 20, 25, 29, 41–46, 49, 54,
    71–73, 75, 87, 104–106, 108,
    117, 118, 149, 188
perceptual tradition
  perceptual core of interaction, 70
Perkins, D, 119
personal leadership, 41
personal management, 54, 65
personal responsibility, 60, 65
personal wellness, 53, 56, 65
perspectives, 5–7, 19, 23, 43, 44, 46,
    49, 60, 62, 64, 85, 99, 101, 105,
    125, 149, 163, 169, 186,
philosophy
Pink, D, 102, 126, 185
Pinker, S, 117, 156, 157, 160, 163
Pirsig, R, 126
places, 17, 19, 22, 23, 63, 65, 66, 76,
    77, 82, 91, 97, 109, 119, 125,
    133, 136, 138–143, 149, 164,
    166, 171, 173–177, 187–189
pleasing habitat, 131, 132
policies, 143
political leadership, 5
politics, 71, 121
Postman, N
  & Weingartner, C, 10
positive expectations, 131, 132, 137

power, 5, 23, 27, 46, 49, 70, 88, 91, 92, 96, 107, 119, 139, 148, 152, 162–164

practical wisdom, 40, 42, 49, 53, 54, 57, 58, 64, 66, 71

practice, 4, 6, 8, 11, 17–20, 22–24, 27, 32, 35, 40, 50, 56, 58, 62, 65, 66, 82, 83, 85, 98, 104–106, 115, 121, 122, 135–137, 142, 148, 150, 152, 153, 164, 172, 176, 179, 185, 187

preparation, 76

processes, 4, 6, 19, 22–24, 26, 27, 35, 39, 42, 44–46, 48, 50, 77, 80, 101, 102, 105, 118, 119, 125–127, 134, 139–141, 144, 145, 149, 165, 173, 175–178, 187, 188

product, 19, 21, 51, 129, 144, 146, 152, 163, 164, 175, 178

programs, 56, 76, 119, 125, 129, 134, 136, 137, 139, 141, 144, 145, 149, 165, 170, 173, 175, 177, 187, 188

Purkey, W., 140, 149, 172, 186

Purpose, 12, 20, 26, 28, 30, 31, 35, 39, 41, 43, 49, 55–59, 62, 65, 74, 75, 102, 105, 133, 152, 153, 172, 185

reality, 5, 6, 8, 14, 15, 25, 39, 42, 43, 48, 49, 54, 60, 61, 65, 70, 86, 96, 97, 127, 129, 144, 156, 159, 160, 164

reflection, 3, 6, 16, 31, 35, 54, 59, 62–66, 76, 88, 94, 95, 98, 110, 123, 62, 179, 186, 187

rejection, 61, 80

relating, 5, 70, 100, 103, 127

relationship(s), 9, 10, 15, 58, 63, 69, 70, 79, 82, 96, 109, 115, 138, 155, 157, 159, 163, 166, 188

respect, 24, 29, 36, 53, 59, 62, 63, 73, 74, 81, 85–87, 94, 114, 117, 122, 130, 131, 134, 137, 138, 144, 156, 179, 185,

responsibility, 20, 27, 32, 60, 65, 81, 88, 93, 101, 108, 109, 123, 135, 138, 162, 165, 166,

right versus right, 121, 122

Rogers, C, Kelly, G, & Combs, A, 71

Rorty, R, 11, 33

Sandel, M, 12, 162

savouring
  educational experiences, 53

schools
  efficient factory, 125, 127, 128
  inviting family schools, 130, 136
  leading, 39, 125, 184, 185
  managing, 39, 125, 184, 185
  mentoring, 4, 6, 7, 11, 14, 15, 19, 22, 25, 35, 50, 53, 65, 82, 96, 109, 122, 136, 151, 165, 178
  taking into the community, 137, 159, 165, 166, 169, 179
  connections to society, 132

Schon, D, 62

Schwartz & Sharpe, 40, 42

self
  inviting oneself personally, 32, 185
  inviting oneself professionally, 32, 185
  perceptions of, 18, 44, 45, 73
  preparing oneself, 75

self-concept as learner, 116, 117, 150, 185

self-concept theory, 22, 25, 116, 185

self-confidence, 27, 63, 82, 120

self-correcting, 6, 8, 9, 11, 13, 15, 75, 105, 118, 176

self-mentoring, 58, 61

self-systems, 46

self-talk
  inner-conversations, 60

Sellars, W, 20

Six-Cs
  Concern, 87–89
  Confer, 89
  Consult, 90
  Confront, 91
  Combat, 92
  Conciliate, 92–94

Snygg, D, 71
social interaction, 118, 119
social responsibility, 13, 187
society
    leadership and, 4, 51, 66, 83, 88,
        179, 207
    management and, 54, 62, 101
    vital connections to, 131, 132
spiral diagram, 46
SPURT-Q, 94–96, 162, 163, 186
stance, inviting, 69, 73–76, 82, 83, 86,
        91, 92, 94, 114, 150, 184, 185, 189
Stanley, P.H., 60, 61
Starfish analogy
    managing, 141
strategies, 71, 77, 85, 104, 116–118,
        146, 149, 153, 162, 172, 178, 187
Sternberg, R, 119, 120
Strategies, 71, 77, 85, 104, 116–118,
        146, 149, 153, 162, 172, 178, 187
stress
    management, 65
structural leadership, 5
structure and freedom, 125–128, 137
sustainability
    doing with, 19, 21, 69, 70, 71, 72, 74,
        75, 77, 82, 90, 114, 187
    following through, 75, 80, 87
symbolic leadership, 5
systemic application, 147

technology, 12, 13, 25, 129
thinking
    all or none thinking, 60
    as a virtue, 105, 115

tribalship/tribalism, 12, 13
Truett Anderson, W, 8
Trust, 18, 28, 40, 53, 63, 66, 69, 73, 77,
        79, 82, 92, 100, 114, 135, 137,
        144, 172, 178, 185

understanding, 11–13, 20, 21, 24,
        34–36, 39, 42–44, 46–50, 53, 55,
        66, 72, 80, 86, 87, 89, 90, 93, 94,
        97–99, 102, 105–108, 110, 111,
        114, 116–118, 127, 128, 136,
        137, 141, 146–150, 156, 160,
        164–166, 179, 187–189
underwhelming, 10, 57, 118
unintentionally disinviting, 26, 28, 185
unintentionally inviting, 26, 29, 185
uniqueness, 5, 13, 19, 42, 74, 79, 81,
        117, 130, 131, 135, 137, 144
Ury, W., 156, 162, 163
values
    core, 160, 175, 178
valued knowledge, 99–111, 114, 116,
        144, 185
values and knowledge
    leading for, 39, 69, 99, 125
    managing, 53, 85, 113, 139, 169
vision, 3–6, 8, 11–15, 82, 125, 164,
        178, 184
virtues, 105, 108, 109, 164

Wasicsko, M.M., 72
Whelming, 11, 118
Wong, P, 151, 171

Zhang, D, 143

ABOUT THE AUTHORS

John M. Novak is Professor of Graduate Studies in the Faculty of Education at Brock University, Ontario Canada. An invited speaker around the world, he has given keynote addresses from north of the Arctic Circle to the bottom of New Zealand. A former public school teacher and three-time chair of his department, he is also a past president of the Society of Professors of Education and has written a dozen books and monographs on invitational education, John Dewey, and educational leadership.

Denise E. Armstrong is an Associate Professor in Administration and Leadership in the Faculty of Education at Brock University and has also worked in a variety of K-12 institutions in Canada and the Caribbean as a professor, administrator, and teacher. Her research and writing focus on ethical leadership and social justice. She is the author of *Administrative Passages: Navigating the Transition From Teacher to Assistant Principal* and co-author of *Inclusion in Urban Educational Environments: Addressing Issues of Diversity, Equity and Social Justice.*

Brendan Browne is a Superintendent of Education with the Halton Catholic District School Board. He has been a classroom, special education, and itinerant teacher in both elementary and secondary schools, and a vice-principal and principal in several diverse and distinct school communities. In addition, he has a Ph.D. in Educational Leadership and has written and presented on Invitational Leadership and Theory around the world. He is interested in the intersection of ideas and ideals in contemporary schools.

CPSIA information can be obtained at www.ICGtesting.com
Printed in the USA
LVOW10s0252150414

381672LV00002B/4/P